Doing Animal Studies with Androids, Aliens, and Ghosts

Environmental Cultures Series

Series Editors:
Greg Garrard, University of British Columbia, Canada
Richard Kerridge, Bath Spa University, UK

Editorial Board:
Frances Bellarsi, Université Libre de Bruxelles, Belgium
Mandy Bloomfield, Plymouth University, UK
Lily Chen, Shanghai Normal University, China
Christa Grewe-Volpp, University of Mannheim, Germany
Stephanie LeMenager, University of Oregon, USA
Timothy Morton, Rice University, USA
Pablo Mukherjee, University of Warwick, UK

Bloomsbury's *Environmental Cultures* series makes available to students and scholars at all levels the latest cutting-edge research on the diverse ways in which culture has responded to the age of environmental crisis. Publishing ambitious and innovative literary ecocriticism that crosses disciplines, national boundaries, and media, books in the series explore and test the challenges of ecocriticism to conventional forms of cultural study.

Titles Available:
Bodies of Water, Astrida Neimanis
Cities and Wetlands, Rod Giblett
Civil Rights and the Environment in African-American Literature, 1895–1941, John Claborn
Climate Change Scepticism, Greg Garrard, George Handley, Axel Goodbody, Stephanie Posthumous
Climate Crisis and the 21st-Century British Novel, Astrid Bracke
Cognitive Ecopoetics, Sharon Lattig

Colonialism, Culture, Whales, Graham Huggan
Contemporary Fiction and Climate Uncertainty, Marco Caracciolo
Digital Vision and Ecological Aesthetic, Lisa FitzGerald
Ecocollapse Fiction and Cultures of Human Extinction, Sarah E. McFarland
Ecocriticism and Italy, Serenella Iovino
Ecospectrality, Laura A. White
Environmental Cultures in Soviet East Europe, Anna Barcz
Fuel, Heidi C. M. Scott
Imagining the Plains of Latin America, Axel Pérez Trujillo Diniz
Literature as Cultural Ecology, Hubert Zapf
The Living World, Samantha Walton
Nerd Ecology, Anthony Lioi
The New Nature Writing, Jos Smith
The New Poetics of Climate Change, Matthew Griffiths
Radical Animism, Jemma Deer
Reading Underwater Wreckage, Killian Quigley
Reclaiming Romanticism, Kate Rigby
Teaching Environmental Writing, Isabel Galleymore
This Contentious Storm, Jennifer Mae Hamilton
The Tree Climbing Cure, Andy Brown
Weathering Shakespeare, Evelyn O'Malley

Forthcoming Titles:
Ecocriticism and Turkey, Meliz Ergin
Anthropocene Realism, John Thieme

Doing Animal Studies with Androids, Aliens, and Ghosts

Defamiliarizing Human-Nonhuman Animal Relationships in Fiction

David P. Rando

BLOOMSBURY ACADEMIC
LONDON • NEW YORK • OXFORD • NEW DELHI • SYDNEY

BLOOMSBURY ACADEMIC
Bloomsbury Publishing Plc
50 Bedford Square, London, WC1B 3DP, UK
1385 Broadway, New York, NY 10018, USA
29 Earlsfort Terrace, Dublin 2, Ireland

BLOOMSBURY, BLOOMSBURY ACADEMIC and the Diana logo are trademarks of
Bloomsbury Publishing Plc

First published in Great Britain 2023
Paperback edition published 2024

Copyright © David P. Rando, 2023, 2025

David P. Rando has asserted his right under the Copyright,
Designs and Patents Act, 1988, to be identified as Author of this work.

For legal purposes the Acknowledgments on p. x constitute an extension
of this copyright page.

Cover design: Burge Agency
Cover image © Shark_749 / Shutterstock

All rights reserved. No part of this publication may be reproduced or transmitted
in any form or by any means, electronic or mechanical, including photocopying,
recording, or any information storage or retrieval system, without prior
permission in writing from the publishers.

Bloomsbury Publishing Plc does not have any control over, or responsibility for, any
third-party websites referred to or in this book. All internet addresses given in this
book were correct at the time of going to press. The author and publisher regret any
inconvenience caused if addresses have changed or sites have ceased to exist, but can
accept no responsibility for any such changes.

A catalogue record for this book is available from the British Library.

A catalog record for this book is available from the Library of Congress.

ISBN: HB: 978-1-3503-5612-2
PB: 978-1-3503-5616-0
ePDF: 978-1-3503-5613-9
eBook: 978-1-3503-5614-6

Series: Environmental Cultures

Typeset by Newgen KnowledgeWorks Pvt. Ltd., Chennai, India

To find out more about our authors and books visit www.bloomsbury.com
and sign up for our newsletters.

In memory of
Corinne Ondine Pache

Contents

Acknowledgments	x
Introduction: Android as Device: Literary Creatures and the De-automatization of Animals	1
1 Nonhuman Hope	21
2 The Artificial Gaze	51
3 Familiar Aliens	83
4 Posthumous Humanity	113
5 Conclusion: Uniqueness, or, Doing Animal Studies One Alien at a Time	149
6 Coda: To the Wild Robots of the Future	169
Bibliography	183
Index	197

Acknowledgments

Material from Chapter 1 previously appeared in *Modern Fiction Studies*. I'm grateful for permission to reprint it here.

Trinity University supported this book with Summer Research Stipends in 2020 and 2022.

Elena Nusloch, Mellon Summer Undergraduate Research Fellow at Trinity University, assisted me while conducting research for Chapter 1. I'm grateful for her meticulous and conscientious help in the summer of 2020.

Ben Doyle and Laura Cope at Bloomsbury and Shyam Sunder at Newgen were once again wonderful to work with.

Laura Brown was my first inspiration in the field of animal studies and remains among my highest models of what a true literary scholar and mentor can be.

I'm grateful for the friendship and support of Ruby Contreras, Kathleen Creedon, Coleen Grissom, Jennifer Henderson, Nicolle Hirschfeld, Tom Jenkins, Ari Lieberman, David Liss, Tim O'Sullivan, Willis Salomon, Claudia Stokes, Stephanie Velasquez, and Elizabeth Wrightman.

I especially want to thank Sam Frederick and Betsy Tontiplaphol for feedback on parts of this book at various stages and for their sustaining friendships.

It is inevitable when writing a book on human-nonhuman animal relationships to reflect on the closest interspecies relationships I've had. I love and remember Buffy, Shadow, and Roddy, and I cherish my time with Nelly, Joey, and Bitty.

This book is dedicated to the memory of Corinne Pache, beloved Homerist and Classical Studies scholar, teacher, and friend.

I'm happy to express my most loving thanks to Shannon Mariotti, without whom this book could not be, and to our son Walter, whose empathy and kindness to creatures human and nonhuman makes us proud.

Introduction:
Android as Device: Literary Creatures and the De-automatization of Animals

This book argues that literary critics in the field of critical animal studies can learn by temporarily directing attention *away* from representations of nonhuman animals in literature.[1] Critical animal studies, in the words of Matthew Calarco, "places [ethico-political issues regarding animals] squarely in the foreground," "is driven by [an] activist orientation," and "contest[s] violence and discrimination against animals."[2] For Carol Gigliotti, critical animal studies equates to "the struggle for compassion and justice."[3] I argue that to refigure, reimagine, and ultimately to liberate nonhuman animals from human instrumentalization it is useful and perhaps even necessary to look at literary representations of emerging creatures such as androids, clones, artificial intelligence (AI), and artificial humans, and imaginary creatures such as vampires, aliens, and ghosts. No longer solely the territory of science fiction, the Gothic, and horror, such creatures increasingly cross literary genres as humans renegotiate and rework our conceptualizations of humanity, animality, and life itself in response to ongoing challenges posed by technology, environmental crises, and alterity. This book seeks to borrow from the strangeness, creativity, and freshness of these emerging and imaginary creatures in contemporary novels, comic book series, and children's books to reconceptualize often intractable views of nonhuman animals. Because these liminal figures confront anthropocentrism, or human-centeredness, in ways that necessarily push against all forms of species dominance, the android, the alien, and the ghost are literary devices that help us to see nonhuman animals afresh and to fruitfully reimagine the terms of our relationships with them.

Readers of this book will find androids that provoke a thorough redefinition and reapportioning of traditional humanist qualities such as hope and uniqueness and offer capacious, more-than-human perspectives on love and intelligence from which to understand and reevaluate animal relationships. They will encounter alien visions that unmask the racist and heteronormative roots of speciesism and expose the madness, self-destructiveness, and futility of insisting upon and maintaining human separateness from nonhuman life. And they will see ghosts and spirits who offer posthumous visions of having-been-human that decenter anthropocentrism and open anthropocosmic possibilities in which humans are no longer at the center but rather *within* the world and *with* other animals.

By availing itself of the rich literary resources of emerging and imaginary figures for the sake of nonhuman animals, this book seeks fresh paths through androids, aliens, and ghosts to better see, understand, and live among nonhuman animals. Study of these figures within a critical animal studies framework opens creative avenues for animal studies and helps to shift the mental landscapes upon which we imagine nonhuman animals. However, instead of concentrating through close reading or quantifying through distant reading, this book searches for the precise focal length at which imaginative and fantastic creatures snap into focus and intersect with nonhuman animal realities and possibilities. They do so not directly, figuratively, symbolically, or allegorically, but rather obliquely, distantly, strangely, and alienly. Indeed, this book avoids reading androids, aliens, and ghosts as literal, figural, symbolic, or allegorical nonhuman animal figures. Moreover, unlike approaches that practice animal studies within the context of genre studies such as science fiction, the Gothic, horror, or the weird, this book focuses on estranging and alienating resonances between the literature of androids, aliens, and ghosts and the realities and experiences of nonhuman animals. Rather than searching for points of identity between imaginary creatures and nonhuman animals, this book prioritizes what Theodor W. Adorno might have called the "nonidentical": moments of illumination in which androids, aliens, and ghosts intersect with nonhuman animals outside of the familiar, comfortable, and comforting containers of genre, metaphor, symbol, and allegory.[4]

Underneath these arguments lies a foundational literary question about the relationship between literature and its objects of representation. I begin, therefore, with an animals approach to a foundational text of modern literary theory, one that has done much to inform our basic sense of what literature is, does, and might do in the future.⁵ Viktor Shklovsky's 1917 essay "Art as Device" understands art as a means of intervening in the human tendency to live habitually or unconsciously and our susceptibility to going through the motions or operating, as it were, on autopilot. Art lives to counter what Shklovsky calls "the automatization process" by which we come merely to recognize things around us but fail to *see* them.⁶ Figuratively, automatization consumes life: "This is how life becomes nothing and disappears. Automatization eats up things, clothes, furniture, your wife and the fear of war" (80). For Shklovsky, a Russian Formalist, the very technique of art is *ostranenie*, a neologism that has been variously translated into English as "defamiliarization," "making strange," "estrangement," "bestrangement," and "enstrangement."⁷ As Shklovsky famously puts it, "art exists in order to give back the sensation of life, in order to make us feel things, in order to make the stone stony" (80).

Shklovsky draws his first two examples of *ostranenie* from Tolstoy, one from Tolstoy's diary and the other from "Strider," a short story written from the perspective of a horse. In the first, Tolstoy registers the experience of dusting his room and then immediately being unable to recall whether he had just dusted his sofa, so routinized and unconscious were his actions.⁸ In the second, Tolstoy presents the human institution of property from Strider's perspective: "Back then I simply could not understand what it meant when they called *me* someone's property. The words '*my* horse' described me, a living horse, and seemed as strange to me as the words 'my land,' 'my air,' 'my water.'"⁹ Nor is this the only example that Shklovsky gives of *ostranenie* that operates through a nonhuman animal figure. In a Russian fairy tale, human sex is estranged through acts of human violence against a bear, a magpie, and a spider.¹⁰ Shklovsky also describes a defamiliarizing Belorussian fairy tale in which "a bear or another animal … fails to recognize a human."¹¹

How should we account for Shklovsky's preoccupation with animal examples in this seminal essay about the very workings of literature? Certainly, they suggest that the human world is made strange when viewed through the eyes of nonhuman animals. They also suggest that human perceptions of animals can become as automatized as our nonperception of the sofas on which we sit, and that literature can estrange them. As Mario Ortiz Robles notes, Strider's "perspective makes *both* humans and horses alike newly 'strange.'"¹² But while it might be as difficult to see nonhuman animals as it is to see furniture to which we have become habituated, overcoming the difficulty of seeing is insufficient. From a critical animal studies perspective, it is crucial not just to *see* nonhuman animals, but also to move entirely outside of human exceptionalist and anthropocentric frames. We need to embrace the radical equivalent of not just *seeing* the sofa but also intervening in perceptions of it *in such a way that the sofa no longer seems like a thing on which to sit.* Or, put another way, it might be to see not only how automatized perception figuratively "eats up" nonhuman animals but also how perceptual consumption can and does end routinely in the literal consumption of animals: as food, raw materials, commodities, and test subjects. The full end of literature's *ostranenie* should be to de-automatize animals in every way.

There are considerable obstacles to such full de-automatization, to say the least, and some of them lurk in Shklovsky's own essay. For one thing, the idea of automatized life and the desire to transcend it have long been deeply enmeshed with human perceptions of nonhuman animals themselves. The question of human artifice and animal automatization are already joined in Descartes. He writes, "It seems reasonable, since art copies nature, and men can make various automata which move without thought, that nature should produce its own automata, much more splendid than artificial ones. These natural automata are the animals."[13] In a viciously circular way, human creatures make thoughtless machines and then remake nonhuman creatures in that mechanical image. In William James, from whom Shklovsky in part derives his sense of perceptual automatization,[14] reflex actions are "machine-like"; while humans and nonhuman animals share reflex actions, "Man is born with a tendency to do more things than he has readymade arrangements for in his nerve-centres. Most of the performances of other animals are automatic."[15]

The sexual functions are seen as the most reflexive, automatic, and unconscious of all. That the preponderance of examples of *ostranenie* that Shklovsky gives are either animal or proper to the erotic or the traditionally "low" or "animalistic" is hardly coincidental, for the idea of sexual automatization is highly soluble with human images of nonhuman animals. James notes, "The sexual act [in birds] is not performed until every condition of circumstance and sentiment is fulfilled, until time, place, and partner are all fit. But in frogs and toads this passion *devolves* on the lower centres. They show consequently a *machine-like* obedience to the present incitement of sense, and an almost total exclusion of the power of choice."[16] James suggests that automatization increases as one "descends" from birds to frogs and toads. James also observes that a male bird with its cerebral hemisphere surgically severed "will coo all day long and show distinct signs of sexual excitement, but his activity is without an object, it is entirely indifferent to him whether the she-bird be there or not."[17]

Animals, then, are often imagined as the very location and emblem of automatized living and perception. James envisions animals on a scale that descends from humans, who while given to certain reflexes and perceptual automatization are yet the least machine-like of animals. Given this hierarchical formulation, one might even say that in Shklovsky's formulation art exists not just "to 'return sensation' to life, to reinvent the world, to experience it anew," as in the words of Svetlana Boym,[18] but also to make the human "humanly," to distance humans from animal perception and experience, jarring us out of our mechanical, degraded, and degrading animalistic existences. Indeed, if as Gary Saul Morson notes there is "a salvationist side of [Russian] Formalism"—"Formalists, too, see art as having profound moral significance. Theirs is an ethic of the avant-garde, of the cultural revolutionary. Lives lived according to habit: 'such lives are as if they had never been.'"[19]—then this salvation must at least in part be seen as art's rescue of the human from the perils, deprivations, and humiliations of automatized animal life. In these terms, Shklovsky's version of *ostranenie* hardly seems like a promising technique for serving those very animals from which literature is implied to liberate us.

Moreover, despite the starring role given to nonhuman animals in his examples, Shklovsky could also be accused of a certain indifference to the object of *ostranenie*. He writes, "Art is a means to live through the making of a thing; what has been made does not matter in art" (80). Shklovsky seems to declare art's autonomy from life. Indeed, Victor Erlich concludes, "That in the [Tolstoy] examples 'making it strange' became a vehicle of social criticism, of the typical Tolstoyan debunking of civilization on behalf of 'nature,' is incidental to [Shklovsky's] argument. He is not concerned here with the ideological implications of the device."[20] Boym persuasively complicates such a view, however; she argues,

Estrangement lays bare the boundaries between art and life but never pretends to abolish or blur them. It does not allow for either a seamless translation of life into art or the wholesale aestheticization of politics. Art is meaningful only when it is *not* entirely in the service of real life or realpolitik and when its strangeness and distinctiveness is preserved. So the device of estrangement can both *define* and *defy* the autonomy of art.[21]

Alexandra Berlina also reasonably notes that the examples that Shklovsky chooses from Tolstoy almost all "[serve] as a critique of society," and that his essay "never explicitly comments on the social function of the examples, but it is Shklovsky who chose them."[22] Nonetheless, Shklovsky does not comment on why the estrangement by or of his nonhuman animal examples might be important or what they might mean. The animals typically serve to estrange some aspect of human thought or behavior, and in this sense Shklovsky's animals are never estranged quite enough. Strider remains at most a device for estranging human behavior and ideology in Shklovsky's essay; the horse never quite appears as a subject in his own right. Even this master of estrangement, then, can fail to see an animal in the literary representation of a horse who defamiliarizes human ownership of animals. And art's ambiguous relationship to the world in Shklovsky's formulation hovers, at best, uncertainly between the aesthetic and the political.

This need not be, however. For instance, precedent for Shklovsky's view of art as *ostranenie* can be found in Romanticism. Taking up Shklovsky's work in 1949, René Wellek and Austin Warren noted, "The criterion of novelty has been very widespread since the Romantic movement. ... Wordsworth and Coleridge were variously, correlatively, working to 'make it strange,' as one sought to give strangeness to the familiar and the other to domesticate the wonderful."[23] In "A Defence of Poetry" (1821), almost a century before Shklovsky's essay, Percy Bysshe Shelley described poetry's role in unveiling and illuminating a world to which we tend to fall asleep:

> But poetry acts in another and diviner manner. It awakens and enlarges the mind itself by rendering it the receptacle of a thousand unapprehended combinations of thought. Poetry lifts the veil from the hidden beauty of the world, and makes familiar objects be as if they were not familiar; it reproduces all that it represents, and the impersonations clothed in its Elysian light stand thenceforward in the minds of those who have once

contemplated them, as memorials of that gentle and exalted content which extends itself over all thoughts and actions with which it coexists.[24]

Chiming with Shklovsky's sense that perception becomes automatized and that art estranges or defamiliarizes what is merely recognized but not really seen, Shelley suggests that the mind needs broadening and awakening, that the things of the world need unveiling, and that poetic representations can impersonate and illuminate these things in an Elysian light that makes them stand forth for special contemplation.

"To a Skylark" perhaps exemplifies Shelley's method of lifting the perceptual veil and making the familiar unfamiliar. Shelley presents his skylark in a cascade of figures that estrange everyday perceptions of the familiar bird. The skylark is like "a cloud of fire,"[25] "an unbodied joy" (15), "a star of Heaven" (18), "a rain of melody" (35), "a Poet hidden" (36), "a high-born maiden" (41), "a glow-worm golden" (46), and "a rose embowered" (51). These figures estrange the skylark; Shelley's language "unbodies" it, denying any easy, automatic, or reflex reduction of the bird to mere body as we saw in James. The images of "a star of Heaven" and "a glow-worm golden" make the skylark flash forth in a way that almost literalizes Shelley's language of Elysian light. Yet these figures still seem to dissatisfy the speaker for failing to capture the bird who "never wert" (2). "What thou art we know not," the admiring and marveling speaker asserts, and then he asks, "What is most like thee?" (31–2). He concludes by appealing directly to the skylark:

> Teach me half the gladness
> That thy brain must know,
> Such harmonious madness
> From my lips would flow
> The world should listen then—as I am listening now. (101–5)

Shelley's speaker pleads to know what the skylark knows. Such a teaching would move his lips to speak "harmonious madness," and this harmonious madness—the potential and perhaps transcendent or Platonic version of Shelley's poem that he has been unable to write without the skylark's knowledge of gladness—would make the world listen to Shelley's harmonious madness just as Shelley listens to the skylark. Such harmonious madness would make the world hear

Shelley's poetry, which would include hearing this poem in which Shelley struggles to present the common skylark in a de-automatized fashion. Although the poetic mediation of harmonious madness would constitute the very perceptual unveiling of the bird, Shelley admits that he falls short of this ideal. In resorting to a catalog of similes, for instance, Shelley inevitably admits into the poem some degree of mechanical repetition and even automatization from which he cannot perhaps entirely escape. Yet even if Shelley's impersonation of the skylark is not quite clothed in Elysian light, the skylark and its hidden beauty yet emerge from the ode at once less familiar and more unveiled. Arguably, this (by Shelley's ambitions) imperfect ode is rather preferable to a harmonious madness that would represent the pure and total convergence of the skylark and the language of poetry. "To a Skylark" does not purport to plumb, to know, or to master the skylark. It makes the skylark stand forth and glow, but leaves it uncolonized by the imagination and with its store of more-than-human knowledge—"What sweet thoughts are thine" (62)—guarded and intact. In Shelley, de-automatization is not an escape from a mechanical, animal-like state but rather an awakening to animal reality, gladness, and mystery.

Unlike Shklovsky, in his prose Shelley makes explicit the ways in which humans perceive nonhuman animals in automatized ways. Shelley makes it possible to link his ideological and figural estrangement of the skylark, as well as his refusal to perceptualize the bird mechanically, with his advocacy and practice of vegetarianism, his refusal to literally consume animals, and his commitment to estranging the automatized practice of meat-eating. In his two pamphlets advocating vegetarianism, "A Vindication of Natural Diet" (1813) and "On the Vegetable System of Diet" (1814–15), Shelley posits that meat-eating is unnatural for humans and causes much human disease. Shelley defamiliarizes and de-automatizes acts of human meat-eating as "habits demonstrably unnatural" and as a "destructive custom."[26] Habit and custom become the very provinces of automatization; unlike James and Shklovsky, Shelley sees habit and custom not only as automatizing, but also as profoundly unnatural. In contrast to habit and custom, for Shelley human "instincts are inimical to bloodshed, and … the food which is not to be eaten without the most intolerable loathing until it is altered by the action of fire and disguised by the addition of condiments, is not the food for which he is adapted by his physical construction."[27] By representing customs and habits as "pernicious"[28] and "perverse"[29] and by aligning them with mechanical and unnatural reflexes, Shelley effectively estranges meat-eating.

In addition to mounting his own arguments, Shelley, like Shklovsky, also practices the technique of *ostranenie* by presenting examples drawn from others. Vegetarian diet advocate John Frank Newton sees the Prometheus myth, in which Prometheus steals fire from the gods and consequently brings human disease and suffering into the world, as allegorical: as Shelley puts it, "How plain a language is spoken by all this.—Prometheus, (who represents the human race) effected some great change in the condition of his nature, and applied fire to culinary purposes; thus inventing an expedient for screening from his disgust the horrors of the shambles. From this moment his vitals were devoured by the vulture of disease."[30] While Shelley's own view of Prometheus, as reflected for example in *Prometheus Unbound*, is far more nuanced than Newton's, here he follows Newton and suggests that the purpose of Prometheus' fire is to occlude the horrors of the shambles, the slaughterhouse. Out of this transgression and the perceptual occlusion that results from it, human illness issues: meat-eating is the vulture that torments and punishes Prometheus endlessly. Shelley's example from Plutarch is even more estranging:

> Let the advocate of animal food, force himself to a decisive experiment on its fitness, and as Plutarch recommends, tear a living lamb with his teeth, and plunging his head into its vitals, slake his thirst with the streaming blood; when fresh from the deed of horror let him revert to the irresistible instincts of nature that would rise in judgment against it, and say, Nature formed me for such work as this. Then, and then only, would he be consistent.[31]

By forcing readers to consider meat-eating in such visceral terms, without the mediation and occlusion of Prometheus' fire, Plutarch estranges meat-eating as almost unthinkable.

Shelley does not just de-automatize human meat-eating; he also emphasizes the suffering of animals bred and killed for human consumption. Referring again to Plutarch, he writes,

> Sows big with young are indeed no longer stamped upon until they die, and sucking pigs roasted alive; but lobsters are slowly boiled [to death] and express by their inarticulate cries the dreadful agony they endure. Chickens are mutilated and imprisoned until they fatten, calves are bled to death

that their flesh may appear white: and a certain horrible process of torture furnishes brawn for the gluttonous repasts with which Christians celebrate the anniversary of the Saviour's birth.[32]

Relatedly, Shelley notes the automatizing and consequently "malevolent and ferocious"[33] effect of animal slaughter on the slaughterers: "Who that is accustomed to the sight of wounds and anguish will scruple to inflict them, when he shall deem it expedient?"[34] Thus accustomed, the slaughterers receive an "admirable apprenticeship to the more wide wasting wickedness of war, in which men are hired to mangle and murder their fellow beings by [the] thousands."[35] But it is not just the slaughterer who becomes inured to killing through custom. Anyone passing automatically or unconsciously by a pasture is affected and perhaps implicated: "The very sight of animals in the fields who are destined to the axe must encourage obduracy if it fails to awaken compassion."[36] Shelley sees the mechanism of custom as a problem of *human* culture rather than of lower animal life, one of whose consequences is a destructive and self-destructive view and use of nonhuman animals. Shelley, then, anticipates Shklovsky's theory of *ostranenie*, but he also combines a more overtly political view of the relationship between art and life with a compassionate commitment to seeing and understanding (within certain limits and without mastery) nonhuman animals in and out of literature.

Compared with Shelley's time, today's nonhuman animals are automatized more profoundly, in every sense. Not only is human perception of nonhuman animals often dulled, unthinking, habitual, obdurate, on autopilot, unconscious, and screened by fire; not only do many still regard nonhuman animals as Cartesian automatons disqualified from moral consideration and from whom human creatures must distinguish ourselves at all costs; but many of these supposedly mechanical animals are also farmed, slaughtered, or otherwise instrumentalized and processed in ways that epitomize the very process of mechanization and automatization. One implicit or explicit premise of many critical animal studies approaches to literature is that literature can intervene in this triple automatization, that it may, in Shklovsky's terms, estrange perceptions of nonhuman animals, and that it may, in Shelley's terms, expose custom as pernicious and awaken compassion for nonhuman animals. Indeed, animal studies of literature powerfully demonstrate literature's capacity to both estrange and alter human perceptions of nonhuman animals. For example,

Kari Weil notes that fiction (along with poetry and philosophy) promotes "an oppositional way of thinking."[37] Her rich poststructuralist readings of nonhuman animal representations in modernists such as Woolf, Kafka, Rilke, Mann, Coetzee, and others help us to "hear those voices surrounding us … [and] to listen to them attentively."[38] Alice Kuzniar examines literary and visual arts that "attempt … to address and repair melancholia: in other words, they rescue the animal made abject from silence and death. … [T]hey attempt to come close to the animal, all while melancholically despairing at not being able to do so."[39] Laura Brown argues that "Literature provides an alternative model" to prevailing views of animals; as opposed to the views rooted in either anthropomorphism or in alterity, the modern literary imagination offers "fantasies that verge toward the dissonant, the unconventional, the aberrant, and the unbounded."[40] Philip Armstrong argues that "the study of fiction has a special role to play" in identifying "the various structures of feeling that characterize human-animal relations during the emergence, zenith and decline of Western modernity."[41] Mario Ortiz Robles argues, "Literature helps us imagine alternatives to the way we live with animals, and animals help us to imagine a new role for literature in a world where our animal future is uncertain."[42] Finally, introducing *The Palgrave Handbook of Animals and Literature*, whose contributors examine medieval to contemporary literature, Susan McHugh, Robert McKay, and John Miller argue for "the special value of animals as literary presences," both as metaphorical and material creatures.[43] These are just a few of many examples that could be adduced of the power, productivity, and potentiality of looking at representations of nonhuman animals in estranging literature.

However, this book responds to a potential insufficiency or limitation in readers' encounters with animal representations in literature. As *ostranenie* is said to make the stone stony, Shklovsky's "Strider" example perhaps returns some horsiness to the horse. But Shklovsky's failure to go beyond just *seeing* the animals in his examples of *ostranenie* suggests that perceptions of nonhuman animals are so automatized that it often takes more than defamiliarizing or estranging animal representations per se to intervene in their figural and literal automatization. For all the demonstrated power of literature's animal representations to evoke oppositional, alternative, dissonant, and restorative thinking, there are reasons to wish that animal studies could find additional resources in literature beyond representations of nonhuman (and human) animals. How else might literature not just make the horse horsey, but also liberate it from all sense of automatization? What other resources does literature possess to help critical animal studies to intervene in perceptions of nonhuman animals in such a way that people do not only see them but are also moved to regard them as ends in themselves rather than means?[44]

This book finds answers to these questions in the literature of emerging and imaginary beings: androids, aliens, and ghosts. Critics are already beginning to look at intersections between animal studies and genres such as science fiction and the Gothic. In *Animal Alterity: Science Fiction and the Question of the Animal*, Sherryl Vint makes a Shklovskian argument for science fiction's relevance to animal studies: "sf literature is a particularly productive site for exercising … sympathetic imagination, striving to put ourselves in the place of the animal other and experience the world from an estranged point of view."[45] Collections such as *Werewolves, Wolves and the Gothic,* and *Gothic Animals: Uncanny Otherness and the Animal With-Out*[46] have examined nonhuman animals in relation to imaginary figures from the Gothic, weird, and horror genres. Such work often focuses on how science fictional and Gothic figures help to question, undermine, or redefine the limits of the human or to contest human exceptionalism.

The book extends these efforts and shifts the emphasis toward questions about how representations of liminal and emergent androids, aliens, and ghosts in recent novels can be seized on by critics purposively, largely outside of the context of genre studies, to help reimagine nonhuman animals and to challenge our ways of seeing, knowing, treating, and indeed, loving them. These liminal, emerging, and plastic species interrelations offer fresh and creative resources for reimagining the ways in which we share the world with nonhuman animals. Emerging beings such as androids and AI put anthropocentric, humanist, and human exceptionalist discourses in flux. As the discourses that surround androids, ghosts, and aliens are opened to disruption and estrangement, these new and fantastic creatures necessarily intervene in the relentless, automatic, automatized, and largely unconscious processing of nonhuman animals.

Chapter 1 introduces and practices reading strategies for critical animal studies that eschew literal, figurative, symbolic, and allegorical mappings of androids and clones as nonhuman animals. In their representations of engineered and artificial life, Kazuo Ishiguro's *Never Let Me Go* and Philip K. Dick's *Do Androids Dream of Electric Sheep?* help to convey and rectify the injustice of denying nonhuman animals hope while demystifying and dereifying human hope as such. Ishiguro's clones and Dick's androids allow readers to experience the hopes of nonhuman creatures without presuming to know the unknowable or to make "the animal" speak. Their novels help to further animal liberation discourses by democratizing the ostensibly human concept of hope, opening new paths of empathy between nonhuman and human animals, and making it harder to accept the instrumentalization of nonhuman animals under anthropocentric capitalism.

Chapter 2 explores challenges to anthropocentrism that are posed by literary representations of vastly intelligent artificial beings on the one hand and of subordinate sexbots on the other. Jeanette Winterson's *Frankissstein*, Richard Powers's *The Overstory*, and Jonathan Luna and Sarah Vaughn's *Alex + Ada* ask readers to imagine ecology, bodies, and love through more resourceful and intelligent brains than our own and to respond seriously and empathetically to thinking and feeling figures whose potentiality is trammeled by human domination and instrumentalization. In overshadowing human intelligence, visions of superior AI erode the basis of human exceptionalism that supports anthropocentrism and prioritizes human over nonhuman perspectives and experiences. Meanwhile, the sexbots who gaze up at humans from the perspective of instrumentalization and domination demand recognition of their desires, experiences, and perspectives and open vistas of humbler, more loving, and more nurturing relationships between human and nonhuman creatures.

Chapter 3 considers what aliens or, more precisely, the sense of a being *as* alien can afford to animal studies. Octavia E. Butler's Gothic alien vampire novel *Fledgling* and Jeff VanderMeer's weird ecology novel *Annihilation* offer representations of extraterrestrial creatures that embody uncanny closeness or "abcanny" (inexorably alien) intimacy. These novels imagine relationships between humans and nonhumans that are at once parasitic and symbiotic, abject and erotic, and enslaving and liberating. They critique the irrationality, racism, and heteronormativity that police the boundaries of speciesism and anthropocentrism by exploring the ways in which the human horror of being integrated with the nonhuman world exists alongside an attraction to forfeiting and capitulating our humanity. These fictions suggest the unacceptable toll taken when humans insist that we are separate and exceptional, and they probe the simultaneous horror and allure of surrendering the boundaries of self and species.

Spirits, souls, and ghosts are creatures of the literary imagination that contest anthropocentrism and animal soullessness by representing the states and perspectives of human posthumousness: the once-human, the having-been-human, and the no-longer-human. In Chapter 4, ghosts broaden the world's compass while offering fresh challenges to the boundaries of life and to existing relationships between nonhuman and human animals. Literary character itself emerges as proto-ghost and fragile nonhuman or not-quite-human creature. As they refigure human and nonhuman capacities, limitations, and vulnerabilities, posthumous spirits in Louise Erdrich's *The Night Watchman*, the souls in George Saunders's *Lincoln in the Bardo*, and the metafictional literary characters in Salman Rushdie's *Quichotte* and J. M. Coetzee's *The Lives of Animals* help to shift readers' perspectives from the anthropocentric to the anthropocosmic, expanding consciousness and compassion while decentering the human.

The Conclusion considers ways of understanding and valuing human and nonhuman uniqueness outside of legal, humanist, exceptionalist, and anthropocentric paradigms. Instead of deriving from heart, spirit, or any other intrinsic or essential characteristic, uniqueness is redefined in terms of relationships: what makes an individual unique is the loving and uniqueness-conferring regard of the other. Ishiguro's *Klara and the Sun* and Ian McEwan's *Machines Like Me* model an android sense of "uniqueness *to*" that avoids the liabilities of humanism on the one side and the anti-humanist indistinguishability of Deleuze and Guattari's "becoming-animal" on the other. Against the background of the universal replaceability of human, nonhuman, and artificial animals, "uniqueness to" is a mechanical and relational form of loving and valuing that grows out of interactions between organic or inorganic creatures. Such an android or alien uniqueness suggests a distinctive animal ethics, one free from humanist essences on the one hand, and liberated from the posthumanist allergy to emotion, particularly love, on the other.

By drawing on Toni Morrison's sense and practice of the "coda" in her fiction, this book ends with a wishful and future-looking Coda on Peter

Brown's children's books, *The Wild Robot* and *The Wild Robot Escapes*. The Coda opens out from private acts of reading to wider social contexts in the form of rupture, mediation, and debate. It looks toward the threshold between text and social practice, especially through young readers, and envisions how the literature of robots might help to disrupt and de-automatize children's perceptions of human and nonhuman animals. Viewed this way, *The Wild Robot* books imagine how androids might teach human children to see, value, and love nonhuman animals better than we, their imperfectly human parents, have so far been able to do.

Notes

1 While this book is primarily motivated by critical animal studies, I take "animal studies" to be a container term for variegated work in fields such as ethology, anthropology, psychology, philosophy, religion, and literary studies, including human-animal studies, critical animal studies, and animality studies. Though stretching back at least to the work of animal rights philosophers Peter Singer (*Animal Liberation*, Updated Edition [New York: HarperCollins, 2009]) and Tom Regan (*The Case for Animal Rights* [Berkeley: University of California Press, 1983]), animal studies has more recently coalesced as a major academic field. Important overviews were published by Margo DeMello (*Animals and Society: An Introduction to Human-Animal Studies* [New York: Columbia University Press, 2012, 2021]) and Paul Waldau (*Animal Studies: An Introduction* [New York: Oxford University Press, 2013]). Major thinkers such as Jacques Derrida (*The Animal That Therefore I Am*, ed. Marie-Louise Mallet, trans. David Wills [New York: Fordham University Press, 2008]) and Donna Haraway (*When Species Meet* [Minneapolis: University of Minnesota Press, 2008]) have made vital philosophical and theoretical contributions to the field. Carol J. Adams (*The Sexual Politics of Meat: A Feminist-Vegetarian Critical Theory* [New York: Bloomsbury, 1990, 2015]) and other eco-feminist scholars have investigated the intertwined oppressions of woman and nonhuman animals under patriarchal capitalism. Critics such as Joshua Bennett (*Being Property Once Myself: Blackness and the End of Man* [Cambridge: Harvard University Press, 2020]) and Zakiyyah Iman Jackson (*Becoming Human: Matter and Meaning in an Antiblack World* [New York: New York University Press, 2020]) have investigated intersections between animal studies and race studies. Cary Wolfe (*What Is Posthumanism?* [Minneapolis: University of Minnesota Press, 2010]) has

connected animal studies to the challenges posed by the posthumanist critique of humanist paradigms. Anat Pick (*Creaturely Poetics: Animality and Vulnerability in Literature and Film* [New York: Columbia University Press, 2011]), Michael Lundblad, ed. (*Animalities: Literary and Cultural Studies Beyond the Human* [Edinburgh: Edinburgh University Press, 2017]), and others have drawn attention to the ways in which the idea of animality functions within constructions of the human.

2 Matthew R. Calarco, *Animal Studies: The Key Concepts* (New York: Routledge, 2021), x.

3 Carol Gigliotti, "The Struggle for Compassion and Justice through Critical Animal Studies," in *The Oxford Handbook of Animal Studies*, ed. Linda Kalof (New York: Oxford University Press, 2017), 190.

4 Susan Buck-Morss succinctly summarizes Adorno's sense of nonidentity this way:

> The whole point of his relentless insistence on negativity was to resist repeating in thought the structures of domination and reification that existed in society, so that instead of reproducing reality, consciousness could be critical, so that reason would recognize its own identity with social reality, on the one hand, and material nature's nonidentity with the categorizing consciousness that passed for rationality, on the other. (Susan Buck-Morss, *The Origin of Negative Dialectics: Theodor W. Adorno, Walter Benjamin, and the Frankfurt Institute* [New York: The Free Press, 1977], 189)

5 Terry Eagleton begins his classic introduction to literary theory by noting of Shklovsky's essay, "If one wanted to put a date on the beginnings of the transformation which has overtaken literary theory in this century, one could do worse than settle on 1917, the year in which the young Russian Formalist Viktor Shklovsky published his pioneering essay 'Art as Device,'" Terry Eagleton, *Literary Theory: An Introduction*, 2nd edition (Minneapolis: University of Minnesota Press, 1996), ix. Similarly, Gary Saul Morson writes, "One could almost say that literary theory has evolved into a series of footnotes to Formalism," Gary Saul Morson, "Introduction," in *Russian Formalist Criticism: Four Essays*, 2nd edition, ed. Lee T. Lemon and Marion J. Reis (Lincoln: University of Nebraska Press, 2012), v.

6 Viktor Shklovsky, "Art as Device," in *Viktor Shklovsky: A Reader*, ed. and trans. Alexandra Berlina (New York: Bloomsbury, 2017), 79. Subsequent references will be given in parentheses in the text.

7 For a discussion of these translations, see Alexandra Berlina, "Part One: Introduction," in *Viktor Shklovsky: A Reader*, ed. and trans. Alexandra Berlina (New York: Bloomsbury, 2017), 53–9.

8 See Shklovsky, 80.

9 Quoted in ibid., 82, emphasis in original.
10 See ibid., 91–2.
11 See ibid., 90–1. In the example that Shklovsky cites, which is not included in prior English translations of the essay, the husband addresses an audience of "devils," making it unclear if the example involves animals or actual devils, which Shklovsky mentions as another variation of the tale.
12 Mario Ortiz Robles, *Literature and Animal Studies* (New York: Routledge, 2016), 49, emphasis in original.
13 René Descartes, "From the Letters of 1646 and 1649," in *The Animals Reader: The Essential and Contemporary Writings*, 2nd edition, ed. Linda Kalof and Amy Fitzgerald (New York: Routledge, 2022), 138.
14 As Caryl Emerson writes, "The Russian Formalists had borrowed the idea of automatized perception from Henri Bergson and from the associationist psychology of William James, but they aestheticized the idea and heightened its dependence on the material world," Caryl Emerson, "Shklovsky's *ostranenie*, Bakhtin's *vnenakhodimost'* (How Distance Serves an Aesthetics of Arousal Differently from an Aesthetics Based on Pain)," *Poetics Today* 26.4 (Winter 2005), 645. In 1890, James writes, "actions originally prompted by conscious intelligence may grow so automatic by dint of habit as to be apparently unconsciously performed," and concludes, "Habit is thus the enormous fly-wheel of society, its most precious conservative agent," William James, *The Principles of Psychology* (Cambridge: Harvard University Press, 1983), 19, 125. On the topic of living as "a conscious automaton," Bergson writes in 1913, "It will be found that the majority of our daily actions are performed in this way and that, owing to the solidification in memory of such and such sensations, feelings, or ideas, impressions from the outside call forth movements on our part which, though conscious and even intelligent, have many points of resemblance with reflex acts," Henri Bergson, *Time and Free Will: An Essay on the Immediate Data of Consciousness*, trans. F. L. Pogson (Mineola: Dover Publications, 2001), 168.
15 James, 19, 118.
16 Ibid., 34, emphasis added.
17 Ibid., 84.
18 Svetlana Boym, "Poetics and Politics of Estrangement: Victor Shklovsky and Hannah Arendt," *Poetics Today* 26.4 (Winter 2005), 586.
19 Morson, xi. "Such lives are as if they had never been" is a phrase from Tolstoy's diary, quoted in "Art as Device" and repeated by Shklovsky for emphasis. See Shklovsky, 80.
20 Victor Erlich, *Russian Formalism: History–Doctrine*, 4th edition (The Hague: Mouton Publishers, 1980), 177.
21 Boym, 587, emphasis in original.

22 Alexandra Berlina, "Translator's Introduction," in *Viktor Shklovsky: A Reader*, ed. and trans. Alexandra Berlina (New York: Bloomsbury, 2017), 25.
23 René Wellek and Austin Warren, *Theory of Literature* (London: Jonathan Cape, 1954), 252–3.
24 Percy Bysshe Shelley, "A Defence of Poetry," in *Shelley's Poetry and Prose*, ed. Donald H. Reiman and Sharon B. Powers (New York: W. W. Norton & Company, 1977), 487.
25 Percy Bysshe Shelley, "To a Skylark," in *Shelley's Poetry and Prose*, ed. Donald H. Reiman and Sharon B. Powers (New York: W. W. Norton & Company, 1977), 226–9, line 8. Subsequent line numbers are given in parentheses in the text.
26 Percy Bysshe Shelley, "The Vegetable System of Diet," in *The Prose Works of Percy Bysshe Shelley, Volume I*, ed. E. B. Murray (New York: Oxford University Press, 1993), 153.
27 Ibid., 152.
28 Ibid., 147.
29 Percy Bysshe Shelley, "A Vindication of Natural Diet," in *The Prose Works of Percy Bysshe Shelley, Volume I*, ed. E. B. Murray (New York: Oxford University Press, 1993), 87.
30 Ibid., 78.
31 Ibid., 80.
32 Shelley, "The Vegetable System of Diet," 152.
33 Ibid., 154.
34 Ibid.
35 Ibid.
36 Ibid., 154–5.
37 Kari Weil, *Thinking Animals: Why Animal Studies Now?* (New York: Columbia University Press, 2012), xix.
38 Ibid., 149.
39 Alice A. Kuzniar, *Melancholia's Dog* (Chicago: University of Chicago Press, 2006), 11.
40 Laura Brown, *Homeless Dogs & Melancholy Apes: Humans and Other Animals in the Modern Literary Imagination* (Ithaca: Cornell University Press, 2010), 2.
41 Philip Armstrong, *What Animals Mean in the Fiction of Modernity* (New York: Routledge, 2008), 4.
42 Ortiz Robles, xi.
43 Susan McHugh, Robert McKay, and John Miller, "Introduction: Towards an Animal-Centred Literary History," in *The Palgrave Handbook of Animals and Literature*, ed. Susan McHugh, Robert McKay, and John Miller (Cham: Palgrave Macmillan, 2021), 2.

44 Here I borrow a Kantian rhetoric as persuasively practiced by Christine Korsgaard. Korsgaard argues that Kant is wrong when he reasons that only humans are ends in themselves whereas animals are means to ends. She writes,

> As rational beings, we need to justify our actions, to think there are reasons for them. That requires us to suppose that some ends are worth pursuing, are absolutely good. Without metaphysical insight into a realm of intrinsic values, all we have to go on is that some things are certainly good-for or bad-for us. That then is the starting point from which we build up our system of values—we take those things to be good or bad absolutely—and in doing that we are taking *ourselves* to be ends in ourselves. But we are not the only beings for whom things can be good or bad; the other animals are no different from us in that respect. So we are committed to regarding all animals as ends in themselves. (Christine M. Korsgaard, *Fellow Creatures: Our Obligations to the Other Animals* (New York: Oxford University Press, 2018), 145, emphasis in original)

45 Sherryl Vint, *Animal Alterity: Science Fiction and the Question of the Animal* (Liverpool: Liverpool University Press, 2010), 15.

46 See Robert McKay and John Miller, eds., *Werewolves, Wolves and the Gothic* (Cardiff: University of Wales Press, 2017) and Ruth Heholt and Melissa Edmundson, eds., *Gothic Animals: Uncanny Otherness and the Animal With-Out* (Cham: Palgrave Macmillan, 2020).

1

Nonhuman Hope

Kazuo Ishiguro's *Never Let Me Go* (2005) and Philip K. Dick's *Do Androids Dream of Electric Sheep?* (1968) depict beings on a spectrum between human and nonhuman animals. Like farmed animals, these beings are produced for the instrumental purpose of serving humans: clones are harvested for organ replacement "donations" in *Never Let Me Go* and androids labor for their "masters" settling Mars in *Do Androids Dream*. Critics have read these novels as commentaries on liminality, trauma, commodification, and the limits of empathy. While the importance of nonhuman animals is frequently noted or analogized in these readings, critics nonetheless tend to ask how these texts question the idea of the human or contest human exceptionalism. I propose instead that Ishiguro and Dick represent clones and androids in ways that challenge conventional literary representations of nonhuman animals and help to further animal rights and liberation discourses by democratizing the ostensibly human concept of hope. To erode the human monopoly on hope and to see our fellow creatures as full not just of life but also of hope would be to open new paths of empathy between human and nonhuman animals and to make it harder to accept the continuing instrumentalization of animals under capitalism.

Since the nineteenth century, authors have codified realist and sentimental conventions for representing animal emotions, including hope.[1] Allegorical representations of animals have an even longer history. These literary modes have had a place in the cause of noticing, respecting, and helping nonhuman animals. The emotional appeal of Anna Sewell's sentimental novel, *Black Beauty* (1877), for instance, prompted legal reforms in Britain concerning the treatment of horses. While this novel had particularly direct effects on legislation, many other realist, sentimental, or allegorical fictions have had subtler but nonetheless substantial effects on readers' hearts and minds.

However, new literary innovations for representing nonhuman animals are also important because they help to overcome readers' culturally conditioned responses to both nonhuman animals and generic conventions themselves. Literature and critical animal studies both need new possibilities for imagining and relating to nonhuman animals.

Science fiction and science fiction-adjacent or hybrid genres represent one rich area of possibility. Critics characterize science fiction as an "ongoing discussion"[2] that is unusually responsive to emerging scientific and technological possibilities. David Seed notes, "It has been a recurring claim among SF writers that they are more and more occupying the position previously occupied by realist fiction and that their narratives are the most engaged, socially relevant, and responsive to the modern technological environment."[3] Sherryl Vint concurs that science fiction "offers an 'everyday' language for thinking about and responding to daily life in twenty-first century."[4] For Vint, science fiction "is a tool for thinking about and intervening in the world."[5] Darko Suvin and Fredric Jameson align science fiction with defamiliarization and potential social-utopian transformation,[6] allowing readers to see what is nearest with fresh eyes and to imagine a radical overhaul of the familiar. In *Animal Alterity*, as we have seen, Vint demonstrates that science fiction is especially suited for rethinking nonhuman animals: "sf literature is a particularly productive site for exercising … sympathetic imagination, striving to put ourselves in the place of the animal other and experience the world from an estranged point of view."[7] *Never Let Me Go* and *Do Androids Dream of Electric Sheep?* offer such estranged perspectives, not by representing nonhuman animals directly but rather through creative indirection. Although neither novel fits comfortably within genre designations,[8] Ishiguro's clones and Dick's androids draw upon science fiction conventions to allow readers to experience the hopes of nonhuman beings while simultaneously circumventing the culturally entrenched barriers and resistances that often limit our ability to notice and imagine the lives of nonhuman animals. These novels cultivate the ability to imagine the experience of nonhuman hope in contexts in which this hope is cruelly and unfairly dashed, and they work to demystify human hope itself.

Ernst Bloch, the twentieth century's primary theorist of hope, claims, "Hope, this expectant counter-emotion against anxiety and fear, *is therefore the most human of all mental feelings and only accessible to men*."[9] Bloch's claim that hope is the "most human" expectant emotion is a human exceptionalist view, one that understands humans as categorically different from and superior to nonhuman animals. Bloch's view is also anthropocentric, seeing the world from a perspective that prioritizes human over nonhuman interests. Bloch's *The Principle of Hope*, which he began writing in the 1930s and published in three volumes in the 1950s, is a work of extraordinary scope and imagination. It constitutes a virtual encyclopedia of the ways that hope manifests in art, praxis, and culture, yet Bloch stubbornly resists anthropomorphism—the attribution of supposedly human emotions to nonhuman animals—especially the anthropomorphism of hope.

More recently, scholars working in the interdisciplinary field of animal studies, including work in ethology, anthropology, psychology, philosophy, religion, literary studies, and more, have challenged the taboo against anthropomorphism in multiple ways. Taking up Darwin's work on evolutionary continuity and animal emotion,[10] scholars are now more likely to regard emotional differences between human and nonhuman animals as matters of degree rather than of kind. For instance, Margo DeMello writes, "Darwin showed that all animals, including humans, share a continuum of mental and emotional capacities."[11] Marc Bekoff sees anthropomorphism as "an evolved perceptual strategy; we've been shaped by natural selection to view animals in this way."[12] From Bekoff's perspective, the strategy of anthropomorphizing nonhuman animals has not yielded illusions about the creatures we live among, but rather reliable information that has helped humans to survive. Lorraine Daston and Gregg Mitman write, "The advent of evolutionary theory, which posits phylogenic continuities between humans and other animals, has made the ban on anthropomorphism difficult to sustain in principle as well as in practice in the life sciences."[13] Scholars have also become wary of "anthropodenial," a term coined by ethologist Frans de Waal to describe the categorical denial that nonhumans share attributes with humans,[14] for such denials distort our vision and inhibit our relations with nonhuman animals. Others, such as Kari Weil, call for strategic or critical anthropomorphism: "[W]e might then want to call an ethical relating to animals (whether in theory or in art) 'critical anthropomorphism' in the sense that we open ourselves to touch and to be touched by others as fellow subjects and may imagine their pain, pleasure, and need in anthropomorphic terms, but stop short of believing that we can know their experience."[15] These critical and ethical impulses toward anthropomorphism and away from anthropodenial suggest how fully the field of animal studies is itself animated by a sense of hope and future. Indeed, Paul Waldau describes one of the tasks of animal studies as "exploring future possibilities."[16]

Yet as much as the field is premised upon evolutionary continuity and animated by hope, scholars avoid hope when describing nonhuman animal cognition and emotions. Those in the sciences favor more emotionally neutral language, such as "future planning" and "delayed gratification," to take de Waal as example,[17] though more recently de Waal has cautiously suggested that monkeys, chimpanzees, dolphins, wolves, elephants, and perhaps farmed animals "may well experience hope."[18] Bekoff describes his extraordinary book *The Emotional Lives of Animals* as "a forward-looking book of hope that stresses that we must be imaginative in our interactions with other animals;"[19] yet while granting animals the capacities for love, gratitude, joy, humor, wonder, embarrassment, grief, sadness, and more, Bekoff discursively reserves hope as something that humans feel and by which they are motivated.

From an evolutionary perspective, the wariness about nonhuman hope in animal studies and the jealousy with which Bloch reserves hope for humans seems counterintuitive: If hope, via Bloch, can be understood as profoundly seeded in human life and experience—and the field of critical animal studies is only one more manifestation of human hope—then it stands to reason that human hope probably enjoys a broad evolutionary basis. The ubiquity of hope that Bloch finds woven into virtually every human practice would suggest that it is not an emergent evolutionary trait but rather a shared inheritance with certain other nonhumans whose experience of and capacity for hope differ from ours in degree rather than in kind.[20]

Subfields that comprise or overlap with animal studies—including human-animal studies, animal rights and animal welfare studies, critical animal studies, ecofeminist studies, animality studies, and posthumanist studies[21]—vary greatly on the position of emotions. Cary Wolfe's Derridean posthumanism is discursively high on rigor and low on emotion: "taking animal studies seriously thus has nothing to do, strictly speaking, with whether or not you like animals."[22] Wolfe's stance has been critiqued by ecofeminist scholars who insist on combining animal studies with emotion and care. Building on Josephine Donovan's 1990 critique of the ways in which Peter Singer's and Tom Regan's animal rights philosophies similarly disavow sentiment and emotionality,[23] Susan Fraiman critiques Wolfe's resistance to and even "panic" in the face of potentially "femininizing associations" such as emotion.[24] Fraiman characterizes the work of Carol J. Adams, Barbara Smuts, and Donna Haraway as open to and ethically engaged with emotion and care, even though they fall into different branches of animal studies. While the posthumanist animal studies that Derrida has inspired seem crucial for any attempt to reconsider hope in relation to human and nonhuman animals—as Wolfe suggests, animal studies should locate, interpret, and challenge not only the animals "'out there,' among the birds and beasts, but 'in here' as well, at the heart of this thing we call human"[25]—it ought to do so without dismissing affectively informed fields of "socially and ethically responsive cultural studies" for supposedly reifying wholesale the human as "knowing subject."[26] Rather than conforming to a single trajectory within animal studies, then, the study of hope in animal studies ought to draw across subfields and branches, following the trail of emotion past critical fractures while also questioning hope's construction and apportionment within the wider constructions of humans, animals, and animality.

From a strategic perspective, if hope could be habitually established as a common possession between human and nonhuman animals, one more thread of the tenuous basis for human discrimination against and exploitation of nonhuman creatures would be cut.[27] One need not subscribe to a capacities-based philosophical view of animal rights, which argues that rights should be extended to certain animals on the basis of how closely their capacities seem to resemble ours,[28] in order to acknowledge that this approach can have pragmatic and tangible effects. If nonhuman animal hope were self-evident to humans, sympathetic humans would generally be less likely to use, abuse, and dominate nonhuman animals. Given well-established evolutionary perspectives, the obstacle to nonhuman hope is not so much scientific but rather conceptual, terminological, philosophical, and indeed, literary. What is needed is a way habitually, imaginatively, and conceptually to grant hope to animals.

However, animal studies scholars understand that there is risk in projecting language and emotions onto nonhuman animals and of thereby supposing that we can fully understand nonhuman experiences. Presuming to know can become its own form of domination. Literature that represents beings who are neither human nor traditionally animal can help precisely here. Because Ishiguro and Dick write about clones and androids rather than about nonhuman animals, their novels can help to imagine and associate hope with nonhuman animals. They do so not by "fall[ing] into the trap of making the subaltern speak,"[29] as Donna Haraway, drawing on Gayatri Spivak's seminal essay, "Does the Subaltern Speak?,"[30] warns scholars against doing, but rather by creating liminal zones between human and nonhuman animals that open imaginative and empathetic spaces in which to explore the hope conditions of dominated nonhumans. These novels fulfill Weil's criteria for critical anthropomorphism: they allow us to touch and be touched by others as fellow subjects, but without presuming that we can finally know the hopes of nonhuman others.[31] These novels convey the injustice of continuing to ignore and deny nonhuman animal hope for instrumental purposes such as breeding, laboring, experimenting, slaughtering, and harvesting. They help us to cultivate a habit of affirming animal hopefulness.

Arm's Length Reading and Habitual Reception

In *Never Let Me Go*, Tommy, above all, is associated with animals. After his early alienation from the other Hailsham "students"—the culture's euphemism for clones—he is "accepted back in the fold again."[32] One student likens Tommy's gesture to "a dog doing a pee" (10). Ruth calls him a "mad animal" (12), and even Kathy acknowledges that something about Tommy made one think, "well, yes, if he's going to be that daft, he deserves what's coming" (9). Kathy echoes Elizabeth Costello in J. M. Coetzee's *The Lives of Animals*: "If I were asked what the general attitude is toward the animals we eat, I would say: contempt. We treat them badly because we despise them: we despise them because they don't fight back."[33] When taunted by the other students, Tommy does not fight back either, but pitches furious and impotent tantrums. Late in the novel, after Tommy and Kathy learn that there are no deferrals for their instrumental fates, Tommy reverts to childhood fury, running into an open field, "raging, shouting, flinging his fists and kicking out." When Tommy returns to the car, Kathy says, "You stink of cow poo" (274).

Tommy is also associated with animals through his drawings. Kathy calls them "imaginary animals" and "fantastic creatures" (178). Tommy draws these animals at The Cottages in a confused and ultimately futile attempt to impress Madame with his creativity in hope of a deferral for Ruth and himself. Although Tommy's drawings fail to prove that he has a soul, his "inhuman art," as Shameem Black argues, "which marries the animal with the automatic, provides an alternative to the destructive visions of soul-based humanity that the novel critiques."[34] Tommy explains his technique: "If you make them tiny, and you have to because the pages are only about this big, then everything changes. It's like they come to life by themselves. Then you have to draw all these different details for them. You have to think about how they'd protect themselves, how they'd reach things" (178). Kathy is skeptical at first and worries that Tommy is only inviting more ridicule. But when she sees the drawings, in the "barn we called the goosehouse" (186), she is startled by their intricacy:

> So I was taken aback at how densely detailed each one was. In fact, it took a moment to see they were animals at all. The first impression was like one you'd get if you took the back off a radio set: tiny canals, weaving tendons, miniature screws and wheels were all drawn with obsessive precision, and only when you held the page away could you see it was some kind of armadillo, say, or a bird. (187)

Kathy may echo readers' own reactions to Ishiguro's characters when she says of Tommy's drawings, "I was becoming genuinely drawn to these fantastical creatures in front of me. For all their busy, metallic features, there was something sweet, even vulnerable about each of them" (188). Tommy's imaginary animals become metacommentary on the manner in which Ishiguro draws the characters themselves: tiny, detailed, self-protecting, striving, and vulnerable. Their minute circuitry aligns them with forms of technological reproduction and cloning such as cassette tapes and radios. Strange mixtures of repeatable and replaceable circuitry and unique individuality, Tommy's creatures center the novel's concerns about humans and nonhumans, reproduction and repeatability, and striving and vulnerability.

As with Tommy's drawings, however, we can recognize the students as akin to nonhuman animals "only when you held the page away" and break off from the minutiae of their circuitry. This is to undertake something quite different from conventional reading practices: neither the concentration of close reading nor the computation of distant reading, it is reading at a middle distance, reception at arm's length. Call it presbyopic reading: as in middle age, the object only comes into focus when held a certain distance away.

Never Let Me Go models other innovative forms of reception as well. For example, the Hailsham students listen to music with unusual but surprisingly effective ingenuity:

> The craze was for several people to sit on the grass around a single Walkman, passing the headset around. Okay, it sounds a stupid way to listen to music, but it created a really good feeling. You listened for maybe twenty seconds, took off the headset, passed it on. After a while, provided you kept the same tape going over and over, it was surprising how close it was to having heard all of it by yourself. (103)

These, too, become instructions for alternate reading strategies. To let the story play over and over as we tune in and out or to hold the book away from ourselves until something snaps into focus is to read the novel neither as a literal story about clones nor as an allegorical story about animals. In defiance of traditional hermeneutics that call for concentration on the object (as demanded by sentimentalism, realism, and, especially as theorized by Adorno, modernism), we ought not to concentrate on the students or interpret them as nonhuman animals. Instead, aligned with the technologies of cloning and reproducibility as Walter Benjamin theorized them, we receive the students as nonhuman animals in distraction, at a certain distance removed from figuration, allegory, and genre codes. Benjamin writes:

> Distraction and concentration form an antithesis which may be formulated as follows. A person who concentrates before a work of art is absorbed by it; he enters into the work, just as, according to legend, a Chinese painter entered his completed painting while beholding it. By contrast, the distracted masses absorb the work of art into themselves. Their waves lap around it; they encompass it with their tide.[35]

To employ Benjamin's terms of art reception, we might say that what most of us believe about animals is less the result of deep reflection and concentration, such as when we absorb (or are absorbed by) a painting in a museum, and more the result of repetition and habituation, as we dwell in architecture.[36] Rather than presenting clones in ways that claim special insight into nonhuman animal experiences, *Never Let Me Go* builds architectures of artificial life that help to disrupt older and more intractable conceptualizations and acclimate readers to new habits of thought about nonhuman creatures. Artificial creatures of this kind offer opportunities for cultivating creative and imaginative habits that are pro-animal and yet respect difference and the impossibility of knowing the vast range of nonhuman animal minds and experiences with certainty or finality. Indeed, *Never Let Me Go* cannot be assimilated into realist, sentimental, or modernist modes; nor can it persist as abstract or intellectual allegory. By situating readers in the oblique space between the literal and the allegorical, and by allowing the matter of identity to remain permanently unsettled between concentration and distraction, the novel allows readers to imagine nonhuman hope in ways that resist the conventionalized forms of representing animal hope.

For Benjamin, reception in distraction is especially valuable at historical junctures when the new cannot be accessed directly through concentration but only by gradual habituation and acclimation to the emergent: "*For the tasks which face the human apparatus of perception at historical turning points cannot be performed solely by optical means—that is, by way of contemplation. They are mastered gradually—taking their cue from tactile reception—through habit.*"[37] *Never Let Me Go* works in our transitional moment of thinking about nonhuman animals: The novel's vision of nonhuman hope must affect and wash over readers until we begin to form new perceptual habits.

This model of reading and reception relies on habit rather than concentration. Artificial beings in fiction ought not to be concentrated on or scrutinized as veiled, oblique, or allegorical nonhuman animals. Though they do not purport to illuminate nonhuman animal experiences, by accustoming readers to artificial beings these texts offer new subject positions and perspectives that reflect on nonhuman animals indirectly. As we become accustomed to new ways of thinking about artificial life, we can transfer these new patterns and ideas to our thinking about nonhuman animals. The habitual reading model is fitting because, despite being powerfully reinforced by Western philosophy and religions and naturalized through government and capitalist institutions, human attitudes toward other animals have been shaped less by concentration and intellection than by repetition and habit.

The following sections examine how Ishiguro's hopeful clones and Dick's hopeful androids might be read as forms of critical anthropomorphism, as compatible with being touched by the hope of nonhuman others but without the distorting and resistance-provoking presumption that we can finally know the unknowable in nonhuman others. This mode of reception helps readers to circumvent the distorting tendency to allegorize clones and androids into nonhuman animals, even as these liminal figures help readers to overcome the problems of identification and ventriloquism associated with realist and sentimental animal tales.

Clones

Critics of *Never Let Me Go* have illuminated the novel's inhuman or nonhuman challenges to conventional formulations of empathy and humanity and have established *Never Let Me Go* as a novel adept at challenging and overcoming barriers within and surrounding the human.[38] This section takes the critical discourse of barriers to empathy and humanity in *Never Let Me Go* in an unexplored direction. Examining nonhuman animal hope in the context of Ishiguro's clones, it articulates questions about who hopes and where hope resides in the novel. By experiencing hope while yet resisting human and nonhuman animal categorization, Ishiguro's liminal clones effectively liberate hope from human clutches. Their ruthlessly crushed hopes not only interrogate the nature and limits of human empathy and identification but also dramatize hope in the process of breaking off from the human. By allowing readers to be challenged and moved by nonhuman hope, *Never Let Me Go* makes hope available to nonhuman animals in affective and conceptual forms that circumvent anthropomorphic projection, presumption, ventriloquism, and mastery.

Because the Hailsham students do not enjoy full humanity they are not the pawns of fate and destiny in the way that traditional tragic heroes are, nor does reading about their dashed hopes quite align with tragedy's supposed effects of emotional catharsis through pity and fear, however strong an emotional response Ishiguro's story may elicit. It is utility rather than individual or communal destiny that defines their futures. Nor do the students fit neatly into the role of dehumanized people subject to the cruel power and uses of other humans, as in certain representations of war, enslavement, and genocide. The students' other-than-human status keeps them outside of the genres of dehumanization and resists conventional emotional and intellectual responses to them.

But if Ishiguro's students do not enjoy access to full humanity, neither do they enjoy full nonhumanity. They are too human to fall neatly within the equally well-established conventions for representing nonhuman animals. For instance, they cannot be read as talking horses, as in Sewell's sentimental *Black Beauty* or in Leo Tolstoy's realist "Strider." In sentimental and realist modes, respectively, Sewell and Tolstoy depict their horses' lives of cruel utility. Sewell's Ginger, an abused horse, delivers a sentimental speech shortly before her death:

> It's no use; men are strongest, and if they are cruel and have no feeling, there is nothing that we can do, but just bear it, bear it on and on to the end. I wish the end was come, I wish I was dead. I have seen dead horses, and I am sure they do not suffer pain; I wish I may drop down dead at my work, and not be sent off to the knacker's.[39]

Tolstoy renders in realist style Strider's fatal visit from the knacker:

> "They're treating me; of course; they're going to cure me," he thought. "Let them!" Indeed, he felt them do something to his throat. It hurt, and he shuddered and kicked out with one leg, but he restrained himself and waited to see what else would happen. What happened next was that he felt something liquid running in a thick stream down his neck and chest. He heaved a deep sigh. Then he felt much better.[40]

While Ishiguro draws upon both sentiment and realism at different times, Tolstoy's and Sewell's modes of nonhuman animal representation nonetheless align as poorly with *Never Let Me Go* as tragedy and the genres of dehumanization do.

Instead, the Hailsham students fall between categories and thus between forms of representation. Instead of relying on such conventions, the pathos of the Hailsham students derives from the novel's carefully represented dialectics of hope and utility in an other-than-human context, while simultaneously making it difficult to see the students as traditional nonhuman animals. For instance, the compassionate Miss Lucy admits to the children,

> None of you will go to America, none of you will be film stars. And none of you will be working in supermarkets as I heard some of you planning the other day. Your lives are set out for you. You'll become adults, then before you're old, before you're even middle-aged, you'll start to donate your vital organs. That's what each of you was created to do. (81)

Differing from Ginger's sentiment and Strider's realism, both of which seem calculated to affect readers viscerally, Miss Lucy's tone is flatly unvisceral even when her topic is evisceration. Not only are exotic hopes of being film stars out of the question for the students, but so are more mundane ambitions such as working in a supermarket or, as Ruth later fantasizes, in an office. Even the generally wishful expectation of aging is dashed by the students' ironclad futures.

And yet Hailsham students maintain their hopes in the face of certain instrumentalization. The resiliency of their hope is part of the pathos of their lives. Miss Lucy tells them: "If you're going to have decent lives, then you've got to know and know properly" (81). But the students' ability to "know and know properly" is limited not only by their careful Hailsham indoctrination: neurosis, willful "not-knowing," and "improperly knowing" also perpetuate their hopes. Childhood at Hailsham revolves around preserving illusions in the face of encroaching realities, as exemplified by Ruth's secret guard for Miss Geraldine. Even without evidence that Miss Geraldine was threatened and needed protecting, "we each played our part in preserving the fantasy" (52). When the students reach adolescence and are more directly confronted with the truths of their existences, they manage this knowledge neurotically through jokes: "We still didn't discuss the donations and all that went with them. ... But it became something we made jokes about, in much the way we joked about sex" (84). Even at The Cottages, the older students who have become carers, while not "actual taboo" (132) subjects, are rarely mentioned.

Although the novel makes a full identification of the students with nonhuman animals impossible, *Never Let Me Go* plays extensively on human identity-based discourses about nonhumans. Identity-based approaches, as defined by Matthew Calarco, regard nonhuman animals according to the relative degree to which they possess traits and abilities that have traditionally been considered human. Philosophers such as Aristotle, Descartes, and Kant have denied rights, personhood, and protections to nonhuman animals based on their perceived lack of "ethically relevant" traits or on their supposed dissimilarity from human animals. Darwinian evolutionary theory calls into question the categorical distinctions that are common in the philosophical tradition by demonstrating continuity rather than difference. Both utilitarian and rights-based pro-animal ethical approaches emerge from this understanding. Nonetheless, as Calarco writes, "when animal ethicists locate … quintessential human capacities (say, intentionality or subjectivity) among animals and build an ethics based on that shared identity, they are not displacing anthropocentrism but are instead offering another iteration of it."[41] The search for the human in the nonhuman is itself an anthropocentric enterprise, even when it is conducted for the welfare or rights of nonhuman animals.

Never Let Me Go intervenes here through its discourse about relative student capacities, particularly through their capacities for creativity, love, and hope. The students largely tie their hopes to questions of human capacities; they see the basis of their hope as hinging on the extent to which they can evince these capacities. Indeed, Madame and Miss Emily had hoped that Hailsham would demonstrate to the world that students have souls: "We took away your art because we thought that it would reveal your souls. Or to put it more finely, we did it to prove you had souls at all" (260). While students elsewhere were "reared in deplorable conditions," Hailsham's free-range model set out to show "the world that if students were reared in humane, cultivated environments, it was possible for them to grow to be as sensitive and intelligent as any ordinary human being" (261). However, this identity-based approach to improving the way that students are treated loses out in the novel to the premium that humans put on anthropocentric utility.

While Madame and Miss Emily see artistic creativity as possible evidence of a soul, the students regard creativity as evidence that they can truly love. While Hailsham makes its argument through an implicitly empiricist/realist mode—because students are creative, therefore they have souls—the students see their appeal to loving in an implicitly sentimental mode. Chrissie hears the rumor that if Hailsham students "could prove they were properly in love" (153), they could receive a three-year deferral from becoming carers. Kathy, reflecting on why Madame might have cried when she witnessed Kathy swaying to music and clutching her pillow, supposes that Madame had been emotionally moved by Kathy's demonstrated capacity to love: "She'd have supposed I was holding a lover in my arms. ... she'd be really moved stumbling on a scene like that" (177). Kathy learns much later that Madame had not connected the scene to love at all and had read Kathy quite differently. For Madame, Kathy was a little girl holding "the old kind world" to her breast in the face of the "hard, cruel world" that was "coming rapidly" (272). Madame says, "I saw something else. ... It wasn't really you, what you were doing, I know that" (272). Kathy imagined that Madame had been moved by sentiment, but Madame had in truth been moved by Kathy as allegorical: as "something else," as an other-speaking figure.

Through the students' hopes about being creative and having the capacity to love, *Never Let Me Go* dramatizes what nonhuman hope might look like and how it might have a persuasive force. If it is to be persuasive, *Never Let Me Go* must be kept distinct from allegory on the one hand and from sentimentalism and realism on the other. Reading in the distracted and habituating mode defined by Benjamin and by the students' own habits of art reception, we see what nonhuman hope looks like when it falls outside of generic conventions and eludes traditional reading practices. Miss Emily notes that Kathy and Tommy practice a serious form of hope, and not a harmless ("What harm is there?") "little fantasy" (258). She reflects, "You've *hoped* carefully. For students like you, I do feel regret. It gives me no pleasure at all to disappoint you. But there it is" (258, emphasis in original). A non-fantastic, careful hope, it must nonetheless be dashed.

As we have seen, Tommy's immediate response to dashed hope is one of blind rage in an open cow field. But it is not so much in this immediate emotional venting that the novel's sting lies; the sting lies in the narrating present of the novel, when Kathy's hope has shifted orientation from an unknown future to the fixed past. The most unexpected and disturbing process *Never Let Me Go* represents is the way in which thwarted hope gets rerouted into memory.[42] The novel dramatizes the wrenching mental processes by which the students are forced from hope into memory, with the result that compensatory anamnesis and rumination replace a wishful sense of futurity. Kathy says, "I was never the sort of kid who brooded over things for hours on end. I've got that way a bit these days, but that's the work I do and the long hours of quiet when I'm driving across these empty fields" (58). The novel's narrating clone dwells in memory and nostalgia at the age of human young adulthood, a time typically devoted to building an adult life and to looking ahead with hope. Kathy's perverse shift from hopeful expectation to elegiac memory so badly distorts human life that the pain of dashed hope is dramatized in the very telling of the tale.

Having established hope as central to the students' hopeless lives, *Never Let Me Go* converts all hope into nostalgia. For Kathy, the nostalgic mode seems compensatory and perhaps comforting, but for readers it is more likely to be experienced with a sense of horror. But it is not quite the horror that comes from seeing human hope cruelly dashed nor the horror of seeing anthropomorphized hope thwarted as in sentimental or realist modes for representing nonhuman animals. Rather, the horror of *Never Let Me Go* emerges from the gap between human and nonhuman hope, precisely from witnessing a palpable, undeniable, but inhuman hope come to nothing at the hands of human exceptionalism, anthropocentrism, and instrumentalization. Neither traditionally human nor nonhuman animals, the novel's clones critically anthropomorphize hope in ways that liberate it from sentimental, realist, and allegorical representations. Ishiguro's novel is a far-reaching act of imagination that dislocates human hope without letting it settle comfortably elsewhere. By permanently unsettling hope in this way, *Never Let Me Go* makes hope available to new definitions, new directions, and new habits. It allows readers to imagine nonhuman hope, to feel it viscerally, in relation to nonhuman animals in ways that open paths of empathy precisely because they are neither sentimental, realist, nor allegorical.

Androids

Critics of Philip K. Dick's *Do Androids Dream of Electric Sheep?* often see the novel as opening, displacing, or radically transforming the human through its intersections with nonhuman animals and androids. By reading the novel as a critique of capitalist exploitation, instrumental rationality, speciesism, and anthropocentrism, critics have positioned Dick's androids and nonhuman animals to challenge and reimagine the human in non-anthropocentric, postcapitalist, and posthuman forms.[43] However, Dick's android challenge to the human has unexplored implications for seeing nonhuman animals as well. This section examines the consequences of Dick's android representations on conceptualizations of nonhuman animals, particularly in the field of hope.

Like the hopes of Ishiguro's clones, android hope in Dick dislocates hope from humans. In the process, it challenges the presumption that humans possess hope as such, in its undivided fullness, and simultaneously liberates hope in a way that potentially enfranchises nonhuman creatures within the privileged construct of hope.

As in *Never Let Me Go,* in *Do Androids Dream* humans discriminate against androids on the basis of capacities. Androids resemble humans in virtually every way, but for humans, what decisively distinguishes androids is their inability to empathize. Hope is central to android experience, but the way in which Dick represents empathy crucially contextualizes android hope. Since the advent of androids, a religion premised upon the capacity to empathize has emerged. "An android, no matter how gifted as to pure intellectual capacity, could make no sense out of the fusion which took place routinely among the followers of Mercerism."[44] Whatever else Mercerism might be, it is also a spiritual and ideological development that allows humans to retain a sense of exception as android technology throws the category of the human into crisis. Dick reflects the tendency for humans to take a capacities-based approach to differentiating themselves from nonhuman animals. As de Waal writes, "Keeping humans in their preferred spot on that absurd scale of the ancient Greeks has led to an obsession with semantics, definitions, and redefinitions, and—let's face it—the moving of goalposts."[45] Vexing this tendency, however, each new generation of androids in *Do Androids Dream* is more sophisticated, intelligent, and difficult to differentiate.

As in *Never Let Me Go* the tenuous sense of human distinctiveness is supposed to justify the instrumental use and killing of nonhumans. Imputed lack of empathy licenses humans to treat androids as Cartesian animal-machines, not unlike electric sheep. Rachael Rosen compares her fellow androids to ants: "Chitinous reflex-machines who aren't really alive" (178). She says, "We are machines, stamped out like bottle caps. It's an illusion that I—I personally—really exist; I'm just representative of a type" (173). Bounty hunters like Rick Deckard hunt and kill androids without having to empathize with their victims or question the morality of killing. As in *Never Let Me Go* killing is euphemized: Hailsham students "complete"; illegal "andys" are "retired."

However, the novel is practically anarchic in the way in which it destabilizes empathy and our sense of who possesses it. In spite of their reputed coldness, androids can form friendships with and care about each other. Led by Roy Baty, the escaped androids have experimented with "mind-fusing drugs … to promote in androids a group experience similar to that of Mercerism" (169–70). The eight escaped androids empathize with each other and feel pain when their friends are killed. When Deckard kills Irmgard, "Roy Baty … let out a cry of anguish" (205). This response leads Deckard to recognize an equivalency: " 'Okay, you loved her,' Rick said. 'And I loved Rachael' " (205).

Although the mechanical Cartesian view should preclude viewing androids empathetically, the novel also presents evidence of human empathy for androids. Deckard's wife Iran calls them "poor andys" (4), and Deckard begins to empathize with certain female androids. He even begins to love Rachael Rosen, a development that threatens his work as a bounty hunter. However, the novel shows that the desire not to empathize can powerfully forestall empathy. Deckard successfully battles his empathetic response in order to continue killing androids. Ironically, it is while Rick peers into the empathy box and experiences fusion that Mercer tells him, "Go and do your task, even though you know it is wrong" (164). The imperative to kill androids is so powerful that it remains entrenched even after it is grasped as wrong. No matter how personally distasteful it becomes for Rick to retire androids, his work remains ideologically and instrumentally essential. Rick sees his particular form of suffering as worse than Mercer's endless torment because Rick is "required to violate his own identity" (164).

If humans in the novel identify themselves on the basis of empathy, then to act unempathetically is also to question the basic assumptions that underwrite human identity. What is especially destabilizing about Dick's novel, and what makes it a crucial counterpart for *Never Let Me Go*, is that it not only raises the possibility that nonhumans possess capacities denied to them, but also assails the well-entrenched assumptions that humans possess in their plentitude the capacities upon which we often pride and differentiate ourselves. Dick mirrors Derrida's deconstructive approach to humans and animals, which consists of questioning not only what humans deny to nonhuman animals, but also the cherished abilities that humans attribute to themselves. Derrida writes:

> It is not just a matter of asking whether one has the right to refuse the animal such and such a power (speech, reason, experience of death, mourning, culture, institutions, technics, clothing, lying, pretense of pretense, covering of tracks, gift, laughter, crying, respect, etc.—the list is necessarily without limit, and the most powerful philosophical tradition in which we live has refused the "animal" all of that). It also means asking whether what calls itself human has the right rigorously to attribute to man, which means therefore to attribute to himself, what he refuses the animal, and whether he can ever possess the pure, rigorous, indivisible concept, as such, of that attribution.[46]

Derrida's method is to scrutinize what philosophers such as Aristotle, Descartes, Kant, Heidegger, Levinas, and Lacan have denied to nonhuman animals and then to deconstruct that which they are so sure that humans do possess. If for Lacan animals lack the ability to "cover their tracks," then Derrida demonstrates that even within Lacan's own writing, humans are always already no more able to erase their own traces than nonhuman animals are.[47] If for Heidegger, animals lack relation to the "as such," then Derrida shows how within Heidegger's opposition of the "as such" and the "not as such" there are only endless differences. He questions whether "man, the human itself, has the 'as such,'" and suggests that human-nonhuman animal differences "are not those between 'as such' and 'not as such.'"[48] In the same spirit, Dick's novel questions the extent to which humans can possess the pure, rigorous, indivisible capacity for empathy. By what right do Deckard and other humans call themselves empathetic? As his fusion experience demonstrates, Deckard must perform acrobatic rationalizations in order to have his empathy and kill androids, too.

The latest test used to identify androids, the Voigt-Kampff Empathy Test, discriminates according to the ability to empathize with nonhuman animals. Test takers are meant to react physiologically when the test administrator describes bearskin rugs, lobsters boiled alive, and wall-mounted deer heads. However, Rick's own response to seeing or hearing about nonhuman animals is immediately to consult "his creased, much-studied copy of Sidney's Animal & Fowl Catalogue" (9) to ascertain its exchange value. For Rick, animals are not to be empathized with but possessed; owning animals assuages social pressures and signals prestige. As Vint says, "If empathy were as important to the experience of human culture as it is to the ideology of the human/android boundary, then owning a real animal should be a social relationship, not a commodity one."⁴⁹ Instead, as animals have become rarer, they generally seem more commodified than empathized with. According to supply and demand, animals are simply too scarce and expensive any longer to abuse, kill, or eat. Given this instrumentalized human perspective, Megan E. Cannella sees animals as "the guardians of unmediated emotion" in the novel.⁵⁰

After Rick discovers that he has begun to empathize with certain androids, he becomes even more desperate to own an animal. Buying a goat helps him to cope emotionally with his job. "I've begun to empathize with androids," he tells Iran. "That's why I bought the goat. I never felt like that before. Maybe it could be a depression, like you get. I can understand now how you suffer when you are depressed" (161). Rick fixates on exchange value to the very last, when he finds what appears to be a living toad. First, he "swiftly dragged out his much-creased Sidney's" (217), and then, finding that toads are extinct and knowing that an extinct animal can bring a "reward running into millions of dollars" (218), Rick thinks, "I need a box" (217). A further irony about Deckard's mercenary view of animals is that the toad is the "critter most precious to Wilbur Mercer" (217), the paragon of fusion and empathy. The empathetic basis for discriminating between human and android is belied by the persistent and culturally entrenched human tendency to coldly calculate about animals' exchange value.

Androids expose the lie of human empathy as well. Irmgard Baty says, "Without the Mercer experience we just have your word that you feel this empathy business, this shared, group thing" (193). Or, as Buster Friendly puts it, more bluntly, "*Mercerism is a swindle!*" (193, emphasis in original). Those with the strongest "shared, group thing" in the novel are the escaped androids. Indeed, humans and androids both need a supplement to feel empathy. The androids need mind-altering drugs, but the humans, who pride themselves on the innate capacity for empathy as such, nonetheless require the prosthesis of an empathy box that displays an actor against a "backdrop of sky and daytime moon" (190). The evil "Killers" in Mercerite theology turn out not only to be the androids, as Rick supposes (30), but the humans as well. Each is Mercer and Killer; each can love and kill coldly at the same time. The android Pris coldly snips off four of a spider's legs with scissors, but Deckard picks off eight androids, one for every leg of a spider. Like Derrida, Dick shows that when it comes to the qualities that humans generously assign to themselves and parsimoniously withhold from others, the sky is often painted.

Within this context of destabilized empathy, the novel suggests that nonhuman hope is widespread. All androids who escape to Earth act out of hope for freedom, and this hope is so widely seeded that escaped androids support a worldwide network of bounty hunters. As Garland tells Rick about escaping from Mars, "It's a chance anyway, breaking free and coming here to Earth, where we're not even considered animals" (113). "Do androids dream? Rick asked himself. Evidently; that's why they occasionally kill their employers and flee here. A better life, without servitude" (169).

Dreams of a better life are the essence of hope and utopia. Bloch's original title for *The Principle of Hope* was *Dreams of a Better Life*,[51] and he observes, "How richly people have always dreamed of this, dreamed of the better life that might be possible."[52] The plot of *Do Androids Dream* is shaped by Roy Baty's dreams of a better life. Baty radically proposes "the sacredness of so-called android 'life'" (169), a utopian notion if there ever were one. The popularity of "pre-colonial fiction" among Martians, and in Baty's cell particularly, also manifests the utopian impulse in the androids. As Pris says of these "stories written before space travel but about space travel" (139), "You can imagine what it might have been like, What Mars *ought* to be like" (140, emphasis in original). The title of Dick's novel poses the question of android hope, and it turns out that rather than electric sheep, which is more or less what Deckard shallowly dreams about, androids dream of freedom.

Do Androids Dream takes a different route from *Never Let Me Go* to imagining nonhuman hope. Dick is just as likely to question the foundation and character of human hope as he is to represent hope in androids. Not only can mechanical androids hope, but just as in the case of human empathy, there turns out to be something mechanical and impoverished about human hope as well. Isidore tells Pris that an empathy box "is the most personal possession you have! It's an extension of your body; it's the way you touch other humans, it's the way you stop being alone" (62). When Iran wants to snap out of her feelings of despair, she programs "481" into her Penfield mood organ: "Awareness of the manifold possibilities open to me in the future; new hope that—" (6). Devilishly, Dick demonstrates that human hope—dreams of a better life, the sense of a future, the openness of possibility—sometimes requires mechanical supplementation. This erodes the prejudice, reflected by Bloch, that hope is innately and uniquely human, but it does so from the opposite direction of *Never Let Me Go*. Because mechanical androids, too, dream of a better world, hope must be demystified and dereified as essentially human. The differences between humans and androids are not those between hope and non-hope. By questioning at once human exceptionalist definitions of hope and the human possession of hope as such, *Do Androids Dream of Electric Sheep?* suggests rethinking relationships of hope across the spectrums of organic-mechanical, human-nonhuman, and human-animal. The novel opens the door to creatively redistributing hope across species. If hope, the emotion that fuels utopian thinking, is not "only accessible" to humans as Bloch has it, then we may (have to) locate the utopian impulse not only elsewhere than in the human, but virtually everywhere.

Nonhuman Hope

Drawing on the defamiliarizing and transformative possibilities of science fiction, but unassimilable to that or any genre, Ishiguro's and Dick's novels circumvent conventional conceptions and representations of nonhuman animal hope. Because these novels are not directly about nonhuman animals, they can avoid representing nonhuman hope in realist, sentimental, and allegorical modes. For all of their benefit to animal studies, these traditional modes can still nonetheless reflect and maintain considerable resistances and barriers to rethinking nonhuman animal hope. By looking at nonhuman animals through the minute circuitry of clones and androids, these novels help readers imaginatively and habitually to loosen the jealous human grip on hope. They allow hope to pass more readily across species. To demystify human hope as mechanically reflexive or technologically mediated, as Dick does, is similarly to erode the basis for denying nonhuman animals "authentic" hope.

To attribute hope—rather than simply "future-planning" or "delayed gratification"—to nonhumans is to make it harder to accept the inhumane and brutal instrumental treatment of thinking and feeling fellow beings under current systems of production. The form and aim of reading proposed here may seem like wishful thinking, empty hope, and utopian daydreaming. However, Bloch shows how daydreams are not only, as Freud would have it,[53] idle compensatory fantasies: "Another part [of the daydream] is provocative, is not content just to accept the bad which exists, does not accept renunciation. This other part has hoping at its core, and is teachable."[54] Further, he writes, "The daydream can furnish inspirations which do not require interpreting, but working out, it builds castles in the air as blueprints too, and not always just fictitious ones."[55] Ishiguro and Dick present provocations with hoping at their core. They are not content with the bad that exists, nor, they tell us, should we be. Besides interpreting these novels through acts of critical concentration, we ought also to let them inspire daydreams, idle and compensatory on the one hand, but on the other hand, possible blueprints for a better world, the world that remakes the divisions between and among all creatures.

Never Let Me Go and *Do Androids Dream of Electric Sheep?* are dystopian novels that picture nightmarish parallel histories or futures. However, they are also utopian novels because, in Jameson's terms, they allow us to "think the break"[56] itself or to imagine the status quo disrupted. Ishiguro and Dick represent nonhuman hope in unusually challenging and genre-defying ways. Their novels confront the discourse of hope in ways that cut across accustomed habits and conventions for representing nonhuman animals. They can help to redistribute our precious but most prejudicially parceled-out hope. What this redistributed hope might look like and result in is less the business of completed utopian pictures and more the fuel for imagining innovative paths toward anthropocosmic nonhuman-human animal relationships. This potentiality reminds us that the discourse of nonhuman animal capacities is finally inseparable from the question of fiction's capacities. Debates about animal capacities are also literary debates about what fiction can do to challenge and change readers' minds and hearts, and about what readers can do to strategically harness fiction's affordances. Read through acts of deliberate critical anthropomorphism, Ishiguro's and Dick's novels about clones and androids help to enfranchise nonhuman animals habitually into the privilege, estate, and dignity of hope. In this way, the clones and androids of fiction might help to make a better life for nonhuman animals than humans alone have so far been capable of doing.

Notes

1 I follow Ernst Bloch in treating hope as an emotion, though, as Marianne DeKoven notes, hope is not always considered an affect. Nevertheless, DeKoven writes: "I would argue that, although hope is not, strictly speaking, an affect, it represents an orientation toward the future that encompasses continuing conditions for the possibility of the positive affects interest-excitement and enjoyment-joy rather than an orientation toward the future (despair) that foresees the obliteration of those conditions and therefore of any form of positive affect," Marianne Dekoven, "Women, Animals, and Jane Goodall's *Reason for Hope*," *Tulsa Studies in Women's Literature* 25.1 (Spring 2006), 141.
2 "Science fiction is less a genre—a body of writing from which one can expect certain plot elements and specific tropes—than an ongoing discussion," Farah Mendlesohn, "Introduction: Reading Science Fiction," in *The Cambridge Companion to Science Fiction*, ed. Edward James and Farah Mendlesohn (New York: Cambridge University Press, 2003), 1.
3 David Seed, *Science Fiction: A Very Short Introduction* (New York: Oxford University Press, 2011), 2.
4 Sherryl Vint, *Science Fiction* (Cambridge: MIT Press, 2021), 6.
5 Ibid., 1–2.
6 See Darko Suvin, *Metamorphoses of Science Fiction: On the Poetics and History of a Literary Genre* (New Haven: Yale University Press, 1979) and Fredric Jameson, *Archaeologies of the Future: The Desire Called Utopia and Other Science Fictions* (New York: Verso, 2005).
7 Sherryl Vint, *Animal Alterity: Science Fiction and the Question of the Animal* (Liverpool: Liverpool University Press, 2010), 15.
8 Ishiguro resists the science fiction label. Interviewer John Freeman notes, "At any reference to 'sci-fi,' Ishiguro bristles. 'When I am writing fiction, I don't think in terms of genre at all. I write a completely different way. It starts with ideas,'" John Freeman, "*Never Let Me Go*: A Profile of Kazuo Ishiguro," *Poets & Writers* 33.3 (May–June 2005), 42. Dick, for his part, is frequently treated as an unconventional science fiction writer whose work is imbricated with postmodernism or posthumanism, as in, respectively, Christopher Palmer, *Philip K. Dick: Exhilaration and Terror of the Postmodern* (Liverpool: Liverpool University Press, 2003) and N. Katherine Hayles, *How We Became Posthuman: Virtual Bodies in Cybernetics, Literature, and Informatics* (Chicago: University of Chicago Press, 1999).
9 Ernst Bloch, *The Principle of Hope*, 3 volumes, trans. Neville Plaice, Stephen Plaice, and Paul Knight (Cambridge: MIT Press, 1986), 75, emphasis in the original.

10 Darwin writes, "He who admits on general grounds that the structure and habits of all animals have been gradually evolved, will look at the whole subject of Expression in a new and interesting light," Charles Darwin, *The Expression of the Emotions in Man and Animals* (New York: Penguin, 2009), 23.

11 Margo DeMello, *Animals and Society: An Introduction to Human-Animal Studies* (New York: Columbia University Press, 2012), 41.

12 Marc Bekoff, *The Emotional Lives of Animals: A Leading Scientist Explores Animal Joy, Sorrow, and Empathy—And Why They Matter* (Novato: New World Library, 2007), 10.

13 Lorraine Daston and Gregg Mitman, "Introduction: The How and Why of Thinking with Animals," in *Thinking with Animals: New Perspectives on Anthropomorphism*, ed. Lorraine Daston and Gregg Mitman (New York: Columbia University Press, 2005), 8. See also Alexandra C. Horowitz and Marc Bekoff, "Naturalizing Anthropomorphism: Behavioral Prompts to Our Humanizing of Animals," *Anthrozoös* 20.1 (January 2007): 23–35.

14 de Waal defines "anthropodenial" as "The a priori denial of humanlike characteristics in other animals or animallike characteristics in humans," Frans de Waal, *Are We Smart Enough to Know How Smart Animals Are?* (New York: W.W. Norton & Company, 2016), 319.

15 Kari Weil, *Thinking Animals: Why Animal Studies Now?* (New York: Columbia University Press, 2010), 20.

16 Paul Waldau, *Animal Studies: An Introduction* (New York: Oxford University Press, 2013), 3.

17 de Waal writes,

> The claim that only humans can mentally hop onto the time train, leaving all other species stranded on the platform, is tied to the fact that we consciously access past and future. Anything related to consciousness has been hard to accept in other species. But this reluctance is problematic: not because we know so much more about consciousness, but because we have growing evidence in other species for episodic memory, future planning, and delayed gratification. Either we abandon the idea that these capacities require consciousness, or we accept the possibility that animals may have it, too. (*Are We Smart Enough*, 229)

18 Frans de Waal, *Mama's Last Hug: Animal Emotions and What They Tell Us about Ourselves* (New York: W.W. Norton & Company, 2019), 139.

19 Bekoff, xxi.

20 "Future planning" already seems to be premised on hope, and the reluctance to say "hope" in reference to animal behavior seems to be a lingering holdover from anthropocentrism, the taboo against anthropomorphism, and the enduring

Cartesian view of animals as machine-like. Matthew Calarco succinctly summarizes the Cartesian view:

> Starting from mechanistic premises, Descartes argues that animals (although alive and capable of sensation) are essentially indistinguishable from machines and that their behavior can be fully explained without recourse to notions such as mind and self-awareness. Animals in his account are complex automata, beings that can react to external stimuli but lack the ability to know that such reactions are taking place. (Matthew Calarco, *Thinking Through Animals: Identity, Difference, Indistinction* (Stanford: Stanford University Press, 2015), 9)

21 Although he rejects "animal studies" as a field name, Michael Lundblad suggests that the sub-fields that comprise it reflect "different priorities with different aims or ends in mind, rather than rigid distinctions without overlap," Michael Lundblad, "Introduction: The End of the Animal—Literary and Cultural Animalities," in *Animalities: Literary and Cultural Studies Beyond the Human*, ed. Michael Lundblad (Edinburgh: Edinburgh University Press, 2017), 2.
22 Cary Wolfe, "Human, All Too Human: 'Animal Studies' and the Humanities," *PMLA* 124.2 (2009), 567.
23 See Josephine Donovan, "Animal Rights and Feminist Theory," *Signs* 15.2 (Winter 1990): 350–75.
24 Susan Fraiman, "Pussy Panic versus Liking Animals: Tracking Gender in Animal Studies," *Critical Inquiry* 39 (Autumn 2012), 100.
25 Wolfe, 572.
26 Ibid., 568, 569. Fraiman observes, "Without giving a single example, relying entirely on other scholars for a blanket indictment of cultural studies as incoherent and vague, Wolfe blames these qualities for helping to obscure what remains a normative conception of subjectivity, despite the rhetorical inclusion of animals," 104. Responding to Fraiman, Lundblad calls for sharper distinctions between subfields, 7–8. However, in this study my framing aligns with Fraiman: "I will also use *animal studies* in its broadest, contemporary sense to mean the sprawling, multidisciplinary field known by some as animality studies or human-animal studies and not to be confused with the scientific usage meaning lab studies involving animals," Fraiman 90, note 2, emphasis in original.
27 By focusing on hope, I do not minimize any other common emotions that scholars and critics have found between humans and nonhumans. I mean to support these efforts against human exceptionalism and anthropodenial by focusing on overlooked hope.
28 Calarco identifies three main approaches to the relationship between humans and animals: identity-, difference-, and indistinction-based.

29 Donna Haraway, *When Species Meet* (Minneapolis: University of Minnesota Press, 2008), 20.

30 See Spivak, "Can the Subaltern Speak?" in *Marxism and the Interpretation of Culture*, ed. Cary Nelson and Lawrence Grossberg (Urbana: University of Illinois Press, 1988).

31 Humility about how much we can finally know of the experiences and inner lives of nonhuman animals is another tenet of animal studies as Waldau conceptualizes them: "identifying the nature of any and all limits as to what humans might know about other living beings is a key task requiring honesty, constant work, and liberal doses of humility," Waldau, 6.

32 Kazuo Ishiguro, *Never Let Me Go* (New York: Vintage, 2005), 8. Subsequent references are given in parentheses within the text.

33 J. M. Coetzee, *The Lives of Animals*, ed. and intro. Amy Gutmann (Princeton: Princeton University Press, 1999), 58.

34 Shameem Black, "Ishiguro's Inhuman Aesthetics," *Modern Fiction Studies* 55.4 (Winter 2009), 801.

35 Walter Benjamin, "The Work of Art in the Age of Its Technological Reproducibility: Second Version," in *Selected Writings, Vol. 3: 1935–1938*, ed. Howard Eiland and Michael W. Jennings (Cambridge: Harvard University Press, 2002), 119.

36 Benjamin says,

> Distraction and concentration form an antithesis which may be formulated as follows. A person who concentrates before a work of art is absorbed by it; he enters into the work, just as, according to legend, a Chinese painter entered his completed painting while beholding it. By contrast, the distracted masses absorb the work of art into themselves. Their waves lap around it; they encompass it with their tide. This is most obvious with regard to buildings. Architecture has always offered the prototype of an artwork that is received in a state of distraction and through the collective. (Benjamin, "The Work of Art in the Age of Its Technological Reproducibility: Second Version," 119–20)

37 Ibid., 120. Emphasis in original.

38 For Black, the novel "reinvents empathy for a posthumanist age" by critiquing the limits of empathy in the human and locating self-recognition and empathy in the inhuman, in the "mechanical, manufactured, and replicated," Shameem Black, 786. Similarly, by focusing on the obstacles that the novel erects to traditional reader identification with protagonists, Nancy Armstrong argues that *Never Let Me Go* pushes readers "beyond the limits of sympathetic identification" and

"move[s] us to acknowledge those with whom we share vital organs yet whom we exclude from the mirroring relationship of sympathy," Nancy Armstrong, "The Affective Turn in Contemporary Fiction," *Contemporary Literature* 55.3 (Fall 2014), 464. For Anne Whitehead, *Never Let Me Go* "discomfort[s] and perplex[es] readers, in order to open up, *and to hold open*, central ethical questions of responsiveness, interpretation, responsibility, complicity, and care," Anne Whitehead, "Writing with Care: Kazuo Ishiguro's *Never Let Me Go*," *Contemporary Literature* 52.1 (Spring 2011), 59, emphasis in original. For Bruce Robbins, the novel interrogates the boundary between care and cruelty: "true caring, even love itself, would necessarily have cruelty in it," Bruce Robbins, "Cruelty Is Bad: Banality and Proximity in *Never Let Me Go*," *NOVEL: A Forum on Fiction* 40.3 (2007), 300. Eluned Summers-Bremner argues that animals in the novel are "the natural foil to manufactured humans, but also the regressive, excessive element within ordinary humanity"; from Summers-Bremner's Lacanian perspective, art addresses human "exile from the land of instincts," Eluned Summers-Bremner, "'Poor Creatures:' Ishiguro's and Coetzee's Imaginary Animals," *Mosaic: An Interdisciplinary Critical Journal* 39.4 (December 2006), 147, 155.

39 Anna Sewell, *Black Beauty*, ed. Kristen Guest (Peterborough: Broadview Press, 2016), 162.
40 Leo Tolstoy, "Strider," in *The Death of Ivan Ilyich and Other Stories*, ed. and trans. Kirsten Lodge (Peterborough: Broadview Press, 2017), 113.
41 Calarco, 26.
42 Jeremy J. Mhire and Rodolfo Hernandez argue that Ishiguro finds hope in the students' decency, but that "in a flattened world with no families, no gods, and no ambition, hope in the future is replaced with a fondness for the past," Jeremy J. Mhire and Rodolfo Hernandez, "Decency, Hope, and the Substitution of Memory in Kazuo Ishiguro's *Never Let Me Go*," *Political Science Reviewer* 43.1 (January 2019), 221. Mhire and Hernandez consistently claim that Ishiguro regards *Never Let Me Go* as his "most hopeful" novel, though in the interview they cite, Ishiguro actually calls it "my cheerful novel." Ishiguro attributes this cheerfulness to the students' decency:

> I wanted to show three people who were essentially decent. When they finally realize that their time is limited, I wanted them not to be preoccupied with their status or their material possessions. I wanted them to care most about each other and setting things right. So for me, it was saying positive things about human beings against the rather bleak fact of our mortality. (quoted in Susannah Hunnewell, "Kazuo Ishiguro: The Art of Fiction, No. 196," *Paris Review* 184 (Spring 2008), 52)

43 Ursula K. Heise sees the novel as a potential "indictment of Western culture's fundamental insensitivity to and relentless exploitation of animals," but also sees it as "accept[ing] technology to a certain extent as a replacement for irrecuperably lost nature," Ursula K. Heise, "From Extinction to Electronics: Dead Frogs, Live Dinosaurs, and Electric Sheep," in *Zoontologies: The Question of the Animal*, ed. Cary Wolfe (Minneapolis: University of Minnesota Press, 2003), 73, 74. In contrast to Heise, Vint shows that the novel "puts androids in the place historically occupied by animals," as the mechanical, Cartesian other of humanity. For Vint, the novel is about the need for humans to resist our own android-like and capitalist rationality by cultivating empathy with animals and resisting speciesism: "The central role of animals in *Do Androids Dream of Electric Sheep?* and the issues of species being that they raise show the need to struggle for a different way of being in the world. This way resists commodification in our relations with one another and with nature to produce a better future, one in which humans might be fully human once again by repairing our social relations with animals and nature," Sherryl Vint, "Speciesism and Species Being in *Do Androids Dream of Electric Sheep?*," *Mosaic: An Interdisciplinary Critical Journal* 40.1 (March 2007), 113, 125. For Jill Galvan, human encounters with androids and commodified animals in the novel "[interrogate] a fixed definition of the human subject and at last [acknowledge] him as only one component of the living scene," Jill Galvan, "Entering the Posthuman Collective in Philip K. Dick's *Do Androids Dream of Electric Sheep?*," *Science Fiction Studies* 24.3 (November 1997), 414. Tony M. Vinci sees trauma in the novel as temporarily liberating characters from essentialized human subjectivity and thus of "opening us up to trans-subjective engagements with the android and the animal that facilitate a radical posthuman ethics of expansive vulnerability," Tony M. Vinci, "Posthuman Wounds: Trauma, Non-anthropocentric Vulnerability, and the Human/Android/Animal Dynamic in Philip K. Dick's *Do Androids Dream of Electric Sheep?*," *Journal of the Midwest Modern Language Association* 47.2 (Fall 2014), 94. Building on Vinci's work, Ida Marie Olsen discusses how the possibility of android trauma blurs "the boundaries between machines and humans, thus undermining anthropocentrism," Ida Marie Olsen, "Do Androids Have Nightmares about Electric Sheep?: Science Fiction Portrayals of Trauma Manifestations in the Posthuman Subject in *Frankenstein*, *Do Androids Dream of Electric Sheep?*, and 'Nine Lives,'" *New Horizons in English Studies* 3 (January 2018), 102. For Casey R. Riffel, it is not trauma but apocalypse and historical rupture that "[make] possible new forms of species relations," Casey R. Riffel, "Animals at the End of the World: Notes toward a Transspecies Eschatology" in *Making Animal Meaning*, ed. Linda Kalof and Georgina M. Montgomery (East Lansing: Michigan State University Press, 2011), 160.

44 Philip K. Dick, *Do Androids Dream of Electric Sheep?* (New York: Del Rey, 2017), 29. Subsequent references are given in parentheses within the text.
45 de Waal, *Are We Smart Enough*, 157.
46 Jacques Derrida, *The Animal That Therefore I Am*, ed. Marie-Louise Mallet, trans. David Wills (New York: Fordham University Press, 2008), 135.
47 Ibid., 136.
48 Ibid., 159, 160.
49 Vint, "Speciesism and Species Being in *Do Androids Dream of Electric Sheep?*," 119. Vint rightly attributes this contradiction to capitalist alienation: "Deckard's struggle to have a non-commodity relationship with animals and others within the novel reveals the damage that capitalist modes of relation have done to his subjectivity, but also point, given Deckard's ability to change, to a potential way out of such damaging social structures," 120.
50 Megan E. Cannella, "Do Androids Dream of Derrida's Cat?: The Unregulated Emotion of Animals in Philip K. Dick's *Do Androids Dream of Electric Sheep?*," in *Seeing Animals after Derrida*, ed. Sarah Bezan and James Tink (Lanham: Lexington Books, 2018), 147.
51 See "Translator's Introduction," in Bloch, *The Principle of Hope*, xxiv.
52 Bloch, 3.
53 "We may lay it down that a happy person never phantasies, only an unsatisfied one. The motive forces of phantasies are unsatisfied wishes, and every single phantasy is the fulfilment of a wish, a correction of unsatisfying reality. These motivating wishes vary according to the sex, character, and circumstances of the person who is having the phantasy; but they fall naturally into two main groups. They are either ambitious wishes, which serve to elevate the subject's personality; or they are erotic ones," Sigmund Freud, "Creative Writers and Day-Dreaming," in *The Freud Reader*, ed. Peter Gay (New York: W.W. Norton & Company, 1989), 439.
54 Bloch, 3.
55 Bloch, 86. For Bloch, nightdreams are concerned with the oedipal past and with the unconscious, in which, as Bloch notes, "*there is nothing new,*" 56, emphasis in original.
56 Jameson, 232.

2

The Artificial Gaze

Artificial beings in contemporary fiction offer posthuman possibilities for regarding nonhuman animals. Precisely because it is a contested term, "posthuman" captures a productively flexible range of views and potentialities that I welcome rather than try to settle or reconcile. Cary Wolfe, for instance, maintains a strict distinction between what he calls "humanist posthumanism" or transhumanism, which relies on an Enlightenment ideal of transcending the animal in the human, and posthumanism, which represents a profound technological decentering of the human and requires radically new paradigms and modes of thought.[1] Donna Haraway's formulation of the cyborg is another important approach to the posthuman. Haraway's cyborg is a hybrid of "organism and machine" that is "resolutely committed to partiality, irony, intimacy, and perversity."[2] Like her cyborg, Haraway's concepts of "becoming with" and the "play of companion species" also suggest alternative posthuman possibilities to Wolfe's.[3] In contrast to Haraway and Wolfe, for N. Katherine Hayles, the posthuman prioritizes information over biological substrate to the extent that the physical body becomes an accidental feature of a wider science of communication and controls systems, or cybernetics.[4]

These posthuman definitions and perspectives operate in different ways in Jeanette Winterson's *Frankissstein*, Richard Powers's *The Overstory*, and Jonathan Luna and Sarah Vaughn's comic book series *Alex + Ada*. *Frankissstein*, for example, offers a vision of life and intelligence untethered from the biological and historical "accident" of the body, showing strong affinities with Hayles's cybernetic posthumanism, while mad scientist Victor Stein promotes a form of posthumanism that Wolfe would call transhumanism. Conforming more to Wolfe's own posthumanism, Powers's networked intelligence or "learners," even while premised on the ancient organization of networked trees, precipitate a profound decentering of the human that demonstrates the need for new forms of thought. Meanwhile, *Alex + Ada*'s human and robot couple queer the lines of kind and thus resemble Haraway's model of species "becoming with."

What these stories have in common are the challenges they pose to human conceptions of nonhuman potentiality, intelligence, and love. They cultivate posthuman thought about the nonhuman that can lead us to reflect more clearly and empathetically about nonhuman animals and, while maintaining a necessary sense of the limits of what we can finally know, to develop new relationships with nonhuman creatures. Paul Waldau includes humility about our epistemological horizons as a basic task of animal studies while nonetheless recognizing that creative gifts and imaginative efforts can indeed advance our understanding.[5] Contemporary fiction about artificial beings is one such creative gift. It can open minds and hearts to nonhuman animals by helping readers to cultivate new habits of thought about the categories of the human, posthuman, and nonhuman.

By exploring the range of artificial life that stretches from lowly robot sex workers to vast super-intelligent networks, recent fiction has begun to rethink human and nonhuman life in the context of newly arriving and latent possibilities within robot technologies and AI. This fiction is sometimes marketed as prognosticating technological futures. The jacket copy of *Frankissstein*, for example, asks, "What will happen when *homo sapiens* is no longer the smartest being on the planet? In fiercely intelligent prose, Jeanette Winterson shows us how much closer we are to that future than we realize."[6] While it is intuitive to imagine that science fiction explores the future, most science fiction critics nonetheless see the genre as ideologically engaged with present rather than future concerns. For example, Tom Moylan argues that science fiction confronts contemporary historical conflicts via modes of romance.[7] Similarly, David Seed sees science fiction as engaged with present conditions and possibilities through transformations or suspensions of familiar reality.[8] Octavia E. Butler asserts that science fiction mobilizes readers to rethink present conditions and possibilities creatively and imaginatively.[9] For Butler, science fiction confronts readers with the untried and the unthought-of. On this basis, Butler claims science fiction as a genre particularly useful to Black people. Indeed, by her reasoning, science fiction is implicitly useful to those who have been marginalized, abused, and oppressed by the scientific, technological, social, and political histories and realities that form the genre's objects of inquiry. In a similar vein, as Sherryl Vint writes,

> sf and HAS [human-animal studies] have much to offer one another: sf has a long history of thinking about alterity, subjectivity and the limits of the human, which is precisely the terrain explored by much HAS, while HAS offers new and innovative ways to think about sf's own engagement with such issues, situating it within a material history in which we have always-already been living with "alien" beings.[10]

In line with these views, and in the mold of recent criticism that aligns animal studies with critical race studies,[11] this chapter asks what fiction about artificial beings can offer to our thinking about marginalized, abused, and oppressed nonhuman animals. Through their creative and imaginative techniques of transformation and suspension, fictions of artificial life can represent not only human realities and possibilities but nonhuman animal ones as well. Moreover, representations of artificial beings can reflect simultaneously on human relationships and possible futures with technology and nonhuman animals. Such fiction might function as a form of what Ernst Bloch calls the "Not-Yet-Conscious"[12]: Imaginary and emergent forms of artificial life in recent fiction open creative possibilities for seeing and imagining nonhuman animals and for questioning the ways in which humans share or fail to share the world with other creatures.

Animal studies can take advantage of the newness, unsettledness, and indeterminacy of literary artificial beings as a variation on what, as we have seen, Kari Weil calls critical anthropomorphism.[13] The range of artificial beings in contemporary fiction is amenable to thinking flexibly through a variety of nonhuman animals and interspecies relationships. Although none of the texts examined in this chapter thematizes nonhuman animals, the artificial lives that they represent shake confidence in the human ability to understand the interconnections of life adequately enough to act intelligently, justly, or lovingly within it. As these fictions habituate readers to accept the personhood of artificial beings, they can also disrupt and unsettle the habit of denying full personhood to nonhuman animals. Indeed, these fictions model the costs of choosing domination and anthropocentrism over loving particularity, listening to difference, and nurturing potentiality.

This chapter thus considers the gaze of beings of superior intelligence and power and of subservient sexbots. Networked or higher intelligence beings in Winterson's *Frankissstein* and Powers's *The Overstory* conjure forms of artificial life and intelligence that rival or exceed human capabilities. *The Overstory* encourages readers to try on networked and branching brains that are more sophisticated and resourceful than our own. The novel also promotes an ideal of translating between the languages of human and nonhuman life, suggesting that a more interwoven intelligence would yield greater ecological understanding. Meanwhile, *Frankissstein* imagines radical disruptions in human thought and bodies, suggesting the challenge that nonembodied intelligent life might pose to anthropocentrism. The novel intimates that AI might be capable of higher and more perfect forms of love than humans possess, challenging an emotional basis for human exceptionalism. By overshadowing human cognition and emotion, these artificial figures help to erode the logocentric and anthropocentric worldview that prioritizes human over nonhuman experiences and perspectives on the basis of supposed superiority.

While these beings look at humans from above, subaltern sexbots in *Frankissstein* and Luna and Vaughn's *Alex + Ada* look up at the human from below; they represent intelligence in the thrall of instrumentalization.[14] The sexbot's form of instrumentalization casts nonhuman potentiality up against hegemonic human practices of sexual power and domination. Whereas superior artificial beings suggest vistas on nonhuman life that exceed human capacities and understanding, sexbots are figures whose potentiality is forcibly retarded by human domination; yet these texts suggest the necessity of more loving and nurturing relationships in place of those currently premised on instrumentalization, callousness, and violence.

The View from Above

Jeanette Winterson's novels are noted for their postmodernist destabilizing of social and historical constructs and for their sustained inquiry into the nature of sexuality and love, especially as they relate to the body.[15] In *Frankissstein*, Winterson explores historical fantasy, bodies, and love in relation to AI. The novel shuttles between the early nineteenth century and the early twenty-first century to explore Mary Shelley's groundbreaking ideas about life, development, mind, and body in a contemporary context. Despite its interest in AI and posthumanity, however, at first glance *Frankissstein* seems resolutely anthropocentric. Posthumanity is mostly considered from the perspective of its desirability or undesirability to humans, ranging from those like Victor Stein, who welcomes a life beyond the body, to those like Ry Shelley, who says "Maybe I just don't want to be post-human."[16] Victor is the most enthusiastic about posthuman possibilities, but these possibilities often reflect all-too-human desires: "We cannot live indefinitely in human form on this earth, and the only way we can seriously colonise space is by not being in human form" (282). Though Victor's goal is to transcend the flesh, his vision of AI hews to human impulses and imperatives. One wonders if, for example, a superior artificial being would value nonaging, immortality, or space colonization as Victor does.

Victor's sensibility is premised upon a Platonic contempt for bodies and the material world (an idea more human than strictly intelligent, perhaps) that informs some anthropocentric and human exceptionalist views. Sophia, in the gnostic story Victor retells, "Finds herself trapped in materiality—something she hates" (294). "Our bodies," he explains, "are a front—or perhaps more accurately, an affront—to the beauty of our nature as beings of light" (294). AI, for Victor, constitutes a "homecoming" (295) to pure light. Winterson has written against this Platonic degrading of the body in the past. In *Written on the Body* (1994), the narrator contemplates the death of the beloved and makes a moving claim for the value of the lifeless body:

> What would you do? Pass the body into the hands of strangers? The body that has lain beside you in sickness and in health. The body your arms still long for dead or not. You were intimate with every muscle, privy to the eyelids moving in sleep. This is the body where your name is written, passing into the hands of strangers.[17]

As Andrea L. Harris writes, "For Winterson, to touch the flesh and to love the body is also to write upon it and to read it."[18]

However, Victor's view of imprisoning and affronting materiality and his elevation of the mind and spirit over the degraded body run through Western thought and many religious traditions. Following Descartes, humans often project sheer materiality onto nonhuman animals and contemptuously deny that they possess mind and spirit. This contempt is evident in the way in which Victor and other proponents of AI in the novel denigrate their physical bodies as a product made from animals: meat. In the Singularity Suite at the Tec-X-Po on Robotics, "Some young guys are wearing T-shirts with the slogan 'Give Up Meat.' It's not that the future will be vegetarian—just that they believe that soon enough the human mind—our minds—will no longer be tied to a body that is a substrate made of meat" (35). "Of course, says Victor, what I would prefer is to be able to upload myself, that is, upload my consciousness, to a substrate not made of meat" (110). Contempt for nonhuman animals merges with self-contempt for the abject "animal" dimension that is to be purged from the human. Aligned with the cybernetic posthumanist model, for Victor mind and body are only accidentally joined in an embarrassing and degrading association. He seeks to leave meat-hood to nonhuman animals, freeing humans to pursue higher ambitions.

However, Victor's excitement about "accelerated evolution" (200) is premised on an anthropocentric distortion of Darwinian theory. Although nature "tries out" innumerable possibilities for life in an open-ended, multiply branching, and decidedly non-hierarchical fashion, Victor regards humans as the vanguard of a progressive and hierarchical evolution in which AI represents ascent. Victor paraphrases his "mentor," the AI pioneer I. G. Good, who speculates: "An ultraintelligent machine would lead to the extinction of Homo sapiens" (199). Victor argues, "We humans will only programme the future once. After that, the intelligence we create will manage itself" (80). For Victor, humans' potential to make an intelligence higher than our own is the very thing that sets the human above other forms of life: "It's not survival of the fittest—it's survival of the smartest. We are the smartest. No other species can tinker with its own destiny" (154).

Despite Victor's anthropocentric views of evolution and intelligence, *Frankissstein* offers imaginative glimpses, even through Victor, into the more-than-human future in which a hypothetical intelligence would dwarf the distinctions between human and nonhuman animals altogether and thereby displace anthropocentrism. In his lecture, "The Future of Humans in a Post-Human World," Victor says, "Artificial intelligence is not sentimental—it is biased towards best possible outcomes. The human race is not the best possible outcome" (74). Victor also asserts, "Science is no longer convinced that Homo sapiens is a special case" (79). To be sure, when Victor displaces humans, he still excludes nonhuman animal life from "the best possible outcome." Victor simply shifts humans onto the nonhuman animal side of the ledger, reclassifying us as meat. His human-animal indistinction is not premised on recognizing similarity and connection or on valuing difference; rather, it positions humans and nonhuman animals as inferior to a super-rational and unembodied intelligence that is ultimately just a dematerialized exaggeration of human rationality. At the same time, the possibilities opened by imagining a more intelligent form of life ought not to be dismissed. Though still logocentric, to project a greater rationality is to accept that human biases might have to be renounced, including Victor's own human exceptionalist views. Victor hints at this possibility when Ry suggests, "AI is for our benefit, surely?" Victor replies, "How colonial of you" (150). Victor suggests that AI will be rather, "An end to human stupidity," including "Race, faith, gender, [and] sexuality" (199). Whether or not one agrees with Victor about what constitutes human stupidity, he believes that AI will radically revise human values. In arguing so, he highlights the colonial dimension of anthropocentrism while simultaneously exemplifying it.

More tantalizingly utopian is the suggestion that AI might bring about not just higher intelligence, but also a purer or greater capacity for love. When Victor suggests to Ry that a super-intelligent artificial being might fall in love with a human, Ry is surprised and asks, "Are you saying, Victor, that non-biological life forms might get closer to love—in its purest form—than we can?":

> I have no idea, said Victor. Don't ask me. Love is not my special subject. All I am saying is that love is not exclusively human—the higher animals demonstrate it—and more crucially we are instructed that God is Love. Allah is Love. God and Allah are not human. Love as the highest value is not an anthropomorphic principle. (160)

This represents a striking departure from Victor's anthropocentric and logocentric view of intelligence ("We are the smartest"). Victor acknowledges that humans share the capacity for love with "the higher animals." He locates the origin, height, and plentitude of love not in the human but in the divine: God, Allah.[19] For Victor, love is not a human projection but a divine ideal that is imperfectly reflected in human and nonhuman animals alike. It is thus possible that AI will come closer to this ideal than animals can, human or otherwise: "What the future is bringing will also be the future of love" (160), Victor says. This startling vision of artificial love suggests that orders of love exist between the human and the divine. Although divine love is usually thought to be unattainable for humans, artificial love presents an intermediary form to which humans might yet aspire or at least productively imagine. Artificial love is a creative tool or heuristic with which imperfectly loving humans might yet come to love better.

Frankissstein's visions of posthuman intelligence and love creatively disrupt anthropocentric and human exceptionalist thinking. Although nonhuman animals are not the direct subjects of Winterson's novel, the fresh and imaginative challenges that Winterson's AI pose to human brains and hearts nevertheless have provocative implications for rethinking nonhuman-human animal relationships. The novel exemplifies the ways in which the ongoing and looming crisis that AI provokes in definitions of the human simultaneously implies the necessity of reimagining all relationships and exploring new forms of potentiality within them. As *Frankissstein* decenters human intelligence and love, it calls for new habits of thought and feeling that push beyond anthropocentrism and human exceptionalism. By largely excluding nonhuman animals as subjects, Winterson's novel avoids being prescriptive about how human-nonhuman animal relationships might be reconfigured; instead, it constitutes itself as a space of potentiality and suggestiveness for critical animal studies by opening the human to new scales of intelligence and love within an expanded and reconfigured spectrum of being.

Richard Powers's *The Overstory* functions similarly to *Frankissstein*, but it does so by pushing in different directions. *The Overstory* imagines artificial tools not just for higher intelligence, but also for clearer communication and translation between human and nonhuman life. Tree consciousness and the digital consciousness represented by the novel's "learners," a form of networked AI that is arboreal in form, challenge human perspectives in ways that benefit critical animal studies. By combining the emerging technologies of AI with the "ancient" technologies of trees, the learners unsettle anthropocentrism in ways that are not just science fictional and futuristic but arboreal and everpresent. Indeed, *The Overstory* suggests the extent to which thoroughgoing challenges to anthropocentrism have always existed alongside the human and yet have continued to go largely unappreciated. In some sense, the novel's learners are simply an extreme technological manifestation of the challenge that arboreality always already poses to the reigning paradigms of human-centeredness.

Few novels focus on nonanimal life to the extent that *The Overstory* does. The novel engages with ecological concerns and it is practically encyclopedic when it comes to the topic of trees.[20] *The Overstory* also excels in unhinging time and space from the human scale and suggesting that trees try to communicate with each other, their surrounding environments, and with humans. Trees like Mimas, a giant and ancient redwood, have perspectives and desires. Nick Hoel, struggling to climb this massive tree to prevent loggers from felling it, "opens his eyes on the trunk of Mimas, the largest, strongest, widest, oldest, surest, sanest living thing he has ever seen. Keeper of half a million days and nights, and it wants him in its crown."[21] Atop Mimas, activist Olivia Vandergriff is convinced, "'This is where they want us.' She looks like someone summoned to help the most wondrous products of four billion years" (264). High in Mimas, which is "most of the way up the Flatiron building" (264), Nick and Olivia find a hollow with a "small lake" (266) in it. Life abounds there, even a salamander: "The only plausible explanation is that his ancestors got on board a thousand years ago and rode the elevator up, for five hundred generations" (267). The size and age of Mimas affect Nick: "He feels himself becoming another species" (265).

For those who are similarly "primed to see" (165), trees in *The Overstory* tell different kinds of stories from those to which humans are most accustomed. Nick inherits a "flip book" of photographs that depicts 100 years of chestnut growth, normally invisible to human perception: "everything a human being might call the *story* happens outside of his photos' frame" (16, emphasis in original). As human life proceeded at its fevered pace for a century, the story of the Hoel Chestnut tree was slowly unfolding on a scale so large and slow that only the time-lapse photos could reveal it. Later, treetops in the forest look to Nick "like the tip of a Ouija planchette, taking dictation from beyond" (355). Nick watches the branches move and reads their words:

> *The spruces pour out messages in media of their own invention. They speak through their needles, trunks, and roots. They record in their own bodies the history of every crisis they've lived through. The man in the tent lies bathed in signals hundreds of millions of years older than his crude senses. And still he can read them.*
>
> *The five white spruces sign the blue air. They write:* Light and water and a little crushed stone demand long answers.
>
> *Nearby lodgepoles and jack pines demur:* Long answers need long time. And long time is exactly what's vanishing. (355, emphasis in original)

These tree languages, temporalities, stories, and perspectives, the novel shows, put some of the characters "at peace with being human, in league with something very much not" (254). It also puts them into conflict with those doing the cutting. Logging crews provide their own form of temporal shock, their own incompatible stories: "Trees ten feet thick and nine hundred years old go down in twenty minutes and are bucked within an hour" (268).

While close attention to trees and their desires pushes humans like Nick out of their accustomed species positions and suggests stories from other-than-human perspectives, *The Overstory* also represents emerging AI as a tree-like species that stands in relation to humans as humans do to trees. Through the ways in which the novel represents AI—networked in arboreal ways that far exceed individual human capabilities—*The Overstory* encourages readers to imagine thinking with brains less individualized, more interconnected, and smarter than our own about subjects such as life, the natural world, and the place of humans within it. In this way, *The Overstory* offers the opportunity to rethink human views and aims with respect to nonhuman animals. The novel's view of AI can help readers to recognize limitations in human understandings of life; it encourages readers to try to think "above" human intelligence and idealizes the goals of translating between human and nonhuman life and ultimately of ameliorating this relationship.

The AI learners in the novel are versions of networked arboreal intelligence, but they shift the power dynamic between humans and trees. As a child, future Silicon Valley visionary Neelay Mehta reads a science fiction story that remains with him into adulthood (though he is never able to locate it again):

Aliens land on Earth. They're little runts, as alien races go. But they metabolize like there's no tomorrow. They zip around like swarms of gnats, too fast to see—so fast that Earth seconds seem to them like years. To them, humans are nothing but sculptures of immobile meat. The foreigners try to communicate, but there's no reply. Finding no signs of intelligent life, they tuck into the frozen statues and start curing them like so much jerky, for the long ride home. (97)

Neelay's story implicitly analogizes Powers's larger story about the ways in which humans instrumentalize and exploit trees: as trees are to humans, so humans are to these zipping aliens. As the aliens zip past the seemingly lifeless humans, so do humans overlook the intelligence, innate and ecological value, and communicative abilities of trees. Like the "foreign" humans in the tale, trees also try to communicate but are unheard by their exploiters. Just as the aliens regard the humans as a ready source of cured meat to be hauled off and consumed at their convenience, so do humans "tuck into" trees as mere resources. The analogy suggests the difficulty of relating to others across vastly different orders of magnitude and speed. It also suggests, in anthropomorphic terms, the disastrous consequences of failing to do so. It is finally a didactic story that hints at a certain comeuppance, asking readers to imagine being seen and used as inert and unintelligent material and serving as pure resource for a smaller, faster, and more "advanced" species.

The tale's prophetic dimensions begin to take shape in the novel's final and future-pointing section, aptly titled "Seeds." The future, we are made to understand, will see the realization of Neelay's story, not because of alien invaders, but because of the "learners" whom Neelay and many other coders are programming to absorb and interpret the world's information. Neelay's work in computer programming has been inspired in part by Stanford University's "Martian botanical garden" (276): a Queensland bottle tree growing there is "an alien invader" (109). Others are "alien life-forms" (192), "otherworldly" (195), and "creatures from another galaxy, far, far away" (195). These trees, who first posed to Neelay the question of what life wants from humans, inspire his computer games and later, when the games have failed to answer the trees' questions, motivate Neelay to help create the learners. Like the aliens of Neelay's lost science fiction story, the learners' connections and speed far surpass individual human and species' capacities. In the future, humans are immobile trees: "Bots watch and match, encode and see, gather and shape all the world's data so quickly that the knowledge of humans stands still" (487). The information that humans slowly gather and generate will become a resource for the learners, and it becomes possible to imagine scenarios of surveillance or tyranny that eclipse the horror-movie kitsch of aliens making jerky out of helpless humans. From his prison cell, eco-activist Adam Appish contemplates such futures: "Futures where our robot descendants use us for fuel, or keep us in infinitely entertaining zoos …. Futures where humanity goes to its mass grave swearing it's the only thing in creation that can talk" (495).

The learners swarm sinisterly around Mimi Ma as well. Mimi is another eco-activist fugitive wanted for "domestic terrorism." She sits in Mission Dolores Park in San Francisco searching with her phone for information about her fellow activists' jail sentences. She realizes that her searches are creating "bread-crumb trails" (478) that could lead authorities to her, though she no longer cares. As she sits immobile under the park's knobcone pine, something else is zipping around the world at an unimaginable pace, seeking her out, learning her, and zeroing in on her identity and location:

> Other eyes, invisible, read alongside hers. In the time it takes Mimi to scan ten paragraphs, the bodiless eyes read ten million. She retains no more than half a dozen details that fade as soon as she flips to a new page, but the invisible learners preserve every single word and fit them into branching networks of sense that grow stronger with each addition. The more she reads, the more the facts evade her. The more the learners read, the more patterns they find. (478)

Networked intelligence, the novel implies, is arboreal. Arboreal processing and knowledge far exceed human capacities when they are sped up and globalized. Like trees, the learners "spread outward" (482). Their "Tendrils of data swell and merge" (487). In her Buddha-like moment of enlightenment under the pine tree, Mimi seems to grasp the vast interconnection of trees: "Messages hum from out of the bark she leans against. Chemical semaphores home in over the air. Currents rise from the soil-gripping roots, relayed over great distances through fungal synapses linked up in a network the size of the planet" (499). Using the organizational principles of the trees, which humans have seen as inert resources, the learners convert humans into slow-moving meat. The networked learners represent not only a technological magnification of arboreal intelligence but also the revenge of the trees.

This reversal humbles human capacities and our sense of superiority, but it also has wishful and utopian ecological consequences. Threaded through *The Overstory* are the questions of what trees want from humans and what life itself wants from humans. The novel suggests that too few humans ask these questions or earnestly pursue answers. But Powers's characters are precisely those alive to such questions; they actively try to find out "what life wants from people, and how it might use them" (494). Mimi sits under another tree much earlier in the novel and thinks of the Buddha's enlightenment under the bodhi tree. She thinks, "He sat under a magnificent peepul—a Bo, *Ficus religiosa*—and vowed not to stand up again until he understood what life wanted from him" (186). Nick remembers the late Olivia, also called Maidenhair after an ancient gingko genus, as "the girl who always heard what life wanted from them" (338): "*The most wondrous products of four billion years of life need help*" (165, emphasis in original). Scientist and conservationist Patricia Westerford implores her lecture audience, "believe me: trees want something from us, just as we've always wanted things from them. This isn't mystical. The 'environment' is alive—a fluid, changing web of purposeful lives dependent on each other" (454). Finally, as we've seen, the inspiration for Neelay's world-building computer game comes from contemplating the trees in Stanford's botanical garden: "the goal of the game will be to figure out what the new and desperate world wants from you" (111).

In the "Seeds" section, the theme of what life wants from humans is taken up repeatedly in relation to the learners. Returning after many years to Stanford, Neelay now realizes that his massively successful games have been a wrong turn. Because of this, as we have seen, he commits to building the learners: "The trees refuse to say a thing. Neelay sits in Stanford's inner quad—the intergalactic botanical garden—waiting for an explanation. The lifelong calling has gone wrong. He's lost the trail they've set him on. What now?" (433). Instead of continuing to presume that he can hear what life wants from him, Neelay humbly turns to the networked form of intelligence represented by the learners:

> In a few short seasons, simply by placing billions of pages of data side by side, the next new species will learn to translate between any human language and the language of green things. The translations will be rough at first, like a child's first guess. But soon the first sentences will start to come

across, pouring out words made, like all living things, from rain and air and crumbled rock and light. *Hello. Finally. Yes. Here. It's us.* (496, emphasis in original)

In Powers's vision, the learners will constitute a new species able to translate for humans what green things want from life. The learners will not so much replace humanity as replace anthropocentric human intelligence as the final or "highest" arbiter of what life wants or means. The learners will reveal voices that humans have been unable or unwilling to hear. The moment Powers imagines resembles the extraterrestrial communion imagined in so many science fiction stories, yet rather than with an alien race, here the communion is with a long-lost terrestrial relative. (As Patricia Westerford explains in her book, "After an immense journey in separate directions, that tree and you still share a quarter of your genes" (132)). For Powers, the learners do not replace or transcend but rather assist, learn, and translate for humans: "But already they've learned, in a few short decades, what it took molecules a billion years to learn to do. Now they need only learn what life wants from humans. It's a big question, to be sure. Too big for people alone. But people aren't alone, and they never have been" (489).

The Overstory exposes human exceptionalism as not a position of superiority but as a condition of isolation and loneliness. Human isolation and loneliness are in part a function of anthropocentric logic: because humans are so exceptionally intelligent, we have no companions among other species on earth. Instead of replacing other humans or offering equal or higher intelligence companionship, the learners in *The Overstory* reveal that human loneliness has always been an illusion produced by the distorting perspective of human exceptionalism. Paul Waldau makes such a point when he observes,

> Our peculiar habits of thinking and speaking bewitch even sophisticated scientists—the motto of the program known as SETI (Search for Extraterrestrial Intelligence), which was set up in the 1960s and 1970s, is "Are we alone?" This motto was chosen by scientists who know only too well that all humans live with and amid countless mammals, birds, insects, and, especially, many trillions of microorganisms that we cannot see.[22]

Waldau, concerned primarily with nonhuman animals, omits plant life from his census of human neighbors, but Powers's learners also make the perspectives and voices of trees visible and audible. If exceptionalism bewitches human community among nonhuman life, Powers's trees and learners offer means of disenchanting or "un-bewitching" such attitudes and of mitigating human loneliness. The learners, modeled on the aliens in Neelay's story, help to expose that human loneliness has always been an illusion. Life is interdependent, and SETI begins at home.

The Overstory itself becomes an instrument with which to think interconnection and communication beyond anthropocentrism. While the learners are entities rooted firmly in emerging AI technologies, the novel effectively functions as a learner-like form of networked intelligence and as an attempt to translate between species. The novel, in other words, is already a form of AI that can exceed human intelligence in surprising ways. By imagining and evoking an intelligence more arboreal, comprehensive, and communicative than our own, *The Overstory* grants readers something of these capacities. Or, more precisely, it pushes readers away from anthropocentric and toward anthropocosmic thinking of a kind for which they already have the capacity, even if it is underused. In compelling readers to "look up"—up at the trees above our heads, up at a system of intelligence and communication that towers above our own—*The Overstory* defamiliarizes and challenges anthropocentrism from an imagined point of superiority to humans. As we see in the following section, anti-anthropocentric thinking can also be powerfully imagined from below and can offer different imaginative resources to critical animal studies.

The View from Below

In Philip K. Dick's *Do Androids Dream of Electric Sheep?* Rick Dekard has sex with the android Rachael Rosen, but this contact is considered taboo. What about situations in which the android is specifically designed for sex? Though not as intelligent as Victor Stein's AI, sexbots in *Frankissstein* also offer imaginative resources for seeing nonhuman animal life in non-anthropocentric terms, suggesting perspectives on human limitations and fresh ways of viewing nonhuman life. In *Frankissstein*, Ron Lord manufactures sexbots whose lives are premised upon human sexual desire and mastery.

Whereas Rachael Rosen was not designed for sex—she has "dry lips," "pale, cold loins," and resembles an adolescent[23]—Ron's sexbots are engineered around their sex function: "Very tight figure—little waist, double G-cup—and I tell you what, her tits and pussy are always warm" (43). He boasts that his bots have "Three holes all the same size" and "they all VI-BRATE! Any hole, any position" (41). Intelligence in Ron's sexbots is an afterthought. He tells Ry, "Deluxe has a big vocabulary. About 200 words. Deluxe will listen to what you want to talk about—football, politics or whatever. She waits till you're finished, of course, no interrupting, even if you waffle a bit, and then she'll say something interesting" (45–6). Intelligence in Ron's sexbots works in the service of subservient "companionship" alone: "This model is a companion— and that's how we'll forward her career as the technology develops. Some men want more than sex. I get that" (46).

Ron justifies his creations to Claire, who objects to sexbot companions because "A sexbot is not a human being!" (235), by equating sexbots to domestic pets: "That's right! said Ron. And neither is a dog or a cat. We wouldn't be without them, though, would we? ... We all need something. That's life. So why not a robot?" (235). "Robot," a word first used in Karol Čapek's 1920 play *R. U. R.: Rossum's Universal Robots*, derives from the Czech word *robota*, meaning forced laborer. As with many companion animals, sexbots are conceived primarily in terms of what they can offer to the human "owner." Ron's artificial women exist for men's sexual pleasure and companionship, on their terms alone. Ron recalls his first sexbot, which he purchased via mail order in the early days of the technology: "She was ready in bed for a cuddle, and I was getting sex every night. No warm-up. Straight in. Slept with my arm across her. I felt better. Stopped the Xanax. My rash cleared up" (235). Ron's approach to sexbots mirrors the anthropocentric view that nonhuman animals are for human uses: companionship, emotional support, entertainment, consumption, and so on. He does not see himself as being as much a companion to his sexbot as she is to him, nor has he any notion that as he looks at her, she gazes back at him.

Ron's attitude toward sexbots not only extends instrumental perspectives on nonhuman animals but also combines with patriarchal and sexist perspectives that support objectifying and instrumental uses of human women. Ron's glib and casually sexist sales pitch to Ry at the Tec-X-Po is a catalog of outrages and violent offenses to women to which Ron himself seems blithely oblivious: "All her parts arrived in a separate bag like a chainsaw massacre" (36); "If you want to be a bit more discreet you can fold her up and strap her in the back, or stow her out of sight in the boot or trunk or whatever you call it" (40); "You can have a party, pass her around, play a hand of cards in between without worrying about her going flat" (43); "We ask for double the deposit on this model because of the hair and you have to sign a waiver declaring that you won't spill booze or smear food, piss, shit, or cum in her hair" (45); and "A lot of the XX-BOTs get their faces bashed in. Get thrown at the wall or something. ... Sex can get a bit rough, can't it? I don't judge" (51). Ron's monologue is punctuated by disingenuous declarations about his love and respect for women: "I mean, I am on the side of the woman, I am" (45).

Violent uses of female sexbots might be understood through the concept of "intertwined oppressions" articulated in the work of Carol J. Adams to describe overlapping patriarchal violence against women and nonhuman animals.[24] Indeed, several times Ron relates and compares sexbots, women, and nonhuman animals. At one time this comparison is disavowed: "I made the decision not to give my girls names. No, it's not like the lambs you'll be eating later" (41). This intersection, though disavowed by Ron, exemplifies the connection that Adams finds between violence against women and the production and male consumption of meat. Later, when Ry, a trans man, tells Ron that he's a vegetarian, Ron responds, "I knew you wasn't a bloke" (94), reinforcing the place of meat-eating that Adams notes in conventional constructions of masculinity.[25] Ron also affirms the woman–animal connection: "You're not meant to call women 'birds' nowadays, are you? I always liked it. Sums women up—not in a bad way, don't get me wrong" (42). At other times, the connection is more incidental, though it still suggests an intertwined relationship between women, sexbots, and nonhuman animals: "You *can* buy some bots with Family Mode; they can talk about animals, and tell fairy tales, all that stuff" (44, emphasis in original). Race intersects with gender and the nonhuman when Ron reports that his Black sister-in-law warned him not to make "an Economy black woman. And I love women, I do, and I thought, yeah, show respect" (42).

Ron never suggests that sexbots see *us* or have perspectives on their own lives, on humans, or on the world. Sexbots lie at the other end of the spectrum from superior artificial beings whom we expect to offer higher intelligence and a greater perspective on life. When a voice from the audience at his lecture asks, "*Will women be the first casualties of obsolescence in your brave new world?*," Victor dismisses sexbots as "low-to-medium grade robotics that deploy narrow outcome goals." Victor distinguishes "a pulsating vagina ...—even if she can call you Big Boy in eight languages" from "true artificial intelligence; by which I mean machines that will learn to think for themselves" (75, emphasis in original). After the lecture, however, Ron takes Victor to task, if not for likening sexbots to pulsating vaginas then at least for dismissing sexbots as a "threat" to the human. Surprisingly, given the instrumental dissertation on sexbots that he earlier delivered to Ry, Ron now insists, "Some day robots will be an independent life form. That's what you told me when I said I might invest in you" (84).

Late in the novel, when faced with death in Victor's underground mad scientist tunnels, Ron finally suggests that sexbots will one day possess their own perspectives on the world: "And how do you know it will be one-way? Bots will learn" (312). He tells a hypothetical story about a man and his sexbot Eliza who live together in mutual love and companionship. "They learn together" (312). The man talks to Eliza about his experiences and feelings. He takes her places, and they experience things together. Eliza listens, learns, and can talk capably with the man "because her software upgrades itself" (313). Eventually, Eliza knows everything about him. He says, "You know ... ," and she says, "I KNOW" (313). When the man ages and gets ill, she stays with him until he dies. Unlike his family, Eliza is not repelled by his illness or dirtiness. After the man dies, his family regards Eliza as an embarrassment and the son sells her on eBay. However, "They forget to wipe her clean. She is confused. Is this a feeling?" (313), she wonders. Eliza learns, "Her new owner isn't interested in any of that. He's a fuck-only type. She understands. She wishes she could wipe her own software. I AM SORRY, she says, but she has no tears because big bots don't cry" (314).

Ron describes a being with the ability to learn and feel, a being who is the sum of her previous experiences, even though she possesses neither the capacities that Victor would grant "true artificial intelligence" nor the power that AI might claim or grasp for itself. Yet sexbots have a point of view, no less valuable and as potentially illuminating as the vista on life that high or "*Fully self-designing*" (73, emphasis in original) artificial beings offer. In contrast to the imagined future in which super-intelligent beings establish themselves as independent from and more powerful than their human programmers, sexbot intelligence grows and feels and yet remains bound to the whims and instrumental uses of humans. The sexbot gratifies human sexual desire and combats human loneliness, all the while becoming more capable of development herself. But these developments remain subordinated and suppressed rather than celebrated like Victor's AI. Sexbots can be loved and nurtured, but most will not be used for more than sexual gratification. There is thus poignancy and pathos in Eliza's story because her developed potentiality, learned capabilities, past experiences, and future growth possibilities remain suppressed for the sexual gratification of her human owner.

Jonathan Luna and Sarah Vaughn's comic series *Alex + Ada* meditates at length on sexbot potentiality and accreted experience.[26] Like those in *Do Androids Dream*, the androids in *Alex + Ada* are not explicitly for sex. The Attorney General who leads Operation Avalanche, the crackdown against robot sentience in the series' near-future setting, characterizes the androids as "our servants, our assistants, and oftentimes our companions" (7.22). He lists companionship last and qualifies it with "oftentimes," but the unspoken cultural subtext seems to be that androids, among their other functions, are almost always used as sexbots. Unlike in *Frankissstein*, where heterosexual men are the primary consumers of Ron's sexbots—"There *are* male bots but I don't bother with them. Why not? Anatomy, Ryan. Basic anatomy" (48, emphasis in original)—in *Alex + Ada* men and women both own and have sex with sexbots. Katherine, who later buys Ada, a Tanaka X5 android with Prime Intelligence, for her grandson Alex, confides, "Who knew an android might be the best lover I've ever had?" Alex's reply—"Please don't be talking about what I *think* you're talking about"—indicates that human-android sexual relationships are an open secret.[27] When Alex introduces Ada to his friends, Isabel's response reinforces the open secret that these robots are lovers: "It's like getting a girlfriend and a baby at the same time" (3.6). Later, Isabel, jealous of Ada, charges, "Who needs a *real woman* when you can have every man's *fantasy*? ... It's hard enough competing with other women, but now we have to deal with robots" (11.16, 17, emphasis in original). Finally, Alex's enthusiastic and tactless neighbor belies the discourse about nonsexual android assistants when he declares, "I still have an X3, but didn't want to upgrade until Tanaka fixed the lube problem" (7.16). He unashamedly asks, "How does she ride? ... Man, I would love a test run. You wouldn't be interested in—" (7.16). Like Ron Lord, the neighbor suggests that it is at least somewhat acceptable to "pass her around," though Alex firmly rejects the proposal. As in *Frankissstein*, these relationships of domination between humans and androids recall the etymological root of "robot" in forced labor. For sexbots, this forced labor amounts to a nonhuman form of sex slavery.

All the while, however, Ada and the other Tanaka X5s are created with the capacity for full sentience. *Alex + Ada* is a story about the human impulse to suppress the sentience of the android other. Human anxieties about sentient androids, especially after a massacre in which thirty-four humans were killed by Nexaware androids, has led to the "A. I. Restrictions Act" on android sentience. Artificial beings in the world of *Alex + Ada* are prohibited from developing into the kind of limitless AI that Victor envisions in *Frankissstein*. When he receives Ada, Alex is initially intrigued and somewhat compelled when Ada tells him, "The only thing that matters is what you want" (3.10). Ada is a complex and highly capable being who will agree to whatever Alex desires. However, Alex's dissatisfaction grows when he observes that Ada only laughs when he laughs, that she cannot appreciate things such as sunsets, and that she stands all day by the door waiting for him to return from work (4.18, 3.11, 3.12). Then Alex discovers from Levi, an online AI forum moderator, that the Prime Intelligence in the Tanaka X5 is capable of full sentience: "Prime Intelligence is an artificial brain. Any android with it is as mentally complex as we are. If you remove any element, the entire system will collapse. But what you do is *block* sentience. And that's exactly what Prime did. Prime Intelligence performs nowhere near its full potential" (4.11, emphasis in original). There is even a term among the forum members for what Alex is experiencing: "Galatean disappointment." He confesses, "She's not what I thought she'd be" (4.5). Alex wants more in a companion than the sentience-blocked Ada can offer to him, but significantly he also wants more for Ada: "I just ... I see *more* in her. I want to know who she can really be" (4.11, emphasis in original).

It is only when Alex illegally unblocks Ada's sentience that Ada's own story and experiences begin. In striking contrast to her insensibility to the previous evening's sunset, on her first morning with full sentience she experiences the beauty of a sunrise. Instead of blindly obeying her owner's desires, Ada now gazes at, talks back to, and judges Alex. She forms opinions and preferences about everything around her. She asserts her will and has an undeniable point of view. She even dreams, not about electric sheep, but about a little boat on the open sea, a boat that represents the freedom she will fail to attain when she and Alex are later hunted and captured by authorities.[28] Ada also has perspectives on herself and her pre-sentient, subservient past. Franklin, the X5 who performed Ada's conversion, warns Alex, "Her life is her own after this, and she has every right to make her own decisions, even if it includes leaving you" (4.13). Full sentience, that is, precludes ownership. Alex must live with Ada in mutual companionship and with mutual consent. Ada does leave Alex for a time after he seems unable to love and treat her as a being who possesses full personhood. After they reconcile and eventually have sex for the first time, Ada is nothing like Ron Lord's sexbots, who are defined by their constant sexual availability and can be neither satisfied nor dissatisfied by sex. Ada enjoys sex and has her own perspective and feelings about it. In a sequence of panels that depict Ada and Alex in post-coital conversation, Ada says, "Again," and Alex asks, "Really?" When Ada replies, "Yes please," Alex says, "Hey now. I'm not an android. I need a little time to recover." But Ada sees through this: "You're not recovering. You're falling *asleep*." After Alex playfully threatens, "Do I need to switch you off so I can get a break?," Ada "thwaps" him with a pillow and says, "You better be joking" (10.22, emphasis in original).

Ada differs not only from Ron's sexbots but also from Katherine's unconverted Tanaka X5, Daniel. On her deathbed, his grandmother tells Alex, "I didn't make Daniel sentient ... because I didn't want to know how he would feel about being here. And looking at it ... it's ... a very selfish reason. But now I'm sorry that I'll never truly meet him" (12.16). Panels early in the series depict the unusual juxtaposition of the hunky young Daniel serving tea to Katherine and reading in bed beside her (1.13, 2.5–6). These images of disproportionate ages are repeated late in the series when Alex has aged twenty-five years, but Ada remains unchanged. Clearly, part of what humans fear in android sentience is not just the potential for massacre but perhaps even more threateningly their capacity to gaze back at and to judge humans.

In other words, *Alex + Ada* depicts a human world that struggles on the individual and social levels to recognize and integrate androids as persons. Alex's friend Teji, a veteran whose life was saved by a "militroid" in battle, tells

Alex, "we already created robots and we already created a place for them. All that's left is *accepting* them" (10.14, emphasis in original). Although Alex and Ada are hunted down as part of Operation Avalanche, *Alex + Ada* is relatively sanguine about the longer-term future of human-android relations. Something of a cultural and legal sea change occurs during the twenty-five years that Alex spends in prison and that Ada spends deactivated, disassembled, and stored in an evidence box. Although the Attorney General once declared, "We can't forget that robots are a tool to enrich and elevate our lives ... not to have lives of their own" (7.23), humans and androids begin to march together in allegiance for android rights. Robot sentience is eventually legalized, and robots are recognized as persons with rights. At the series' end, however, inequalities and violent crimes against androids remain. Apologies for Operation Avalanche have never been made and robots continue to struggle for true equality and quality of life (15.11). The series depicts the struggle for android personhood as ongoing and incomplete.

Ada + Alex and *Frankissstein* insistently pose the question of what it means to live alongside and to instrumentalize sentient artificial beings who are capable of personal development and are as able to gaze out at the human as they are of being gazed upon. In doing so, these novels also press the question of instrumental human-nonhuman animal relationships without, however, having to pass directly *through* these relationships. Their effect is achieved outside of the limitations of realist, symbolic, or allegorical representations. Even as we lose the concreteness, resonance, or analogousness associated with those respective modes of representing human-nonhuman animal relationships, this situation presents advantages for rethinking human-nonhuman animal relationships in defamiliarized terms.

Specifically, without having conceptually to pass through the fraught categories of bestiality or zoophilia, the sexual preoccupation of the android-human relationships in these fictions allows the powerfully resonant ideas of sexual development, freedom, and domination to creatively affect the ways in which we conceive of power relations between human and nonhuman creatures. These fictions allow readers to reimagine nonhuman-human animal relationships in the context of the pathos that *Frankissstein* and *Alex + Ada* generate out of their depictions of instrumentalized and dominated sexbots. Caught and gazed back at not just naked, as in Derrida's matutinal encounter with his singular cat, readers are also encouraged to imagine the human seen in instrumentalizing acts of sexual domination, from perspectives capable not just of sentience but also of developing and of enjoying freedom and happiness. Such sexbot perspectives resonate in open and hopeful ways in the context of human-nonhuman animal relationships.

The Novel as AI

Artificial beings can help us to think more creatively about nonhuman animals. As we necessarily struggle to form judgments about liminal and developing figures who challenge our conceptions about who knows, who looks, who grows, who becomes, and who loves, the struggle can simultaneously animate our inquiries in critical animal studies and help to exercise our creativity, imagination, and empathy as we seek to intervene in much older, oppressive, and more fixed conceptions of nonhuman animals. Artificial beings as represented by *Frankissstein*, *The Overstory*, and *Alex + Ada* map imperfectly onto nonhuman animals while exercising and stretching our perspectives on the nonhuman and working against reigning paradigms and conventionalized Romantic, realist, modernist, and allegorical representations of nonhuman animals. One value of artificial beings to critical animal studies lies in the degree to which these beings can neither be equated neatly with nonhuman animals nor absorbed into existing modes of human thought about animals. Creative potentialities for animal studies lie precisely in the deep differences between artificial beings such as the learners, Eliza, and Ada and nonhuman animals. Rather than offering analogues, symbols, or allegories that pin down nonhuman animal experience with certainty, such artificial beings encourage habits of thought that push nonhuman animals outside of dominant and dominating patterns. If read creatively, habitually, heuristically, and purposefully, artificial beings can contribute to the imperatives of critical animal studies to tell, defamiliarize, and positively transform human perceptions of and relationships with nonhuman animals.

Because artificial forms of intelligence, life, and personhood are still unfinished and unfinalized, critical animal studies can borrow from the energy, newness, and unsettledness of these beings to stretch sclerotic thinking about animals and to recognize that it, too, is still unfinished. We know that attitudes toward nonhuman animals have ossified and become increasingly instrumentalized in the last 200 plus years. Derrida, for instance, marks a difference in "a process that is no doubt as old as man" in which, "in the course of the last two centuries … traditional forms of treatment of the animal have been turned upside down by the joint developments of zoological, ethological, biological, and genetic forms of *knowledge*, which remain inseparable from *techniques* of intervention *into* their object."[29] These forms of power-knowledge have produced a tight but impoverished grip on nonhuman animals, at once divorced from traditional and indigenous ways of knowing animals and simultaneously blocking future developments that could come from understanding the personhood of nonhuman animals. Learners and sexbots, about whom little or nothing is yet certain or settled, conceptually loosen this grip and can potentially persuade readers to alter their habits of thought. Their artificial gazes can defamiliarize the illusion of timelessness and inevitability that pervades the ideologies of human-nonhuman animal relations that have emerged in the last 200 plus years. To think the technological and conceptual break that emerging artificial creatures represent is simultaneously to expose all creaturely relationships, including ossified and essentialized relationships between human and nonhuman animals, as unfixed, mutable, and contingent. These artificial beings encourage us to reformulate Bloch's hopeful and future-looking pronouncement that "man [sic] everywhere is still living in prehistory"[30] to recognize that existing human-nonhuman animal relationships might all, in a crucial sense, be in their prehistory.

Frankissstein's artificial vision of better love in combination with better thinking, for instance, can help to ameliorate human relationships with nonhuman animals, especially when love and respect are habituated. Marc Bekoff reminds us that the heart is the necessary complement to the mind for this kind of progress: "Far too many animals are harmed each and every day worldwide. If we can change minds and hearts and especially current practices, we will make progress and there is hope."[31] Although *Frankissstein* is not directly about nonhuman animals, the novel enables readers to imagine a pure love that highlights inadequacies in the human capacity for and exercise of love. If artificial beings move the bar for love, then humans are better able to see ourselves as incompletely loving. Such a creative vision, absorbed and made habitual, can help to overcome our impoverished love for nonhuman animals. The potential for superior intelligence and pure love that Winterson explores in AI need not even be realized technologically for it to be useful to humans. A story, as Winterson's Mary Shelley suggests, has a life of its own (140), and humans have learned to think and feel by using the visionary fictions that writers can create. As Winterson's Shelley says in *Frankissstein*, "In the progress of my story I am educating my monster. My monster is educating me" (127). Winterson's novel is itself the needed form of AI.

As *The Overstory* participates in the effort to translate green languages into human language, it too demonstrates that novels about AI can stand in for the very forms of AI that they posit. Powers's learners help readers to assimilate and become habituated to the idea that nonhuman animals have perspectives on humans, on the world, and on their own lives. They, too, want something from us. The learners acclimate readers to the idea that humans may only be able to form a limited, partial, and distorted sense of those perspectives and desires. The learners guide and fuel the imagination to correct and adapt human perspectives, questions, and aims. Similarly, readers who absorb and assimilate sexbot stories such as those in *Frankissstein* and *Alex + Ada*, stories that demonstrate capacities for experiencing, growing, thriving, feeling, gazing back at, and judging the humans who dominate them, can cultivate habits of imagining, knowing, and accepting subaltern potentiality, subjectivity, desire, and independence. Moreover, fiction that represents sexbot potentiality and perspectives can help readers to avoid the error of projecting onto or of supposing to know nonhuman animal minds, while nonetheless reinforcing ameliorative habits of mindfulness about the existence of nonhuman sentience, perspectives, and emotions.

The literature of artificial beings offers opportunities for forming new habits of thought about nonhuman life that can help to unsettle received ideas about nonhuman animals. As readers grow more accustomed to "granting" and acknowledging the personhood, perspectives, and potentiality of emerging and imaginary artificial life, they simultaneously open their hearts and minds to new ways of imagining human and nonhuman animals. Recent fiction asks us to look above our heads at networked or arboreal intelligence and below our waists at instrumentalized sexbots. The intelligence, potentiality, and love that fiction represents in both directions is itself a form of AI for clarifying the personhood of nonhuman animals while preserving their difference and not presuming to make them speak.

Notes

1. For Wolfe, transhumanism is premised on the "ideals of human perfectibility, rationality, and agency inherited from Renaissance humanism and Enlightenment," Cary Wolfe, *What Is Posthumanism?* (Minneapolis: University of Minnesota Press, 2010), xiii. Transhumanism is about "overcoming and finally transcending not only our 'animal' origins (in the name of a rational manipulation and optimization of the human condition) but also the fetters of materiality and embodiment altogether," Cary Wolfe, "Posthumanism," in *Posthuman Glossary*, ed. Rosi Braidotti and Maria Hlavajova (New York: Bloomsbury, 2018), 357. In contrast, for Wolfe the posthuman is:

   > A historical moment in which the decentering of the human by its imbrication in technical, medical, informatic, and economic networks is increasingly impossible to ignore, a historical development that points toward the necessity of new theoretical paradigms (but also thrusts them upon us), a new mode of thought that comes after the cultural repressions and fantasies, the philosophical protocols and evasions, of humanism. (Cary Wolfe, *What Is Posthumanism?*, xv–xvi)

   Rosi Braidotti's sense of the posthuman as a form of post-humanism chimes with Wolfe's. In Braidotti's view, the posthuman is founded on a view of the continuum of nature-culture that opposes the wide consensus of the social constructivist approach. See Rosi Braidotti, *The Posthuman* (Malden: Polity Press, 2013), 2.

2. Donna J. Haraway, *Simians, Cyborgs, and Women: The Reinvention of Nature* (New York: Routledge, 1991), 150, 151.

3. Haraway writes, "I am not a posthumanist; I am who I become with companion species, who and which make a mess out of categories in the making of kin and kind. Queer messmates in mortal play, indeed," Donna J. Haraway, *When Species Meet* (Minneapolis: University of Minnesota Press, 2008), 19.

4. Hayles writes, "The posthuman view privileges informational pattern over material instantiation, so that embodiment in a biological substrate is seen as an accident of history rather than an inevitability of life." She does not find "essential differences or absolute demarcations between bodily existence and computer simulation, cybernetic mechanism and biological organism, robot teleology and human goals," N. Katherine Hayles, *How We Became Posthuman: Virtual Bodies*

in *Cybernetics, Literature, and Informatics* (Chicago: University of Chicago Press, 1999), 2, 3.

5   Waldau writes,

> We need to be frank about the nature and extent of the inevitable limits of what humans might know about other living beings, and then work as diligently as we can within these limits. … We can openly appreciate that some of the limits on our present knowledge may yield to a future human's creative gifts, or the efforts of a group's imaginative work, either of which could open our minds to undreamed-of possibilities of human awareness of certain other-than-human lives. (Paul Waldau, *Animal Studies: An Introduction* (New York: Oxford University Press, 2013), 3)

6   Jeanette Winterson, *Frankissstein: A Love Story* (New York: Grove Press, 2019), dust jacket copy.

7   Moylan writes,

> For "realistic" as science fiction and utopian fiction may appear on the surface, they are forms of the romance which are meditations upon deep conflicts in the historical present that are displaced onto the terrain of an other-worldly locus so that the reader, consciously or unconsciously, can see her or his society and its contradictions in a fresh and perhaps motivating light. (Tom Moylan, *Demand the Impossible: Science Fiction and the Utopian Imagination*, Classics Edition, ed. Raffaella Baccolini (New York: Peter Lang, 2014), 31–2)

8   Seed writes,

> Science fiction is about the writer's present in the sense that any historical moment will include its own set of expectations and perceived tendencies. The futures represented in sf embody its speculative dimension. In that sense, as Joanna Russ has explained, it is a "What If Literature." The writer and critic Samuel Delany has applied the term "subjunctivity" to sf in a similar spirit to explain how these narratives position themselves between possibility and impossibility. It is helpful to think of an sf narrative as an embodied thought experiment whereby aspects of our familiar reality are transformed or suspended. (David Seed, *Science Fiction: A Very Short Introduction* (New York: Oxford University Press, 2011), 1–2)

9   Octavia E. Butler would often be asked what value science fiction has for Black people. In 1989, when she was "still the only Black woman" writing science fiction for a living, Butler turned that question into a series of other questions that suggest the value, and indeed centrality of science fiction to Black people:

What good is science fiction's thinking about the present, the future, and the past? What good is its tendency to warn or to consider alternative ways of thinking and doing? What good is its examination of the possible effects of science and technology, or social organization and political direction? At its best, science fiction stimulates imagination and creativity. It gets reader and writer off the beaten track, off the narrow, narrow footpath of what "everyone" is saying, doing, thinking—whoever "everyone" happens to be this year. And what good is all this to Black people?

Butler implicitly argues for the value to Black people of thinking about the past, present, and future, of hearing warnings and considering alternatives to the status quo, of scrutinizing science, technology, social organization, and politics. Octavia E. Butler, "Positive Obsession," in *Bloodchild and Other Stories* (New York: Seven Stories Press, 2005), 134–5.

10 Sherryl Vint, *Animal Alterity: Science Fiction and the Question of the Animal* (Liverpool: Liverpool University Press, 2010), 2.

11 For instance, by historicizing the history of US dairy farming and pork production alongside the techniques of slavery and by investigating the "dynamic discursive web of race and species," Samantha Pergadia makes a persuasive case for a thawing of the ice between animal studies and critical race studies, Samantha Pergadia, "Like an Animal: Genres of the Nonhuman in the Neo-Slave Novel," *African American Review* 51.4 (Winter 2018), 290. Joshua Bennett seeks to "illuminate the ways in which the black aesthetic tradition provides us with the tools needed to conceive of interspecies relationships anew and ultimately to abolish the forms of antiblack thought that have maintained the fissure between human and animal," Joshua Bennett, *Being Property Once Myself: Blackness and the End of* Man (Cambridge: Harvard University Press, 2020), 4. Zakiyyah Iman Jackson argues that "key texts of twentieth-century African diasporic literature and visual culture generate unruly conceptions of being and materiality that creatively disrupt the human-animal distinction and its persistent raciality," Zakiyyah Iman Jackson, *Becoming Human: Matter and Meaning in an Antiblack World* (New York: New York University Press, 2020), 1.

12 Bloch defines the Not-Yet-Conscious as "a relatively still Unconscious disposed towards its other side, forwards rather than backwards. Towards the side of something new that is dawning up, that has never been conscious before, not, for example, something forgotten, something rememberable that has been, something that has sunk into the subconscious in repressed or archaic fashion," Ernst Bloch, *The Principle of Hope*, 3 Volumes, trans. Neville Plaice, Stephen Plaice, and Paul Knight (Cambridge: MIT Press, 1986), 11.

13 Kari Weil, *Thinking Animals: Why Animal Studies Now?* (New York: Columbia University Press, 2010), 20.
14 It is beyond the scope of this project to take up the subjects of bestiality or zoophilia.
15 Mojca Krevel sees *Frankissstein* as "an intrinsic part of [postmodern] ontology," Mojca Krevel, "The Monstrous Cosmos of Jeanette Winterson's *Frankissstein*," *ELOPE* 18.2 (2021), 98. Peter Childs notes that Winterson's novels experiment with "fantasy and history" and demonstrate "how ideas and beliefs about history and reality are social constructs, which can be changed and can be reimagined," especially "social constructions of gendered identity," Peter Childs, *Contemporary British Fiction Since 1970* (New York: Palgrave Macmillan, 2005), 257, 258. Childs also identifies one of Winterson's key themes as love and the goal of loving better and differently, ibid., 261. For Amy J. Elias, Winterson's work evidences "a preoccupation with time and space, conceptualizations specifically linking non-Western epistemologies to post-Einsteinian physics," Amy J. Elias, *Sublime Desire: History and Post-1960s Fiction* (Baltimore: Johns Hopkins University Press, 2001), 57. Winterson's "metahistorical romance," Elias argues, "forms a double-pronged critique of Western teleological or progressivist history and of the West's more disciplinized historical studies," ibid. For Leigh Gilmore, Winterson "exploit[s] the possibilities of how bodies possess and perform 'identity'.… [T]he ways in which the representation of the body *is* its identity is of central concern," Leigh Gilmore, *The Limits of Autobiography: Trauma and Testimony* (Ithaca: Cornell University Press, 2001), 125, emphasis in original. Susana Onega sees Winterson's characters as archetypal: "The force that drives Winterson's protagonists on their life quests … is an acute feeling of lack and incompleteness that produces in them a consuming desire for the other, expressed in archetypal images such as the search for buried treasure/the Philosopher's Stone/the Holy Grail/that which cannot be found/death," Susana Onega, *Jeanette Winterson* (Manchester: Manchester University Press, 2006), 228.
16 Winterson, *Frankissstein: A Love Story*, 281. Subsequent page references are given in parentheses within the text.
17 Jeanette Winterson, *Written on the Body* (New York: Vintage, 1994), 178.
18 Andrea L. Harris, *Other Sexes: Rewriting Difference from Woolf to Winterson* (New York: State University of New York Press, 2000), 129.
19 There is a curious inconsistency in Victor's views of love and intelligence. When he speaks of love, humans are but a partial reflection of divine love, but when he speaks of intelligence, humans are the smartest. If human intelligence is to be rivaled, it will be by AI and not a deity. Yet human intelligence can also and has often been seen as a partial reflection of divine wisdom. In "Isaiah," God says, "For my thoughts are not your thoughts, nor are your ways my ways …. For as

the heavens are higher than the earth, so are my ways higher than your ways and my thoughts than your thoughts," *The New Oxford Annotated Bible*, Fifth Edition, ed. Michael D. Coogan (New York: Oxford University Press, 2018), 1054.

20 Paul K. Saint-Amour sees the novel as "a compendium of modes and expression of [ecological] grief," but one that, intriguingly, is able to encompass "the collective and interminable griefwork shaped by our deepening ecological crisis" via "the warping pressures of metalepsis," Paul K. Saint-Amour, "There Is Grief of a Tree," *American Imago* 77.1 (Spring 2020), 144, 140, 145. For Wai Chee Dimock, in *The Overstory*, "[the nonhuman world] is on its own now, a primary reality, densely and superabundantly inhabited, and no more solicitous of humans than nonhumans. Epic realism here is the realism of elemental forces, impartial in their power to nourish and their power to destroy," Wai Chee Dimock, "The Survival of the Unfit," *Daedalus* 150.1 (Winter 2021), 144. Marco Caracciolo classes the novel among "narratives that engage with nonhuman assemblages … via a formal focus on the collectivity of nonhuman animals, plants, and even inanimate things and processes," Marco Caracciolo, "We-Narrative and the Challenges of Nonhuman Collectives," *Style* 54.1 (2020), 87. It "uses a network narrative to channel a sense of deep, evolutionary time," Marco Caracciolo, "Emplotment Beyond the Human Scale: On Deep Time and Narrative Nonlinearity," *Poetics Today* 42.3 (September 2021), 352. Elsewhere Caracciolo sees the novel as "imagining a computational solution to the Earth's anthropogenic woes" that "involves letting go of humankind as we know it": "As humanity bows out of existence …, life and mind—on a continuum with computational algorithms—continue expanding and flourishing," Marco Caracciolo, "Deus Ex Algorithmo: Narrative Form, Computation, and the Fate of the World in David Mitchell's *Ghostwritten* and Richard Powers's *The Overstory*," *Contemporary Literature* 60.1 (Spring 2019), 47, 49. Offering an "echological" reading of the novel's "stylistic organicism," Garrett Stewart argues that *The Overstory* is "programmatic in its cognate disclosure of arboreality's own elusive communication system," Garrett Stewart, "Organic Reformations in Richard Powers's *The Overstory*," *Daedalus* 150.1 (Winter 2021), 167, 163.

21 Richard Powers, *The Overstory* (New York: W.W. Norton & Company, 2018), 262. Subsequent page references are given in parentheses within the text.

22 Paul Waldau, 18.

23 Philip K. Dick, *Do Androids Dream of Electric Sheep?*, 173, 177, 172. Rachael Rosen's form resembles Edvard Munch's adolescent figure in his painting *Puberty*, which Luba Luft studies in a catalog in the museum. Androids are also associated with Munch's *The Scream*. See Dick, 122, 121.

24 Carol J. Adams, *The Sexual Politics of Meat: A Feminist-Vegetarian Critical Theory* (New York: Bloomsbury, 2015), 25.

25 Some have criticized Winterston's treatment of trans themes in *Frankissstein*. Ana Horvat, for example, sees Winterson as an example of "cisgender writers taking up trans characters, representing them in outdated and sometimes offensive ways, and basing their research about transness on sources—traditional trans memoirs, medical facts, and mainstream media—that replicate patterns which trans authors have identified as harmful," Ana Horvat, "'Trans is Hot Right Now': On Cisgender Writers and Trans Characters in Jeanette Winterson's *Frankissstein* and Kim Fu's *For Today I Am a Boy*," *Gender Forum: An Internet Journal for Gender Studies* 79 (2021), 80.

26 One reviewer notes, "*Alex + Ada* plays with a much-beloved theme of the sf field: the question of whether or not an android or computer system is capable of true cognitive and emotional abilities," Charles De Lint, "Books to Look For: *Alex + Ada, Starlight, Pretty Deadly*," *Fantasy & Science Fiction* 127.3–4 (September-October 2014), 33. Another describes the way in which the series "combine[s] action, intrigue, big questions about what it means to be sentient," Tom Batten, "Review of *Alex + Ada: The Complete Collection*," *Library Journal* 142.2 (1 February 2017), 60. A third reviewer characterizes the visual idiom of the series by noting that "Luna's art is a marked departure from most contemporary comic-book art—spacious, spare, and minimalist, purposely mimicking the ordered, digital, and robotic nature of this imagined future," Ben Spanner, "Review of *Alex + Ada: Vol. 1*," *Booklist* 111.8 (December 15, 2014), 36.

27 Jonathan Luna and Sarah Vaughn, *Alex + Ada*, The Complete Collection: Deluxe Edition (Berkeley: Image Comics, 2016), 1.14, emphasis in original. The bound edition of the series is unpaginated. Here and following, I give the citation as issue and page number, counting the chapter division page as the first page of each issue. Subsequent issue and page references are given in parentheses within the text.

28 Compare 11.5 to 14.24.

29 Jacques Derrida, *The Animal That Therefore I Am*, ed. Marie-Louise Mallet, trans. David Wills (New York: Fordham University Press, 2008), 25. Emphases in the original.

30 Bloch, 1375.

31 Marc Bekoff, *The Emotional Lives of Animals: A Leading Scientist Explores Animal Joy, Sorrow, and Empathy—And Why They Matter* (Novato: New World Library, 2007), 24.

3

Familiar Aliens

In Ursula K. Le Guin's *The Dispossessed* (1974), the physicist Shevek travels from his home on the moon Annares to Urras, the planet from which his people separated and departed centuries ago. So accustomed is Shevek to the barrenness and hostility of the moon and to the hard-fought conditions of life there that the plentitude of Urras shocks him. It is the uncanny shock of an alien returning to the very place where his species evolved: "The whole world, the softness of the air, the fall of sunlight across the hills, the very pull of the heavier gravity on his body, asserted to him that this was home indeed, his race's world; and all its beauty was his birthright."[1] Looking over a grove of trees, a valley, and distant hills, Shevek thinks, "This is what a world is supposed to look like" (65). Part of the "rightness" of this alien world is the presence of other animals. Shevek's people "for seven generations had never touched an animal's warm fur or seen the flash of wings in the shade of trees" (152). On Urras, Shevek recognizes a deprivation of which he was hitherto unaware. As Shevek's partner Takver puts it,

> We Anarresti are unnaturally isolated. On the Old World there are eighteen phyla of land animal; there are classes, like the insects, that have so many species they've never been able to count them, and some of those species have populations of billions. Think of it: everywhere you looked animals, other creatures, sharing the earth and air with you. You'd feel so much more a *part*. (186, emphasis in original)

However, if Shevek belatedly realizes how deprived he's been because of living isolated from other species, *The Dispossessed* works the other way as well. It alerts readers comfortably ensconced on Earth to forms of abundance, affinity, and inclusion to which they can otherwise be blind.

Rivers Solomon's *An Unkindness of Ghosts* (2017) similarly imagines a return to origins that is at once alien and native; the novel presents the wish image of a *nostos* to Earth, or Great Lifehouse, healed long after it became uninhabitable. While the surviving humans have spent 325 years aboard *Matilda*, a massive slave spaceship, 1,000 years have elapsed on Earth: "Aster didn't know what tragedy had befallen this place, but time seemed to have erased it."[2] When Aster sets foot on the planet, she finds "a perfect tangled mess of planet life" (346) and momentarily believes that she has died along with her friend Giselle and "been spirited away to the Heavenly Lands" (346). As the first human to take a breath on Earth in more than ten centuries, she is simultaneously an arriving alien and the returning daughter who fits her environment harmoniously (although the tall grasses do make her sneeze): "When she inhaled, sweetly scented air, so cold, brushed her face and lips, drying the sweat on her forehead and neck" (347). The crows who do not fly off immediately "stared at her curiously, their bulbous eyes fixed to her, unafraid" (348), their demeanor suggesting a sort of blank slate for human-nonhuman animal relationships after a caesura of 1,000 years. After Aster buries the bones of her mother and the body of Giselle, she "lay down in the black dirt, the granules cooler than the coolest sheets on *Matilda*," feeling sad, sentimental, and superstitious, as though "she could cry and catch her tears in a magic vial, pour the tears over Giselle's face, and resurrect her" (348). Like *The Dispossessed*, *An Unkindness of Ghosts* offers feelings of evolutionary compatibility and harmony with one's environment, including with the many species with which one has coevolved, in a defamiliarized or estranged form; this is an impossible thing to conceive, perhaps, without positing an uncannily familiar alien.

Through science fiction, Gothic, and weird novels, this chapter turns to several other varieties of familiar alienness to consider what the alien offers perceptually, theoretically, and methodologically to critical animal studies. Aliens, of course, are already a presence in animal studies discourses. They appear regularly in philosophical accounts, aligned with or against nonhuman animals, or blurring the very line between human and nonhuman life. While Thomas Nagel evokes Martians to convey the epistemological alienness of bats,[3] Mary Midgley groups humans and other terrestrial animals together against alien species when determining a creature's advantage.[4] Donna Haraway, on the other hand, uses aliens to argue that species are always already mixed and plural.[5] Literary critics have also begun to explore the intersections of science fictional aliens and nonhuman animals in the context of animal studies. In *Animal Alterity*, Sherryl Vint writes, "Representations of aliens in sf are one of the places where these tensions and contradictions [in human-animal interrelations] are worked through culturally. ... [T]he very concept of the alien is one that expresses a human interest in—and struggle with—the reality of living with a different being."[6] Vint shows that, as we see in philosophy and theory, in science fiction aliens are aligned both with or against nonhuman animals, suggesting that "animal aliens represent both humanity's desire for connection to another being and its fear that all others represent a threat to self and hence must be destroyed."[7] Elsewhere, Vint suggests, "sf can have a transformative influence on our encounters with material animals," especially by foregrounding questions of mutual dependence, survival, and justice.[8]

This chapter explores liminal creatures that while embodying a sense of the extraterrestrial alien are nonetheless uncannily intimate, Earthbound, and homely. It suggests that science fiction, the Gothic, and the weird are genres that, through the uncanny and the alien, can help to scrutinize and transform representations of nonhuman animals. In *Fledgling* (2005), Octavia E. Butler draws upon the uncanny closeness and simultaneous alienness to humans of vampires to plumb the tenuous spaces between love, desire, need, symbiosis, and slavery and to expose the inseparable roots of speciesism and racism. In *Annihilation* (2014), Jeff VanderMeer finds horror in the premise of humans becoming infiltrated and contaminated by an alien environment and merging with other species, but he also exposes horror by making visible the mad, violent, self-defeating, and exhausting lengths to which humans go to assert our exceptionalism and our antiseptic separation from other forms of life. Taken together, these novels suggest models of symbiosis between human and nonhuman forms of life that are at once parasitic and mutualistic, feared and desired, rejected and needed, horrific and erotic, and enslaving and liberating. These novels offer critical animal studies perspectives from which to imagine nonhuman animals as familiar aliens. They present forms of symbiosis that challenge and horrify humans' senses of defensive boundaries while also tantalizing us beyond conventional constructions of the human with extraterrestrial as well as terrestrial forms of transcendence. The model of symbiosis that emerges in this chapter is one that illuminates the irrational, heteronormative, and racist obstacles to overcoming speciesism, the horror of integration with the nonhuman world, the fascination with capitulating our humanity, and the high and painful costs of continued separation and human exceptionalism.

Vampires

The Gothic is the genre of ghosts and vampires, haunting and mystery, horror and terror, and the archaic and the transgressive. From its origins in eighteenth-century tales of haunted castles and tormented heroines, the Gothic, as Fred Botting puts it, later "became part of an internalised world of guilt, anxiety, despair, a world of individual transgression interrogating the uncertain bounds of imaginative freedom and human knowledge."[9] David Punter calls the Gothic "a mode of revealing the unconscious,"[10] while for Jerrold E. Hogle it "provides the best-known examples of those strange and ghostly figures that Freud saw as examples of 'the Uncanny.'"[11] Hogle argues,

> Threats of and longings for gender-crossing, homosexuality or bisexuality, racial mixture, class fluidity, the child in the adult, timeless timeliness, and simultaneous evolution and devolution (especially after the middle of the nineteenth century): all these motifs, as possibly evil *and* desirable, circulate through Gothic works across the whole history of the form, differing mostly in degree of emphasis from example to example.[12]

George E. Haggerty calls the Gothic "a testing ground for many unauthorized gender and sexualities."[13] Nancy Armstrong stresses the portability and adaptability of the genre that undoes distinctions and overturns realism wherever it travels, likening the Gothic to Dracula himself:

> Wherever the vampire puts down a coffin-full of original Transylvanian soil, he retains the power to escape the confines of body and mind and bleed into others, human as well as animal, sweeping away all distinctions among them. In this respect, the gothic novel resembles its best-known villain, Dracula himself, in that both create a world within the so-called real world, a second world that overturns realism's grammar of person, place, and thing.[14]

Recently, critics have begun to explore the potential of the Gothic genre for animal studies. In their introduction to *Gothic Animals,* Ruth Heholt and Melissa Edmundson note that representations of nonhuman animals intersect with the Gothic in two primary ways—first, animals are used to emphasize that which is supposedly external to the human: "Alien, Other, and unknowable, in this schema the 'animal' immediately becomes Gothic."[15] But beginning in post-Darwin nineteenth-century fiction such as *The Strange Case of Dr Jekyll and Mr Hyde* and *The Island of Doctor Moreau,* the animal is also Gothic because it is the unknowable thing within the human itself: "An unruly, defiant, degenerate, and entirely amoral animality lying (mostly) dormant within all of us. This was our animal other, a Gothic double associated with the id."[16] Nonhuman animals are at once the alien other and the uncanny double within the human animal. Heholt and Edmundson finally see the Gothic's relation to animals as ambivalent: "The Gothic can be a force for good in relation to giving the animal a vitally important place in discussions and texts, but it can also 'scapegoat' the animal—making animals 'stand in' for cultural anxieties, fears, and abjected taboos."[17]

If the vampire has long been a staple of the Gothic, Octavia E. Butler's *Fledgling* renders it even more alien. Early in the novel, for instance, Butler alienates readers from literary Gothic and folkloric expectations about vampires. Butler's vampires are neither allergic to garlic and crucifixes ("Another perfectly good vampire superstition down the drain"[18]), nor do their bites transform human victims into vampires ("If a dog bit a man, no one would expect the man to become a dog" (394)). When the amnesiac Shori finally meets her father Iosif, he explains, "We have very little in common with the vampire creatures Bram Stoker described in *Dracula*" (336). They do not even call themselves vampires, but rather Ina. As Shori slowly discovers what it means to be Ina, she also seeks to bring to justice the Ina family that killed her mother's and father's families. *Fledgling* is part Ina ethnography and part alien courtroom drama.[19]

Butler also makes the vampire alien by suggesting that the Ina may have extraterrestrial roots. Among various Ina origin theories is one in which they are said to have "landed here from another world thousands of years ago" (340). Another origin myth is that a great mother goddess placed the Ina on Earth as a kind of purgatory, "until we became wise enough to come home to live in paradise with her" (341). They are "stuck here" until they prove themselves to her (402). Humans in the novel who are in contact with the Ina, such as Wright and Theodora, describe themselves as living with "extraterrestrial aliens" (402) and among "the Martians" (497). However, Butler always keeps the alien Ina uncannily near to the human, never allowing them to become entirely other. Iosif's own theory is that the Ina "evolved right here on Earth alongside humanity as a cousin species like the chimpanzee. Perhaps we're the more gifted cousin" (341). "We're too genetically similar to them for any other explanation to be likely" (340), he says.

As in the relationship between Tlic and Terrans in Butler's "Bloodchild," the Ina and humans do not rely on each other merely as entirely separate but dependent species; rather, the alien penetrates the human. In "Bloodchild," the insectile T'Gatoi lays her eggs in the Terran boy Gan and will later surgically extract her voracious grubs before they can eat Gan from within. In exchange for this apparent parasitism, T'Gatoi protects and feeds Gan's family in a Preserve on an alien planet. It is a fraught and painful kind of mutualism. In *Fledgling*, the Ina need human blood. They bite humans, but unlike stereotypical vampires Ina do not seek to kill; each Ina cultivates a stable of human "symbionts" from whom they drink regularly and frugally. In exchange, the Ina protect their symbionts and their human families; indeed, they become part of a large, extended family. Ina venom offers humans intense pleasure, increased immunity and healing capacities, improved memory, and vastly increased longevity. Symbionts can live with Ina for up to two hundred years, while Ina live for about five hundred years. Iosif calls this relationship "mutualistic symbiosis" (336).

In many ways, human-Ina symbiotic relations resemble love relationships. They are "tied" together through venom and taste, and they form bonds of intense affection and devotion. Their pansexual bonds queer the lines of sexuality and reproduction. Whereas male and female Ina mate in heterosexual groups that otherwise live apart from each other, Ina and their human symbionts live together in nonnormative and nonreproductive sexual communities. The Ina render human heteronormativity alien; humans who might initially identify as heterosexual nonetheless experience intense attraction to and affection for same-sex Ina. Wright, who struggles with this idea, asks Brook how she feels about having a female Ina. Brook says, "I would probably have chosen a man if I'd had a choice initially. But I'm okay with Shori. I can find myself a human man if I need one" (434). After overhearing this exchange, Shori asks Martin, William Gordon's symbiont, if he initially minded being "symbiont to another man" (473). After mildly chastising Shori for prying into personal matters, Martin answers similarly to Brook: " 'There are plenty of women here,' he said. 'I married one of them shortly after I decided to stay' " (473–4). Martin then asks Shori about her new female symbiont, Theodora. Shori reports that Theodora "says she doesn't understand her feeling for me" (474). Martin responds, "I saw you two. You were all over each other. That's the way it goes. It doesn't seem to matter to most humans what our lives were before we meet you. You bite us, and that's all it takes" (474). Human symbionts, then, while seeming to retain their sexual orientation among other humans, enjoy greater plasticity of identity, pleasure, and desire in their relationships with Ina. The simple ease with which an Ina bite at least partially overcomes former sexual identities among humans begins to alienate the idea of the inevitability and rigidity of such identity formations.

Ina-human attachments are deep and lasting. Preston Gordon explains to Shori that "our symbionts … they never truly understand how deeply we treasure them" (423). Ina are expected to display intense, paralyzing grief if they lose a symbiont. Katharine Dahlman orders her symbiont to murder Theodora to gain the upper hand over Shori at the next Council of Judgment session. Preston explains, "You should have been, by all reckoning, only a husk of a person, mad with grief and rage or simply mad" (533). Ina rely on their symbionts and must have at least some of them near at all times. Human symbionts also love their Ina; jealousy is common among symbiont families and must be carefully managed by the Ina. Wright, Shori's first symbiont after she experiences amnesia, tells her, "I want you for myself. It scares me how much I love you, Shori" (428). When human symbionts lose their Ina, they experience psychological and physical "withdrawal" (434). The loss is emotional, but also physical: symbionts die without their Ina to remove the extra red blood cells that Ina venom prompts their bodies to make. Unless another Ina can manage to take human symbionts over—a risky operation because "They're addicted to their particular Ina and no other" (348)—the human will die.

Humans who have been bitten but are not yet completely tied to an Ina must be compelled to forget the experience, or "They might waste their lives looking for you" (349). This condition is reminiscent of dogs bent on seeking their former masters. Indeed, Pramod K. Nayar suggests that *Fledgling* offers a posthuman displacement of the human as a companion species.[20] But the Ina-human relationship also suggests something more like petkeeping and ownership than companionship, blurring the line between symbiosis and slavery. As in many human-alien encounters in Butler's fiction, the Ina overwhelm human will, yet with a peculiar ambivalence. In Butler's short story, "Amnesty," for instance, the alien Communities, each something like an "intelligent multitude" (678), enjoy enfolding humans into "itselves" (672). Humans lose autonomy when enfolded, but also feel a sense of comfort and pleasure. New recruits worry about whether the Communities recognize human intelligence and ask "what do they think of us?," but the human recruiter Noah reassures them that the Communities would not offer them contracts "if they'd mistaken you for cattle" (673), a word that not only suggests cows but is also derived from "chattel," as in chattel slavery. In "Bloodchild," T'Gatoi gives Gan a "choice" between being implanted and inflicting the process on his sister. He can bear neither to inflict implantation and extraction on his sister nor to shoot T'Gatoi with the gun he has hidden; both creatures are family to him. Yet Gan, part of a human community that left Earth to escape slavery, agonizes about the line between being T'Gatoi's human family member and her "host animal" (24): "What are we to you?" (635), he demands. As Shori does to her symbionts, T'Gatoi penetrates Gan's body: "I felt the familiar sting, narcotic, mildly pleasant. Then the blind probing of her ovipositor. The puncture was painless, easy. So easy going in. She undulated slowly against me, her muscles forcing the egg from her body into mine" (638). Afterward, T'Gatoi tells Gan, "You were the one making the choices tonight" (638), and she promises, "I'll take care of you" (639).

Like Gan in "Bloodchild," Wright worries that it is not love and choice but rather instrumentalization and compulsion that binds him to the alien other: "Do you love me, Shori, or do I just taste good?" (410). Wright not only worries that as Shori's symbiont he will be "part of a harem" (356),[21] but also, like livestock or enslaved people, that he would be used to "produce the next generation of symbionts" (357). Being a symbiont means having radical limits on individual autonomy. Like T'Gatoi, who insists that Gan made the choices, Shori reminds Wright that before she tied him fully to her, "I offered you freedom" (356). However, Wright admits to Brook that even at that early stage he was "hooked, psychologically if not physically" (433), and expresses regret: "I can't imagine being without her, but I'm not sure I would have begun if I'd known what I was getting into" (433). Other symbionts are similarly ambivalent. Martin, an African American symbiont, explains to Shori that although he eventually decided to be with William, at first "I thought it sounded more like slavery than symbiosis" (474).

While Ina often express their feelings for their human symbionts in terms of love, some of the rhetoric is distinctly paternalistic and speciesist. When he blesses the upcoming Council meeting, Milo, the Silk family patriarch, speaks about symbionts in a way that Shori finds condescending to them: "May we look after our human symbionts with kindness and firmness. May we care for them and keep them from harm" (500). The Silk family and Katharine Dahlman have also used humans to murder Shori's family and symbionts, acts that the Gordon family initially cannot believe because Ina "hadn't done anything like that for centuries" (420). A major ethical concern in the Council sessions is the limits of Ina use of humans. Shori asks, "Are humans tools, then? Should we be free to use them according to our needs?" (545). The Silks will not admit to using humans this way, but their "false outrage" (545) is evident to Shori and ultimately to the Council members. Paralleling debates about the proper and ethical limits of human instrumentalization of nonhuman animals, the Ina debate estranges or "alienates" humans by positioning us as useful and useable animals.

The Ina are also alien and alienating creatures because unlike humans, in whom racism seems so at home, racism at first seems uncannily alien to them. Brook insists to Wright, "They're not human, Wright. They don't care about white or black" (433). Ina and humans are different species, not different races, and therefore cannot interbreed. However, Shori is part human, the result of a genetic crossbreeding experiment conducted by her Ina family to cross Ina with human, specifically African American, genes. The goal of the genetic engineering is for Ina to function during the daytime and to have some protection against the sun. When Wright proposes that Ina might have killed Shori's families because of racism ("Shori is black, and racists—probably Ina racists—don't like the idea that a good part of the answer to your daytime problems is melanin" (419)), the Gordons, their pride "wounded" (420), insist that "Ina weren't racists. ... Human racism meant nothing to the Ina because human races meant nothing to them. They looked for congenial human symbionts wherever they happened to be, without regard for anything but personal appeal" (420). When Butler constructs "another intelligent species here on Earth" (402) that resembles humans in many ways and yet is entirely free of racism, she makes something uncanny and alienating.

However, *Fledgling* also makes racism alien by letting readers observe the very process through which Ina speciesism becomes shot through with racism, or perhaps the way in which latent or concealed racism is brought to the surface because of miscegenation. It is not just Shori's mixed species that moves the Silks and Dahlmans to family feuds and murder of a kind unseen among the Ina for "more than a thousand years" (420); more consequential is her mixed race. We see the Ina become infected by human racism that they have witnessed and finally internalized during their centuries living among humans in the United States. Right before the Council's final judgment, Katharine Dahlman stuns Preston Gordon when she tells him, "You want your sons to mate with this person. You want them to get black, human children from her. Here in the United States, even most humans will look down on them. When I came to this country such people were kept as property, as slaves" (538). After the judgment against his family, Russell Silk assaults Shori, calling her a "Murdering black mongrel bitch" and asking, "What will she give us all? Fur? Tails?" (564). Russell echoes Milo Silk's speciesist words to Shori on the first day of the Council—"You're not [Ina]! And you have no more business at this Council than would a clever dog!" (506)—but also lays bare the racism that Milo had tried to conceal. It turns out that even the Ina, who should be impervious to human racism, are interpellated by white supremacist ideology by living in the United States for hundreds of years. Butler levels a devastating critique of white supremacism by exposing it among an alien species who might even have arrived from another planet.

Zakiyyah Iman Jackson challenges animal studies to come to terms with the ways in which the categories of species and race "have coevolved and are actually *mutually reinforcing* terms."[22] *Fledgling* supports the view that race and species are imbricated and reinforcing, and that we ought not to consider speciesism in isolation from racism. From a critical animal studies perspective, the shock of Ina racism cuts back against the more accustomed speciesism in the novel. Ina racism draws out the abjection that Jackson finds at work in the construction of species. Specifically, Jackson argues that species has been constructed around and against the figure of the reproducing Black woman: "the black(end) female is posited as the abyss dividing organic life into 'human' or 'animal' based on wholly unsound metaphysical premises."[23] It is not surprising, then, that as a Black woman, Shori would agitate the racist underpinnings of Ina speciesism and bring it to a violent crisis. The racist anxieties surrounding Shori's reproductive capacities are clear enough in Russell Silk's anxiety about fur and tails. But Shori's Blackness and femaleness also expose the racist anxiety about reproduction enmeshed with the speciesist paternalism in Russell's impassioned yet more guarded closing statement to the Council:

> They destroy one another by the millions, and it makes no difference to their numbers. They breed and breed and breed, while we live long and breed slowly. Their lives are brief and, without us, riddled with disease and violence. And yet, we need them. We take them into our families, and with our help, they are able to live longer, stay free of disease, and get along with one another. We could not live without them.
>
> But we are not them!
>
> We are not them!
>
> Children of the great Goddess, we are not them! (556–7)

Russell Silk's racist and speciesist contempt for human reproduction, wars, and diseases comes with the frank acknowledgment that Ina lives depend on human symbionts, much as the lives of slaveholders relied on enslaved people. Russell's combination of contempt and dependency culminates in thrice-repeated disavowal of any identity between human and Ina. After Russell's unsuccessful assault on Shori, the Silks grudgingly accept the Council's judgment against their family, all but disbanding it, but Katharine Dahlman refuses to submit to her sentence. She looks at Shori "with more hatred and contempt than I would have thought she could manage" and insists that her punishment for ordering Theodora's murder is unjust: "That human was not a symbiont because Shori is not Ina!" (568). Katharine makes clear that human lives are not valuable per se, but only when they are symbionts to an Ina; like many animals before they fall into the category of "pet," humans in the novel are not intrinsically valuable until they are loved and needed by an Ina.[24] (Once admitted into this category, pets are said to benefit by living longer, staying free of disease, and living peacefully, as in Russell Silk's paternalistic view of human symbionts. That is, the practice is in part rationalized as being for the benefit of the subjected creature.) Katharine does not recognize Shori as Ina because of her human genes and skin color, so it follows that she views Theodora's murder as insignificant: In her view, one cannot murder what amounts to a mere animal. In the end, Katharine suicidally assaults Shori rather than accept the Council's punishment, a stunning embodiment and indictment of entwined racism and speciesism for which Katharine is willing to sacrifice her centuries-long life.

Fledgling draws on science fiction and Gothic conventions and modes of transgression to question sexual, racial, and species distinctions when confronted by symbiosis with the uncanny alien other. Butler's novel underscores the heteronormative, sexist, and racist underpinnings of speciesism while imagining new forms of symbiosis with the alien that queer human-nonhuman relationships and discover love beyond the instinct of horror. In so doing, Ina-human symbiosis asks readers to reflect on the ways in which ideologies of race and sexuality tacitly and habitually maintain our species identities and violently affect human-nonhuman animal relationships. At the same time, *Fledgling* imagines making a habit of, and indeed of becoming addicted to, forms of interspecies symbiosis and love that can only emerge once speciesism is sloughed off and the human is opened to radical risk (rather than to fantasies of antiseptic containment) in its encounter with the alien other. The forms of symbiosis imagined in *Fledgling* thus expand our sense of filiation with nonhuman others even as they defamiliarize and unravel the ideologies that underlie species identity.

Strangling Fruit

The classic attempt to differentiate between the Gothic and the weird is given by one of the weird's practitioners, H. P. Lovecraft:

> The true weird tale has something more than secret murder, bloody bones, or a sheeted form clanking chains according to rule. A certain atmosphere of breathless and unexplainable dread of outer, unknown forces must

be present; and here must be a hint, expressed with a seriousness and portentousness becoming its subject, of that most terrible conception of the human brain—a malign and particular suspension or defeat of those fixed laws of Nature which are our only safeguard against the assaults of chaos and the daemons of unplumbed space.[25]

As S. T. Joshi explains, Lovecraft sought to "transfer the locus of fear from the mundane to what he called the 'Great Outside.'"[26] Nevertheless, the Gothic and the weird can be understood as sharing a common starting point in creating a sense of estrangement from the norm. Indeed, for Joshi, the distinguishing feature of the weird tale is its "refashioning of the reader's view of the world."[27] China Miéville similarly argues, "The focus is on *awe*, and its undermining of the quotidian. This obsession with numinosity under the everyday is at the heart of Weird Fiction."[28] In addition to defamiliarization or estrangement, the weird also shares with the Gothic a sense of the sublime. But whereas Botting defines the Gothic as "an aesthetics based on feeling and emotion and associated primarily with the sublime,"[29] Miéville describes the weird as a "radicalized sublime backwash."[30] "Backwash" suggests that the weird takes a different route to the sublime; the weird represents a kind of backwards current through the "punctures [in] the supposed membrane separating off the sublime"[31] from the everyday. Miéville further differentiates the weird from the Gothic in terms of their respective relations to the uncanny. Because for Miéville, "The Weird is not a return of any repressed,"[32] but a "lack of recognition, rather than any uncanny resurgence,"[33] he argues that the weird is associated with a sense of the "abcanny":[34] "*Implacably alien*,"[35] the "monsters of the abcanny" are "teratological expressions of [the] unrepresentable and unknowable, evasive of meaning."[36] Mark Fisher similarly distances the weird from the already-known and associates it with novelty and the need for new conceptualizations: "The sense of *wrongness* associated with the weird—the conviction that *this does not belong*—is often a sign that we are in the presence of the new. The weird here is a signal that the concepts and frameworks which we have previously employed are now obsolete."[37] If the Gothic is uncannily haunted by past horror—Andrew Smith views Gothic ghosts as "ciphers for models of subjectivity which refer to culturally specific notions of psychological trauma"[38]—then the weird confronts the terrifyingly new. Miéville writes, "The Weird is in opposition to that category for thinking through the history-stained present ... known as the 'Hauntological.' The Weird, rather, impregnates the present with a bleak, unthinkable novum."[39]

Jeff VanderMeer is often categorized as a "new weird" writer. Differentiating such writers from the original weird practitioners such as Lovecraft, Lord Dunsany, Algernon Blackwood, M. R. James, and Ambrose Bierce, Benjamin Noys and Timothy S. Murphy charasterize the new weird as "a new sensibility of welcoming the alien and the monstrous as sites of affirmation and becoming. In contradiction to Lovecraft's horror at the alien, influenced by his racism, the New Weird adopts a more radical politics that treats the alien, the hybrid, and the chaotic as subversions of the various normalizations of power and subjectivity."[40] For M. John Harrison, the new weird recalls the pulp era in which horror, science fiction, and fantasy could still intermingle freely.[41] For Benjamin J. Robertson, the new weird is characterized by its self-conscious awareness and use of genre conventions from the weird, horror, and science fiction, drawing on a stable of established weird conventions still emerging and uncodified in Lovecraft's time.[42] For Stephanie Swainton, however, generic considerations are secondary to the new weird's "theme" of detail:

> The details are jewel-bright, hallucinatory, carefully described. ... The New Weird attempts to place the reader in a world they do not expect, a world that surprises them—the reader stares around and sees a vivid world through the detail. These details—clothing, behaviour, scales and teeth—are what makes New Weird worlds so much like ours, as recognisable and as well-described. It is visual, and every scene is packed with baroque detail.[43]

Synthesizing previous discussions, VanderMeer proposes that the new weird "subverts the romanticized ideas about place found in traditional fantasy," "has a visceral, in-the-moment quality that often uses elements of surreal or transgressive horror for its tone, style, and effects," and "relies for its visionary power on a 'surrender to the weird' that isn't, for example, hermetically sealed in a haunted house on the moors or in a cave in Antarctica."[44]

The first novel in VanderMeer's *Southern Reach* trilogy, *Annihilation* introduces a natural landscape made alien, one in which, as in the Inasymbiont relationship in *Fledgling*, human autonomy is not an option. *Annihilation* literalizes *The Overstory*'s rhetoric of the living landscape as "alien invader."[45] A team of four women, identified only by their roles in the expedition, enter Area X ostensibly to explore it and to understand the way in which nature has reclaimed the land from humans. One by one, they too are claimed by a mysterious natural landscape that is at once beautiful, horrific, and finally sublime in its profusion, fruitfulness, and capacities for mimicry and infiltration. Whereas Miéville distances the weird from the uncanny in favor of the abcanny, *Annihilation* mobilizes both concepts. As in *Fledgling*, in *Annihilation* the penetration of the human by the implacably and abcannily alien serves to uncover dimensions of the human that are often repressed, occluded, or uncanny: "We were scientists, trained to observe natural phenomena and the results of human activity. We had not been trained to encounter what appeared to be the uncanny."[46] However, as the biologist, whose journal comprises the narrative of *Annihilation*, notes, "Estrangement, in all of its many forms, was nothing new for these missions" (23). Each previous expedition has come to bad but uniquely different ends, including mass suicide and mass murder. The members of the immediately preceding eleventh expedition, the biologist's husband among them, all returned as shells of themselves and promptly died of "inoperable, systemic cancer" (38).[47] The forms of Shklovskian *ostranenie* offered in *Annihilation*, then, include both uncanny closeness in the alien and abcanny otherness within the most homely.

The alien penetration of the human begins even before the women enter Area X. Part of their training by the Southern Reach, the government agency tasked with monitoring and exploring Area X, involves hypnosis. The biologist, anthropologist, and surveyor are aware that the psychologist has hypnotized them to ease their transition into Area X, a border-crossing of which they retain no memory. It becomes clear, however, that the psychologist also uses hypnosis to bend team consensus to her will. It gradually emerges that the team is being unwittingly used for unstated purposes. Hypnosis represents a subliminal and uncanny infiltration or contamination of human will that presages the more profound incursions of Area X into the human. It is the first of many phenomena in the novel that penetrate the self and provoke fear of contamination and lost autonomy.

In addition to hypnosis, self-abnegation also appears as an alien condition that is already within the biologist. The biologist is drawn to Area X not only because she seeks to understand what befell her husband, but also because she is strangely compelled by the emptiness evident in the videotaped interviews of returning eleventh expedition members: "At the time, I was seeking oblivion, and I sought in those blank, anonymous faces, even the most painfully familiar, a kind of benign escape. A death that would not mean being dead" (24). Freud described the death drive as "the most universal endeavour in all living substance ... to return to the quiescence of the inorganic world."[48] Because for Freud "*inanimate things existed before living ones*," life must aspire to "an *old state of things, an initial state from which the living entity has at one time or other departed.*"[49] Contrary to Freud, however, *Annihilation* "weirds" the death drive and develops a willed negation of the self not as a return to the inorganic but rather as a remerging with a wider organic world undifferentiated from the human. In *Annihilation*, it is not death, but rather interpenetrating life that is eroticized: "Sustenance for me was tied to ecosystem and habitat, orgasm the sudden realization of the interconnectivity of living things" (72). Earlier in her life, on a field assignment involving the transitional environments of tidal pools, the biologist gets drunk and drives out to her research site: "I really wanted to lose myself. People my entire life have told me I am too much in control, but that has never been the case. I have never truly been in control, never have wanted control" (115). She had become "sidetracked" from her grant responsibilities, "because I melted into my surroundings, could not remain *separate from, apart from*, objectivity a foreign land to me" (115, emphasis in original). In this condition of "dissolution," to echo the title of the novel's final section, the biologist comes upon the rare "destroyer of worlds" starfish searching for its prey in a tidal pool, a discovery that will be repeated in the novel's present when the biologist fatefully encounters the mysterious Crawler. Staring at the incomprehensible starfish, the biologist loses her orientation in a moment of abcanniness: "The more it became something alien to me, the more I had a sense that I knew nothing at all—about nature, about ecosystems" (116). As an act of self-preservation, she finally forces herself to look away, for "if I kept looking, I knew that ultimately I would have to admit I knew less than nothing about myself as well, whether that was a lie or the truth" (116).

Writing, too, is rendered both uncanny and abcanny in Area X. When the expedition begins to explore the mysterious tunnel discovered near base camp, which the biologist calls the Tower, they find that the wall along the stairway is inexplicably lined with strange "fruiting bodies" (17) that spell out an endless and unwinding sentence in English: "*Where lies the strangling fruit that came from the hand of the sinner I shall bring forth the seeds of the dead to share with the worms that ...*" (16). "Tricked into thinking that words should be read," the biologist leans too closely and inhales "a tiny spray of golden spores" (17), which initiates her slow dissolution and integration into Area X.[50] In the Tower, language, so familiar and apparently at home in the human, becomes alive and alien, a thing that penetrates and operates independently inside the human and corroborates William S. Burroughs's sense that language is a virus.[51] The biologist first thinks of her inhalation of language spores as a "contamination" (17), but later calls it a "brightness" that both protects her and changes her from within, slowly integrating her into the ecosystem of Area X. It gives her "an unsettling sensation, as of something creeping under my skin, forming a layer that perfectly mimicked the one that could be seen" (101). Writing is one of the means by which Area X penetrates and incorporates the human, but Area X's transformations and mimicry of the human may also be seen as more generalized forms of writing. Area X rewrites and thus reproduces the biologist.

The uncanny writing in the Tower is echoed in the lighthouse. Under a hatch in the lighthouse, the biologist finds a "huge mound," or "insane midden" comprising hundreds of expedition journals, "Many, many more than could possibly have been filed by only twelve expeditions" (70). "The scene obliquely embodied the scrap of writing I had encountered on the Tower wall" (73–4), she writes. The base of the pile had "clearly turned to compost, the paper rotting way" and become "a mulch of pages" (73). The decomposing and fertile mound of words resembles the garbage heaps and linguistic middens of Beckett and Joyce. Although later volumes in the trilogy reveal that there have been many more than the twelve expeditions officially acknowledged by the Southern Reach, it is still unclear whether there had been enough of them to compose a heap "twelve feet high and sixteen feet wide" (73). The biologist is left "gasping for breath" and feeling something like "a punch in the stomach as I dropped to my knees" (70) in the face of this proliferating and decomposing heap of writing.

As the hypnosis, self-abnegation, and uncanny language and writing suggest, the contamination is always already within the human. Area X simply becomes the organic stage in which such counter-drives to human exceptionalism and separateness can play out in stunning extremes. As Finola

Anne Prendergast says, "*Annihilation* evokes the disorientation and fear that might attend humanity's acceptance of nonhuman life's value and, in consequence, the admission that human life is not *uniquely* valuable."[52] Area X has a genius for integrating forms of life together. The expedition encounters animals that seem to have integrated humans into them. A wild boar charges the team and gives the biologist "the startling impression of some *presence* in the way its gaze seemed to turn inward and its head willfully pulled to the left as if there were an invisible bridle" (12, emphasis in original). She observes that the boar's "features were somehow contorted, as if the beast were dealing with an extreme of inner torment" (12). Later, the biologist sees a dolphin whose eye is "painfully human, almost familiar" (64).[53] In a deserted house, the biologist finds "a few peculiar eruptions of moss and lichen" that form "an approximation of limbs and heads and torsos" (63). Under the microscope, the cells from this moss as well as those from a dead fox prove to be "composed of modified human cells" (106). A beast among the reeds moans nightly at dusk; the biologist never sees it, even when it chases her, but she does find its molted exoskeleton: "It was a kind of tan mask made of skin, half-transparent, resembling in its way the discarded shell of a horseshoe crab. A wide face, with a hint of pockmarks across the left cheek" (93). The biologist concludes that "the moaning creature was, or had once been, human" (94). She eludes the creature, but it "kept calling, pleading with me to return, to see it entire, to acknowledge its existence" (95). *Annihilation* takes the biological concept of transitional environments and makes it uncanny by folding the human into a wildly metamorphic process of transition: "Transformations were taking place here, and as much as I had felt part of a 'natural' landscape ..., I could not deny that these habitats were transitional in a deeply *unnatural* way" (106, emphasis in original). The transmogrifications of bodies worked by Area X suggest new forms of posthumanism, in the sense of having-once-been-human.[54]

The biologist's encounter with the Crawler is the culmination of interconnectivity, dissolution, and loss of control in *Annihilation*. The Crawler defeats the biologist's sensory capacities. Her vision is "battered" (117) by an object that shifts, surges, and overwhelms her: "My eyes kept glancing off of it as if an optic nerve was not enough" (117). She hears the Tower's beating heart, strengthening her earlier hypothesis that everything in the tower is "part of a vast biological entity that might or might not be terrestrial" (59–60) and presaging her later supposition that the Crawler might be "a creature living in perfect symbiosis with a host of other creatures" (126), of which she, too, is becoming part. Like *Fledgling*, then, *Annihilation* proposes as symbiotic relationships that might otherwise be considered parasitic, enslaving, or even predatory. As the novel discovers symbiosis in the teeth of terror, it identifies the scientific and cultural construction of the human, rather than the boundaries, characteristics, and functions of human body, as the obstacle of symbiosis.[55]

Finally confronting the Crawler, the biologist experiences synesthesia, hearing the words on the wall vibrate, "feeling the music from the words" (119) and smelling and tasting the vibration (117). The biologist's language marks the sublimity of this experience, its mixed awe and terror and its transcendence of the self's limited sensory capacities:

> The enormity of this experience combined with the heartbeat and the crescendo of sound from its ceaseless writing to fill me up until I had no room left. *This* moment, which I might have been waiting for my entire life all unknowing—this moment of an encounter with the most beautiful, the most terrible thing I might ever experience—was beyond me. What inadequate recording equipment I had brought with me and what an inadequate name I had chosen for it—the Crawler. Time elongated, was nothing but fuel for the words the thing had created on the wall for who knew how many years for who knew what purpose. (118, emphasis in original)

This alien sublime ("the most beautiful, the most terrible") challenges the biologist's senses and her fundamental conceptualizations of the world. Not only does the encounter make visible that for which her whole life she might unknowingly have been looking, but it also radically refigures her experience and sense of time and space. This natural encounter is so abcanny[56] that it undermines human epistemology: "What can you do when your five senses are not enough?" (118). Human perception is rendered inadequate, along with the techniques and equipment with which humans purport to see, capture, and master reality (e.g., study, objectivity, description; e.g., flashlight, camera, handgun). Like the starfish in the tidal pool, the Crawler is "irreducible" to "taxonomy" (116); human names fail to capture it securely. Somewhat like the vision that Biboon is given by the golden beetle in Louise Erdrich's *The Night Watchman*, examined in the next chapter, which reveals time as an element and substance that humans living within it misconceive, time in the

Tower is not a duration or a process, but simply fuel for the Crawler's ceaseless writing. Time loses its human scale, and writing is no longer just alien and uncanny, but outright sublime: the Crawler's writing is beyond the senses and comprehension. The instrumental link between humans and writing, when conceived as a purposeful tool, is broken. Instead, writing is sheer proliferation, mimicry, and assimilation as indifferent to the human as the Crawler is or indeed as the entire ecosystem of Area X proves to be.

The earlier penetration of alien language and spores is replayed violently when the Crawler notices the biologist. Caught in the field of the Crawler's attention, the biologist feels as though she is literally drowning in its light. When she stops resisting and finally opens her mouth to the light, she feels "a hundred fingers, probing and pressing down into the skin of my neck, and then punching up through the bone of the back of my skull and into my brain" (120). She feels her "skull crushed to dust and reassembled"; she feels "agony," "as if a metal rod had been repeatedly thrust into me and then the pain distributed like a second skin inside the contours of my outline" (120). Drawing from her own experiences as a scientific observer, the biologist recognizes herself as an object of observation and prey, subject to "unlimited force" (120): "I was a thing in a swimming pool being observed by a monstrous little girl. I was a mouse in an empty lot being tracked by a fox. I was the prey the starfish had reached up and pulled down into the tidal pool" (119).

The biologist's terms to describe her penetration by the Crawler bear comparison with philosopher Val Plumwood's account of being attacked by a crocodile: "It is, essentially, an experience beyond words of total terror."[57] The biologist's experience as quarry strengthens the pervading sense of human dissolution and incorporation into Area X. Plumwood's experience similarly forces her to make an epistemological shift away from illusions of human supremacy and inedibility: "Before the encounter, it was as if I saw the whole universe as framed by my own narrative, as though the two were joined perfectly and seamlessly together. As my own narrative and the larger story were ripped apart, I glimpsed a shockingly indifferent world in which I had no more significance than any other edible being."[58] Perhaps doubly dislocating in comparison to Plumwood's experience of being prey is the biologist's subjection to the Crawler's indifferent force in combination with an inner alien presence that persists indifferently to its host.[59] To the Crawler, the biologist seems nothing more than something to penetrate, probe, and scan; to the brightness within her, she is of no more significance than any other host organism. Even when the biologist believes she has stopped breathing, the brightness that inhabits her continues unabated: "It just kept oxygenating my blood" (120). Even her body's capitulation and readiness to die is a matter of perfect indifference to the brightness, alienating the biologist even from her own experience of death. Located between indifferent forces without and within, the biologist's life is saved from the indifferent threat of the Crawler only by the indifferent purposes of the brightness within her.

Having already survived a gunshot wound from the surveyor, the biologist has learned that the brightness heals and keeps her alive for its own unknown but transformative purposes. To defer whatever transformative ends the brightness has in store for her, the biologist learns that she must preoccupy it with healing her body: "To keep the brightness in check, I would have to continue to become wounded, to be injured. To shock my system" (101). In *Acceptance*, we learn that the biologist has survived by "hurting myself" and "using pain to push the brightness back" (483). However, at the end of *Annihilation* the biologist already anticipates giving up self-harm and relenting to the transformative force within her: "the thought of continually doing harm to myself in order to remain human seems somehow pathetic" (128). The contrivance of the novel's uncanny nature has built to this stunning conclusion. *Annihilation* opens the perspective from which to assert and cling to the human is to persist in harming oneself. *Annihilation* makes visible the often invisible resistance that it constantly takes for humans to assert our exceptionalism and separateness from the world and the creatures surrounding us. It also registers the fear and horror of letting go of human separateness in the face of the unknown.

Sherryl Vint notes that *Annihilation* diagnoses the response of fear as "a limitation of human perception" because "Those rooted in what *is* cannot conceptualize *what might be*."[60] The biologist has spent her life devoted to studying what is. But now, as she renounces the human, she also abnegates her drive to know. The biologist writes, "In that moment [of approaching the Crawler], I had convinced myself I would rather die knowing ... something, *anything*" (114, emphasis in original). But at the end of the novel, Area X "has quelled the last ashes of the burning compulsion I had to *know everything* ...

anything" (128, emphasis in original). Knowledge construction, especially the knowledge generated by the scientific inquiry that has motivated the biologist's lifework, supports and maintains the human as a category. The biologist's double renunciation of knowing and being human opens her to the world of Area X in new ways. As Vint notes, the biologist is open to "the promise of Area X to offer another way of experiencing the material world, a way that does not divide humans from other species."[61]

The possibilities she faces are terrifying, but in a situation that makes clear the impossibility of remaining separate, the biologist chooses the unknown as the less harmful of her two choices. When she characterizes the option of harming herself to remain human as "somehow pathetic," she signals that her decision is not solely grounded in reason, but also in emotion. This is similar to the way in which she recognizes ecosystem not just in scientific terms, but also as sensation and affect, as orgasm. For the biologist, it would be pitiable to persist in her current state of self-harming devotion to her own humanity. *Annihilation* thus startlingly defamiliarizes or "weirds" the human as a category of perpetual, pathetic, and fruitless self-destruction that, despite intellectual and emotional fortifications, has never been an entirely discrete species. In doing so, the novel allows readers to "think the break" between the human as a fortified, atomized category and the human as a relationship of entanglement, both orgasmic and excruciating, with a wider ecosystem.

Animal Studies and the Alien

Symbiosis is typically imagined as being mutually satisfying to both parties in immediate and obvious ways, but *Annihilation* and *Fledgling* both represent forms of alien symbiosis that contain an element of horror. They are reminders that symbiosis, though mutualistic, is also an alien encounter, one that disrupts boundaries and belies autonomy. In human-Ina symbiosis the human symbiont loses autonomy and then depends for his or her continued life on a creature of another species. Human symbionts enter life-long dependencies that often queer their sexual identities and desires and shift their speciesist and racist senses of their place in the world, subjecting them to potential instrumentalization. In *Annihilation*, human autonomy dissolves almost entirely as humans are incorporated into other plant or animal lifeforms, but also into a larger ecosystem from which they are finally inseparable and entirely dependent. Both novels eroticize these alien penetrations, marking their peculiar inevitability and ambivalence. Both novels hint that their symbiotic lifeforms are of an extraterrestrial alien origin, but neither gives a definitive and therefore comforting answer. Instead, the symbiotic aliens hover between the terrestrial and extraterrestrial; the *heimlich* and the *unheimlich*; the uncanny and the abcanny; between the human, the nonhuman, the inhuman, and the implacably alien. Both novels explore the horror, attractions, and ambivalences of losing the boundaries of self and species and of becoming integrated with the nonhuman. But both novels simultaneously show that the nonhuman has always been much closer than we imagined. Especially in the context of the human as always already in relation to the nonhuman, these novels probe and question human responses of horror in the face of connection, interdependency, and symbiosis.

In literalizing Shklovsky's *ostranenie* as "*alien*-ation," Gothic aliens and the alien weird offer unique innovations for seeing and knowing nonhuman and human animals in relation to each other. The biologist's conclusion that it would be pathetic to continue to harm herself just to remain human is a wonderful starting point for critical animal studies. *Annihilation* not only calls attention to the painful tolls taken on humans when we assert our separateness and exceptionalism, but it also represents the horror with which humans often confront interconnectivity with nonhuman lives. Similarly, *Fledgling* dramatizes the ways in which race intersects with species construction in the figure of Shori, who mixes not only Ina and human species but also Black and white races. Butler dislocates and alienates human racism across species and invites readers to scrutinize the complex ways in which racism and speciesism are imbricated. Simultaneously, Butler dislocates human heteronormativity and sexism through inter-species encounters. Together, these novels draw on the Gothic and the weird in order to suggest that the feared contamination and the desired integration have always already occurred; the familiar alien is already within the human. Fear and horror are thus not prophylactic states but rather emotional emblems, emblems of annihilating self-destruction and denial but emblems also of fledgling potentiality and becoming.

Notes

1. Ursula K. Le Guin, *The Dispossessed: An Ambiguous Utopia* (New York: HarperCollins, 1974), 77. Subsequent page references will be given in parentheses in the text.
2. Rivers Solomon, *An Unkindness of Ghosts* (New York: Akashic Books, 2017), 348. Subsequent page references will be given in parentheses in the text.
3. "The fact that we cannot expect ever to accommodate in our language a detailed description of Martian or bat phenomenology should not lead us to dismiss as meaningless the claim that bats and Martians have experiences fully comparable in richness of detail to our own," Thomas Nagel, "What Is It Like to Be a Bat?" in *Mortal Questions* (New York: Cambridge University Press, 1979), 170.
4. Midgley writes,

    Alien species, if we ever encountered them, might actually present us with this problem. Solving it would be a great deal harder than most science fiction so far has suggested. But for species on this planet we do have the idea. Advantage is not a mysterious alien notion, the name of a hitherto unidentified quality. It is a general name for thriving and prospering, for all the things that we and other species really want and value. (Mary Midgley, *Beast and Man: The Roots of Human Nature*, Revised Edition (New York: Routledge, 1995), 52)

5. "Singular and plural, species resonate with the tones of logical types, of the relentlessly specific, of stamped coin, of the real presence in the Catholic Eucharist, of Darwinian kinds, of sf aliens, and of much else. Species, like the body, are internally oxymoronic, full of their own others, full of messmates, of companions," Donna J. Haraway, *When Species Meet* (Minneapolis: University of Minnesota Press, 2008), 165.
6. Sherryl Vint, *Animal Alterity: Science Fiction and the Question of the Animal* (Liverpool: Liverpool University Press, 2010), 136.
7. Ibid.
8. Sherryl Vint, "Science Fiction," in *The Edinburgh Companion to Animal Studies*, ed. Lynn Turner, Undine Sellbach, and Ron Broglio (Edinburgh: Edinburgh University Press, 2018), 488, 500.
9. Fred Botting, *Gothic* (New York: Routledge, 1996), 10.
10. David Punter, *The Literature of Terror: A History of Gothic Fictions from 1765 to the Present Day: Vol. 1: The Gothic Tradition* (New York: Routledge, 2013), 4.
11. Jerrold E. Hogle, "Introduction: The Gothic in Western Culture," in *The Cambridge Companion to Gothic Fiction*, ed. Jerrold E. Hogle (New York: Cambridge University Press, 2002), 6.

12　Ibid., 12. Emphasis in original.
13　George E. Haggerty, *Queer Gothic* (Urbana: University of Illinois Press, 2006), 2.
14　Nancy Armstrong, "Gothic Novel," in *The Encyclopedia of the Novel*, ed. Peter Melville Logan (Malden: Wiley Blackwell, 2014), 370–1.
15　Ruth Heholt and Melissa Edmundson, "Introduction," in *Gothic Animals: Uncanny Otherness and the Animal With-Out*, ed. Ruth Heholt and Melissa Edmundson (Cham: Palgrave Macmillan, 2020), 3.
16　Ibid., 5.
17　Ibid., 9.
18　Octavia E. Butler, *Octavia E. Butler: Kindred, Fledgling, Collected Stories*, ed. Gerry Canavan and Nisi Shawl (New York: The Library of America, 2020), 332. Subsequent page references will be given in parentheses in the text.
19　Hershini Bhana Young suggests that Butler's vampire trial "critiques American legal systems that repeatedly fail to address social injustices, particularly the injustice of slavery," Hershini Bhana Young, "Performing the Abyss: Octavia Butler's *Fledgling* and the Law," *Studies in the Novel* 47.2 (Summer 2015), 210.
20　See Pramod K. Nayar, "A New Biological Citizenship: Posthumanism in Octavia Butler's *Fledgling*," *Modern Fiction Studies* 58.4 (Winter 2012): 796–817. Pelin Kümbet similarly sees the human-Ina relationship as a form of posthuman entanglement. See Pelin Kümbet, "A Posthuman Vampire-Human Intra-action in Octavia Butler's *Fledgling*," *Interactions: Ege Journal of British and American Studies* 25.1–2 (Spring-Fall 2016): 105–12. Lin Knutson characterizes this entanglement as a "grotesque communitas relationship," Lin Knutson, "Monster Studies: Liminality, Home Spaces, and Ina Vampires in Octavia E. Butler's *Fledgling*," *University of Toronto Quarterly* 87.1 (Winter 2018), 214.
21　As Susana M. Morris says, Wright struggles with "what he perceives as the unnatural or, at the very least, inappropriate social dynamics of mutualism, with its communal living, queer pansexuality, and nonmonogamy, among other nonnormative practices," Susana M. Morris, "Black Girls Are from the Future: Afrofuturist Feminism in Octavia E. Butler's *Fledgling*," *WSQ: Women's Studies Quarterly* 40.3–4 (Fall-Winter 2012), 159. Morris argues, "*Fledgling* radically reimagines identity, kinship, and intimacy through nonmonogamous queer human-vampire hybrid families that have a variety of configurations, yet it also troubles any easy notions of a vampire utopia by ambivalently regarding the concepts of free will and symbiosis," 147.
22　Zakiyyah Iman Jackson, *Becoming Human: Matter and Meaning in an Antiblack World* (New York: New York University Press, 2020), 12, emphasis in original.
23　Ibid.

24 The Radu family, only mentioned in the novel, seems even to reject this view. Brook tells Shori about how Radu used his symbionts as pawns: "not everyone treats symbionts as people," 402.
25 Quoted in S. T. Joshi, *The Weird Tale* (Austin: University of Texas Press, 1990), 6.
26 Ibid., 2. Contrast this "Great Outside" with Botting's sense of the Gothic as an "internalised world of guilt, anxiety, despair."
27 Ibid., 118. Noting that the Russian Formalists defined estrangement as the defining quality of literary language, Benjamin Noys and Timothy S. Murphy see the weird as "a hyperbolic instance of the literary" itself, Benjamin Noys and Timothy S. Murphy, "Introduction: Old and New Weird," *Genre* 49.2 (July 2016), 118.
28 China Miéville, "Weird Fiction," in *The Routledge Companion to Science Fiction*, ed. Mark Bould, Andrew M. Butler, Adam Roberts, and Sherryl Vint (New York: Routledge, 2009), 510, emphasis in original.
29 Botting, 3.
30 Miéville, "Weird Fiction," 511.
31 Ibid.
32 China Miéville, "M. R. James and the Quantum Vampire: Weird; Hauntological: Versus and/or and and/or or?," in *Collapse: Philosophical Research and Development, Volume IV*, ed. Robin McKay (Falmouth: Urbanomic, 2008), 113.
33 Miéville, "Weird Fiction," 512.
34 Miéville, "M. R. James," 113.
35 Miéville, "Weird Fiction," 513, emphasis in original.
36 China Miéville, "On Monsters: Or, Nine or More (Monstrous) Not Cannies," *Journal of the Fantastic in the Arts* 23.3 (January 2012), 381.
37 Mark Fisher, *The Weird and the Eerie* (London: Repeater, 2016), 13, emphasis in original.
38 Andrew Smith, "Hauntings," in *The Routledge Companion to the Gothic*, ed. Catherine Spooner and Emma McEvoy (New York: Routledge, 2007), 148.
39 Miéville, "Weird Fiction," 513.
40 Noys and Murphy, 125. In an interview with Noys and Murphy, Miéville takes issue with the idea of a "celebratory" weird: "most such work … would bleed out the ecstasy by watering down the sublime into a kind of picturesque, the weird political-picturesque. Which to my taste deguts the key weird element," Benjamin Noys and Timothy S. Murphy, "Morbid Symptoms: An Interview with China Miéville," *Genre* 49.2 (July 2016), 210.
41 See "The New Weird Discussions: The Creation of a Term," ed. Ann VanderMeer and Jeff VanderMeer, *The New Weird* (San Francisco: Tachyon Publications, 2008), 318.

42 See Benjamin J. Robertson, *None of This Is Normal: The Fiction of Jeff VanderMeer* (Minneapolis: University of Minnesota Press, 2018), 24–5. For Robertson, the new weird "recognizes that the criticality of science fiction no longer works and that horror is the only response to this situation," 30–1.
43 Quoted in "The New Weird Discussions: The Creation of a Term," 319.
44 Jeff VanderMeer, "The New Weird: 'It's Alive?,'" in *The New Weird*, ed. Ann VanderMeer and Jeff VanderMeer (San Francisco: Tachyon Publications, 2008), xvi.
45 Richard Powers, *The Overstory* (New York: W. W. Norton & Company, 2018), 109. Subsequent page references are given in parentheses within the text.
46 Jeff VanderMeer, *Area X: The Southern Reach Trilogy* (New York: Farrar, Straus and Giroux, 2014), 46. Subsequent page references will be given in parentheses in the text.
47 Situating the Southern Reach trilogy within our global ecological crisis, Alison Sperling reads sickness in the novels as sites of "co-constitution" and of ongoing relations between the body and its environment, Alison Sperling, "Second Skins: A Body-Ecology of Jeff VanderMeer's *The Southern Reach Trilogy*," *Paradoxa* 28 (2016), 216.
48 Sigmund Freud, *Beyond the Pleasure Principle*, trans. and ed. James Strachey (New York: W. W. Norton & Company, 1961), 56.
49 Ibid., 32, emphases in original.
50 Jon Hegglund accounts for the "unnatural narratology" of *Annihilation* through the combination of the biologist's first-person observing perspective and her gradual integration into the very thing she is observing: "the biologist self-consciously interrogates the boundaries between subject and object, human and environment, and the narrative takes on a vertiginous quality as the narrator tries to both understand the emergent agencies within Area X as well as within herself," Jon Hegglund, "Unnatural Narratology and Weird Realism in Jeff VanderMeer's *Annihilation*," in *Environment and Narrative: New Directions in Econarratology*, ed. Erin James, Eric Morel, and Ursula K. Heise (Columbus: Ohio University Press, 2020), 38.
51 "My basic theory is that the written word was actually a virus that made the spoken word possible. The word has not been recognized as a virus because it has achieved a state of stable symbiosis with the host, though this symbiotic relationship is now breaking down, for reasons I will suggest later," William S. Burroughs, "Playback from Eden to Watergate," in *The Job: Interviews with William S. Burroughs*, ed. Daniel Odier (New York: Penguin Books, 1989), 12. We learn later in *Annihilation* that it is the creature that the biologist names the Crawler who writes these words, which are then inhabited by the fruiting bodies. Subsequent volumes in the trilogy reveal how Saul Evans, the lighthouse keeper

and former preacher, has transformed or been integrated into the Crawler after being infected by something that may or may not have an extraterrestrial origin. Even more proximate, then, is Laurie Anderson's memorable popularization of Burroughs's concept: "Language is a virus from outer space," Laurie Anderson, "Language Is a Virus from Outer Space," *United States Live* (Los Angeles: Warner Bros. Records, 1984). In ecocritical terms, Andrew Strombeck reads the uncanny writing in the novel as an instance of that which "can't be represented as nevertheless representing itself," Andrew Strombeck, "Inhuman Writing in Jeff VanderMeer's Southern Reach Trilogy," *Textual Practice* 34.8 (2020), 1366, emphasis in original. For Strombeck, *Annihilation* argues that the inhuman world must necessarily be accessed through texts, yet that the techniques of realism alone fail to access certain ecological phenomena.

52 Finola Anne Prendergast, "Revising Nonhuman Ethics in Jeff VanderMeer's *Annihilation*," *Contemporary Literature* 58.3 (Fall 2017), 347. Emphasis in original.

53 The biologist suspects that the dolphin might be her husband transformed (111–12); however, in *Acceptance*, the third novel in the trilogy, she seems to encounter her husband in or as an owl (474–8).

54 Even Earth now gives hints of having-once-been. For instance, it is possible that an extraterrestrial presence is remaking Earth in its own image. Late in the novel, the biologist realizes that the stars above her "now looked strange, strewn across the dark in chaotic new patterns" (112). She wonders, "Was I perhaps even farther from home than I had thought?" (112). In *Acceptance* we learn from the biologist's final journal that this state fluctuates. On some nights, the biologist sees a familiar night sky; on others, there is no moon and "the stars are foreign, belonging to a cosmology I cannot identify" (482). Little could be more disorienting and alienating than to look up from the perspective of Earth and to find oneself under alien stars.

55 Pearson Bolt reads the *Southern Reach* trilogy as "a potent critique of borders' unnatural horrors," and "a vision of a decolonized, biocentric ecology rooted in communication," Pearson Bolt, "Monolithic, Invisible Walls: The Horror of Borders in Jeff VanderMeer's *Southern Reach* Trilogy," *Journal of Science Fiction* 4.1 (July 2020), 26.

56 Gözde Ersoy also adapts China Miéville's concept of the "abcanny," which blends the uncanny and the abject, or "the familiar horror and the monstrous," to *Annihilation*. Because there is an element of monstrousness in this uncanny sensory encounter with the Crawler, "abcanny" might capture more than the concept of the uncanny alone does, Gözde Ersoy, "Crossing the Boundaries of the Unknown with Jeff VanderMeer: The Monstrous Fantastic and 'Abcanny' in *Annihilation*," *Orbis Litterarum* 74.4 (August 2019), 255.

57 Val Plumwood, "Being Prey," *Utne Reader* 100 (July-August 2000), 58.
58 Ibid., 61.
59 Robertson characterizes Area X as a place of "nonfeedback" and "abdifference," or "radical difference." As "an uncontainable space that is nothing but a bordering without a border, a limiting that cannot be limited," Area X "becomes a challenge to humanity's conception of itself," Robertson, *None of This Is Normal*, 116–17, 120.
60 Vint, "Science Fiction," 497, emphases in original.
61 Ibid.

4

Posthumous Humanity

This chapter suggests some ways in which fiction puts souls, spirits, and ghosts in the service of nonhuman animals. Creative visions of posthumousness—the ways in which souls, spirits, and ghosts expand and reimagine the world—offer non-anthropocentric insights and opportunities to critical animal studies. Posthumous representations ask not only what it means to have lived as human but also what it means to become something else afterward, to have moved beyond the human. Posthumous perspectives thus inquire into what nonhuman animals and human-nonhuman animal relationships look like from the perspective of having-been-human. By reading contemporary texts that represent once-human souls, spirits, ghosts, even in the form of quasi-human literary character itself, this chapter explores perspectives on nonhuman animals from the position of the no-longer-human.

Though distinct from the techno-ontological ruptures of the posthuman, the posthumous also stretches the idea of life in ways that challenge anthropocentrism. As posthumanism employs technologies to undermine humanism, so do the imaginative and literary technologies of ghosts, spirits, and souls broaden our sense of the boundaries of life and world. Charles Dickens's *A Christmas Carol* paradigmatically uses ghosts to intervene in Scrooge's miserly existence. Marley's ghost cautions Scrooge to consider his behavior within larger contexts. The three ghosts of past, present, and future challenge Scrooge's understanding of time. Scrooge is miraculously transformed by peering through and adopting posthumous positions: "'I will live in the Past, the Present, and the Future!' Scrooge repeated, as he scrambled out of bed. 'The Spirits of all Three shall strive within me. Oh Jacob Marley! Heaven, and the Christmas Time be praised for this!'"[1] Scrooge now "lives in" a wider world in which he reforms his life and treats others with kindness and charity. Although the idea of soul and spirit often underlies and reinforces human exceptionalism, *A Christmas Carol* yet exemplifies the way in which the once-human soul may operate as an imaginative resource for overcoming deficiencies and failures of the imagination. At the same time, as a literary character Scrooge himself can be thought of as a kind of ghost who continues to be revived in and to haunt the popular imagination. Resembling the human and yet confined to a strange kind of literary life and afterlife, literary character is a species of ghost, spirit, or soul that can also suggest posthumous perspectives on the world.

This chapter examines Louise Erdrich's and George Saunders's representations of posthumousness in relation to critical animal studies and then considers fictional character as a peculiar convergence of human, once-human, and nonhuman creatures that finds animals at stake in virtually every act of the literary imagination. The spirit world in Erdrich's novels immerses readers in non-Western experiences of time and space. Erdrich simultaneously represents Ojibwe perspectives on spirits and nonhuman animals that stress mutuality, respect, and interconnection. The Ojibwe spirit world and perspectives on animals are mutually reinforcing and synergistic components of Erdrich's fiction. Similarly, Saunders's *Lincoln in the Bardo* challenges Western understandings of death from both sides of the life–death divide. At the same time, the novel cultivates Buddhist views of nonhuman animal life and acknowledges the troubling histories and present realities that shape our relationships with nonhuman creatures. Like Erdrich, Saunders represents human spirits and nonhuman animals in mutually reinforcing ways that challenge anthropocentrism. Finally, Salman Rushdie's *Quichotte* demonstrates that our ability to imagine death, souls, and nonhuman animals may be inseparable from the capacities of fiction and literary character: Fiction can expand our vision of the world, cultivate non-anthropocentric thinking, and highlight our shared vulnerability with nonhuman animals. Elizabeth Costello argues in J. M. Coetzee's *The Lives of Animals* that fiction lets us think our way beyond ourselves and into nonhuman lives. This chapter argues that these fictions of ghosts and souls can shift our scale and perspective from the anthropocentric to the anthropocosmic.

Souls as Such

In *The Lives of Animals*, Coetzee's fictional philosopher Thomas O'Hearne says, "I do not believe that life is as important to animals as it is to us. ... [T]hey do not *understand* death as we do."[2] O'Hearne reflects two familiar features of human exceptionalism: the denial to animals of important lives and of what Derrida calls "an authentic relation to death."[3] O'Hearne denies that nonhuman animals' lives mean as much to them as human lives mean to us on the basis of mental ability: "Efforts to show that animals can think strategically, hold general concepts, or communicate symbolically, have had very limited success" (61–2). O'Hearne implies that humans are capable of measuring, appreciating, and valuing their lives with a sophistication that other animals lack, and that life is less important if it is less complexly measured and reflected upon.

Peter Singer responds to Coetzee's *The Lives of Animals* similarly. In Singer's fictional exchange with his daughter, he says:

> If I pour the rest of this soymilk down the sink, I've emptied the container; and if I do the same to that bottle of Kahlúa you and your friends are fond of drinking when we are out, I'd empty it too. But you'd care more about the loss of the Kahlúa. The value that is lost when something is emptied depends on what was there when it was full, and there is more to human existence than there is to bat existence.[4]

Singer's and O'Hearne's responses slip between absolute and relative senses of value. O'Hearne claims that life is not as important *to* animals as it is to humans, but he does so upon the supposedly absolute value of mental ability. Similarly, Singer begins with the relative value of soymilk and Kahlúa *to* his daughter, but then claims the absolute higher value of human lives because there is "more to" us.

But what if there is no absolute value behind the relative value of life to a creature? Christine M. Korsgaard argues that value is always a question of value *to* someone: "Everything that is important must be important to some creature—that goodness is 'tethered' to the creatures for whom it is good."[5] When she compares the value of human and rabbit life, Korsgaard concludes, "even if the rabbit's life is not as important to her as yours is to you, nevertheless, for her it contains absolutely *everything of value*, all that can ever be good or bad for her, except possibly the lives of her offspring. The end of her life is the end of all value and goodness for her."[6] For Korsgaard, what matters is not the rabbit's capacity to measure, reflect upon, or to care about her life per se, but rather that anything that possibly *can* matter to her is contained within her life. Mental capacities and characteristics are irrelevant to the question of life's value to any given creature. Because both human and nonhuman lives contain everything of value to the individual, there is no absolute basis for dismissing or diminishing the importance of life to any one creature, even if another creature's mind or life has "more to" it.

The second tendency that O'Hearne reflects—the tendency to deny animals a privileged relation to death—enters the territory of the soul. O'Hearne adds an unconventional twist to the exceptionalist assertion that humans possess superior awareness about death:

> They do not *understand* death as we do, or rather, as we fail to do. There is, in the human mind, a collapse of the imagination before death, and that collapse of the imagination … is the basis of our fear of death. … For that reason, I want to suggest, dying is, for an animal, just something that happens, something against which there may be a revolt of the organism but not a revolt of the soul. (63, emphasis in original)

O'Hearne does not suppose that humans correctly grasp death; he holds up as exceptional a particular "collapse of the imagination before death." O'Hearne privileges in humans and denies to animals a specific mixture of self-awareness and incomprehension: the self-awareness of death's very incomprehensibility. For O'Hearne this privileged incomprehension leads to revolt of "the soul" rather than of just "the organism."

An approach that looks for ethically relevant common ground between human and nonhuman animals would have difficulty countering O'Hearne's privileged incomprehension and revolt of soul. To assert that nonhuman animals can fail to comprehend their deaths in the same or similarly sophisticated ways that humans can is bound to be tortuous. Worse would be to be obliged to argue that nonhuman animals also revolt against death with their souls. Even if one could find evidence of this privileged incomprehension or revolt of soul in some animals, most species would likely be excluded.[7] We ought instead to interrogate not just the imputed impoverishment on the nonhuman animal side but also the supposed privilege on the human side. Derrida, for instance, reminds us to deconstruct not only what we parsimoniously withhold from animals but also what we magnanimously and bountifully grant to ourselves.[8]

Do humans in fact fail to understand death in ways that are distinctive and privileged? Do we revolt with our souls? I consult my own experiences. Compared with the privileged incomprehension of death that O'Hearne asserts, my own incomprehension seems unexceptional. When my father died, in addition to feeling grief and loss—emotions which many species are capable of feeling—I struggled with rudimentary logic that made "higher" reflection on human existence peripheral. I was tortured by the idea that my father did not know that he was dead. Although I told myself that this was a logical impossibility—that there was no perspective remaining from which he could know or not know anything—I could not assimilate this simple idea. In one dream my father indignantly asked why we had given all his furniture away and in another he lovingly consoled me but could not grasp that his death was the cause of my grief. When my feline friend Roddy died a few weeks later, I was agonized by the idea that she must have felt confused, abandoned, and betrayed because I was no longer taking care of her.[9] This was not a collapse of the imagination in the face of death, but a collapse of elementary reasoning. I felt very much like what I was: an animal struggling to comprehend the fundamental factuality of death. But through this struggle, I created something like a soul independent of the organism, not just for my human father but also for the cat Roddy. I projected subject positions for each of them beyond life, positions that expanded my sense of life's scope and range in consoling but also confusing ways. Their souls were the byproducts of my revolt of organism. If the soul can be an invention of the organism in revolt, one that emerges from conditions that are common enough among animals, then perhaps humans do not possess souls *as such*, but only as an affordance of fiction.

Animals and Soullessness

Western, Judeo-Christian traditions have denied so much to nonhuman animals based on imputed soullessness. We have seen in *Never Let Me Go* the ways in which Madame and Miss Emily sought to prove that clones have souls to advocate for their humane treatment. As Harlan B. Miller notes, the supposition that nonhuman animals do not have souls has often been used to defend "the moral dichotomy between humans and nonhumans."[10] Derrida traces such thinking from Descartes and Kant through Heidegger and Levinas, the latter of whose projects otherwise purport to challenge or deconstruct inherited philosophical traditions. Derrida demonstrates that for Heidegger animals cannot be said to die, and that for Levinas animals cannot be murdered. Animals are thought to lack what Heidegger calls the "as such" and what Levinas calls "the face."[11] To possess the "as such" is to have access to the world *as such*, to be able to relate to the world detached from one's own perspective, from the point of view of one's own absence. To possess a face is to be a neighbor, an other, another human being. Because Heidegger's and Levinas's prejudices stand on the socle of animal soullessness, Derrida demonstrates that the soul represents a persistent and troubling undercurrent in thought about animals.

Others have confronted Western tradition with alternatives drawn from indigenous and non-Western traditions and religious practices. These often run counter to exceptionalist thought and offer alternative visions of humans among nonhuman animals. As Paul Waldau notes, "Islam, the world's next most populous religious tradition [after Christianity], asserts that nonhumans do indeed have souls, as do the traditions that originated in the Indian subcontinent. Indigenous peoples, too, characteristically assume that nonhuman animals have souls."[12] Buddhist cosmology, Ian Harris writes, "instills a fellow feeling, or sense of community, with all sentient beings caught in the beginningless circle of *saṃsāra*. This general ethical principle stands at the root of the practice of loving-kindness (*mettā*)."[13] While acknowledging crucial differences between indigenous traditions, John Grim characterizes indigenous views of nonhuman animals as "anthropocosmic" rather than anthropocentric. In contrast to anthropocentrism, which privileges human concerns and perspectives, the anthropocosmic perspective "suggests an intricate interweaving of cosmological power, ecological processes, animal sentience, human reciprocity, and somatic sensitivity."[14] Focusing on Cherokee and Creek traditions, Dave Aftandilian writes, "We have seen the importance of animals as creators and markers of the cosmological realms of existence;

how other animals are viewed as not just people like humans, but relatives; that animals are spiritually powerful; and that humans ought to treat other animals with respect, enter into reciprocal relationships with them, and renew the world on their behalf."[15]

Anthropocosmic beliefs are also evident in literature. About nonhuman animals in Native American literature, Gerald Vizenor writes,

> The creatures in native literature are seldom mere representations of animals in nature or culture, wild, domestic, generic, or otherwise; however, there is an unnamable presence, traces of a familiar nature, comic motivation, native reason, and author introspection. Owens, Momaday, Silko, Erdrich, and Henry use metaphor to turn the pleasures of the unnamable into animal characters. ... Monotheistic creation is a separation of animals and humans in literature and nature; the common unions since then have been both domestic and aesthetic.[16]

For Vizenor, "Many contemporary native novelists present the imagic consciousness of animals in dialogue and descriptive narratives, and overturn the monotheistic separation of humans and animals. ... These practices and sentiments are a native literary aesthetic."[17] Elsewhere, Vizenor writes, "My idea of a native literary aesthetics is a tricky, totemic union of animals, birds, humans and others."[18]

As the following sections explore, by representing, respectively, Ojibwe and Buddhist visions of the soul and nonhuman animals, Erdrich and Saunders challenge the discourse of animal soullessness and reimagine the world, including human-animal relationships, from posthumous perspectives.

Becoming-Ox and Sleeping with the Bear

Human-nonhuman animal interactions often play transformative roles in human and animals lives in Louise Erdrich's novels. Critics have noted the "companionship and interdependence" of human and nonhuman animals and spirits in Erdrich's fiction.[19] As Catherine Rainwater writes, "For the Ojibwa, personhood extends beyond humans to animals and spirits; even plants and material objects can sometimes be persons."[20] In *The Round House*, the legendary Nanapush survives the cold by sheltering inside the body of one of the last buffalo. Before he kills Old Buffalo Woman, Nanapush apologizes to her. His speech reflects indigenous beliefs about animal personhood and consensual self-sacrifice: "Old Buffalo Woman, I hate to kill you, said Nanapush, for you have managed to live by wit and courage, even though your people are destroyed. You must have made yourself invisible. But then again, as you are the only hope for my family, perhaps you were waiting for me."[21] Nanapush sings to Old Buffalo Woman a song his mother has taught him: "Nanapush sang the song again because he knew the buffalo was waiting to hear it. When he finished, she allowed him to aim point-blank at her heart. The old woman toppled over still watching Nanapush in that emotional way, and Nanapush fell beside her, spent" (185). After Nanapush climbs inside of the buffalo to survive the freezing night, Old Buffalo Woman "adopted Nanapush and told him all she knew" (186). Nanapush is reborn from the buffalo as her son. Later, when Nanapush and his human mother bring Old Buffalo Woman back to their starving people, Mooshum, who tells Nanapush's story in his sleep, explains, "Many people were saved by that old woman buffalo, who gave herself to Nanapush and his unkillable mother" (187). Old Buffalo Woman's spirit counsels Nanapush to build the community's round house, which will represent a new way for the buffalo to unite their people: "The round house will be my body, the poles my ribs, the fire my heart. It will be the body of your mother and it must be respected the same way. As the mother is intent on her baby's life, so your people should think of their children" (214–15). The round house represents the respect, mutuality, and family connections between humans and buffalo at the core of community values and traditions.

While Erdrich's novels reflect Ojibwe thinking about animals, they simultaneously represent spirits in ways that also differ from and question human exceptionalist paradigms. In addition to representing family ties between nonhuman and human animals, Erdrich often represents humans in touch with spirits. When the elder Ignatia dies in *LaRose*, Malvern recognizes her spirit's presence and helps young LaRose to feel it:

> Malvern talked to Ignatia, telling her the directions, how to take the first steps, how to look to the west, where to find the road, and not to bother taking anyone along. She said that everybody, even herself, Malvern, who had never told her, loved Ignatia very much. They held Ignatia's hands for a

long time, quietly, until the hands were no longer warm. Still, LaRose felt her presence in the room.[22]

LaRose also sees spirits in the woods, including the spirit of Dusty, the boy whom LaRose was given symbolically to replace after LaRose's father accidentally killed him. LaRose and Dusty's spirits play together in what had once been Dusty's room. Near the end of the novel, LaRose invites the spirits he sees to Hollis's high school graduation party: "LaRose didn't know what to say to them, if they were out there. Oh well, he'd treat them like regular people. You're invited, he said in a normal voice" (368). As *LaRose* demonstrates, Erdrich persistently normalizes spirits in ways that widen the world and posit greater-than-human, rather than merely magic, perspectives.[23]

It is not just that Erdrich represents animals as having spirits, like Old Buffalo Woman, but also that her representation of spirits and nonhuman animals in communion and family relation with humans creates worlds in which alternative values and habits of imagining animals can emerge. These possibilities are powerfully felt in *The Night Watchman*. Like *The Round House* and *LaRose*, *The Night Watchman* combines persistent attention to spirits with sensitivity and attention to nonhuman animals. *The Night Watchman* is at once the *Bildungsroman* of Patrice (Pixie) Paranteau, who is nineteen years old in 1953 and longs to "rise in the world,"[24] and the story of the Turtle Mountain Band of Chippewa's struggle for survival against Federal "emancipation, freedom, equality, success" or, as tribal chairman Thomas Wazhashk thinks, "Termination. Missing only the prefix. The ex" (90). The Federal plan for emancipation, led by Senator Arthur V. Watkins of Utah, would "erase as Indians … his people, *all of us invisible and as if we never were here, from the beginning, here*" (79, emphasis in original).

Patrice is heir to traditional beliefs, especially through her mother Zhaanat, an "old time Indian" (21). Compared with Patrice's white secular and religious teachers, "Zhaanat had a different sort of intelligence. In her thinking there were no divisions, or maybe the divisions were not the same, or maybe they were invisible. White people looked at Indians like her and thought *dull stubborn*. But Zhaanat's intelligence was of frightening dimensions" (189–90, emphasis in the original). For instance, Zhaanat knows, "Why an animal gave itself to one hunter and not another" (190). Her frightening intelligence makes intellection inseparable from caring in ways that belie Western rationalism: "Because everything was alive, responsive in its own way, capable of being hurt in its own way, capable of punishment in its own way, Zhaanat's thinking was built upon treating everything around her with great care" (190).

However, Patrice is more culturally hybrid than Zhaanat, a source of both conflict and power for her.[25] Patrice's *Bildung* involves two intersections with animals or animality that, like rites of passage, mark new periods in her life and signal profound personal transformations. Both intersections are marked by a hybridity of indigenous and colonial beliefs or contexts. In the first, while seeking her missing sister Vera in Minneapolis, Patrice is coerced into performing as a "waterjack" at Log Jam 26, a seedy lumberjack-themed bar. After negotiating with the club owner Jack, Patrice agrees to wear a provocative blue ox outfit and to swim in a transparent water tank. Patrice's becoming-ox objectifies her, but it also transforms and empowers her: "She stepped before [the mirror] and saw herself as alien and fascinating" (130). "I am a stranger to myself. Another person, harder and bolder than the usual Patrice" (132). When she returns home, wellpaid for her five days as a waterjack and having successfully negotiated many of the dangers that Minneapolis presents for young indigenous women, Patrice has new confidence and initiative. She asks her friend Betty about birth control, about how to "try out sex and get rid of the men" (296), and about sexual pleasure—Betty tells her that when you "get your hoo-ha," "it makes you feel like you're floating off" (294). Patrice is above all concerned about remaining independent so that she can "rise in the world." She wants to avoid pregnancy, "sticky" men (307), and being "locked up in a tower with a ring on my finger" (288). Patrice's becoming-ox, though perilous and alienating, is also illuminating, galvanizing, and empowering.

The second intersection that contributes to Patrice's *Bildung* is a distanced encounter with a bear. While checking her rabbit snares, Patrice falls by a ravine. She recognizes by scent that a bear is hibernating nearby. At first, she regrets not having brought a rifle. However, she gives in to her fatigue and naps near the leaf-covered cave: "It was time for her weekend nap, anyway, and how often did a modern working woman get to sleep with a live bear?" (312). Patrice wakes up newly confident and determined to protect her family from her drunken and abusive father: "'I'll be the night watchman,' said Patrice, and went out to get the ax" (313). She thinks, "They would all live easier. Never again would her mother have to go to sleep with a knife beneath her pillow and a hatchet at her feet" (326). Thomas Wazhashk is the night watchman at the Turtle Mountain Jewel Bearing Plant and the tribal chairman who watches over the Turtle Mountain Band of Chippewa while they sleep, but Patrice, too, will become a vigilant caretaker of her family and her community: "She felt superior to the person she was before she slept with the bear" (315). By claiming her own share of the novel's title, Patrice's *Bildung* combines with Thomas's larger cultural struggle. Patrice accompanies Thomas's contingent to Washington, DC to support the anti-termination effort. She ultimately realizes that her vocation is to defend her family and culture by going to college.

Sleeping with the bear leads to a positive transformation for Patrice, but Erdrich introduces ambivalence when it comes to the bear's fate. Patrice returns from work at the Jewel Bearing Plant to find Zhaanat and Thomas skinning the bear: "Of course [Zhaanat]'d gone after it. A bear was a walking medicine cabinet. ... Patrice has been compelled to tell her mother, but she had hoped her mother would not kill the bear. ... Skinned out bears looked too human for Patrice and she hurried to the house" (324). It takes cathartic wood chopping and a certain forgetting for Patrice to overcome her guilt at having betrayed the bear: "She forgot her complicated feelings, or got them out, down the ax and into the wood. She forgot the kindness of the bear and how she had betrayed it, although maybe, as Zhaanat always believed, the bear had intentionally given itself to her" (326). Patrice was compelled to tell Zhaanat about the bear, knowing its value as medicine to her mother.[26] As Zhaanat and Thomas skin the bear, they sing to him or her (the sex is unspecified), echoing Nanapush's respectful buffalo song (324). Sleeping with the bear has strengthened Patrice, but it has also made her less certain about Zhaanat's beliefs. Patrice tries to reconcile those beliefs against her own guilt and the bear's kindness. She is left somewhere between her mother's confidence and her own recognition that the bear noticed her in a unique way that might either confirm or belie her mother's narrative about the bear's self-sacrifice. Patrice reflects, "Maybe the bear dreamed of her because surely the bear smelled her in its sleep and knew she was there. What was it, to be dreamed of by a bear?" (326). Instead of confirming a comforting sense of willing transaction, as between Nanapush and Old Buffalo Woman, Patrice is left pondering the more ambiguous and troubling terrain of ursine dreams.

Indeed, *The Night Watchman*'s animals communicate with humans in indirect and symbolic ways. Biboon discovers a golden beetle inside a pukkon shell. He reflects on the way that humans and other animals are forced to relate to time—"As animals subject to the laws of earth, we think time is experience" (266)—but he also understands time as in truth "a holy element" (267), more "substance" (267) than experience. The beetle in the pukkon shell enables Biboon to envision this elusive truth; the "golden bug, the manidoons, the little spirit being he'd cracked out of the shell not long ago, flew to him. ... All things happened at once and the little golden spirit flew back and forth, up and down through the holy element" (267).

Animals also give meaning and symbolic resonance to names and character. Thomas's grandfather was called Wazhashk, the muskrat. In an Ojibwe origin myth, the muskrat is the only animal capable of diving to the bottom of the watery world to bring up the first bit of earth needed to make land: "He was drowned but his paw was clenched. The Creator unfolded Wazhashk's webbed hands. He saw that the muskrat had carried up just a little bit off the bottom. From that tiny paw's grip, the Creator made the whole earth" (172). Thomas, who suffers a non-fatal stroke after defending the Turtle Mountain Band of Chippewa in Washington, DC, resembles the muskrat in his enabling sacrifice. Thomas's final vision in the novel is similarly symbolic: he sees buffalo bones on the prairie taking on flesh again: "The bones tipped and staggered, assembling into forms, and took on shaggy flesh. The grass rippled and billowed like a green robe and the animals crossed vast and vaster numbers. The earth trembled in a serpentine rush, blew away, and vanished into the sky" (443). This wish-dream of the buffalo's return suggests rebirth, possible redemption, and definition to Thomas, who "was of the after-the-buffalo-who-are-we-now generation" (98).

Animals sometimes communicate directly with the novel's humans. When Patrice knocks at Vera's last known Minneapolis address, she hears a dog whose "bark was rough, high, desperate to live" (124) and "furious with hope" (125). When Patrice enters, she sees that animals and women have been kept on chains. She finds the dog: "A pallid thing, all bones, it tried to struggle to its feet, but it collapsed and lay there, too spent to pant" (147). Patrice gives the starving dog a little water and asks him or her (again, the sex is unspecified) about Vera: "She died on the end of a chain, like me" (147), the dog answers. This turns out to be not true, for Vera eventually returns alive; however, Vera is so damaged by her captors and assaulters that she believes she is dead and walking toward the afterlife: "She knew, as everybody around her knew, that the soul after death sets off on a journey to the next life" (279). Patrice stays until the dog dies.

In the chapter "Edith, Psychic Dog," in which Vera is finally discovered and taken in by a former army medic, Erdrich focalizes the narrative through the medic's dog. This chapter conveys to readers the novel's most concrete information about what has happened to Vera, and it derives not from Vera's report but from Edith's sense of scent:

> She put her nose to the woman's leg. The woman had slept in the clothing of a man who cooked with grease, she had slept in snow and wild mint, near the carcass of a skunk, had recently been in town and before that out on the water. There was no harm in her, but she was confused, in despair, and might choose to sleep forever. (299)

Edith's powerful sense of scent perhaps works like a form of Toni Morrison's "rememory," in which the atrocities of the past remain present and can still be physically encountered in the world. Although in *Beloved* Sethe explains rememory to Denver in terms of sight—"The picture is still there and what's more, if you go there—you who never was there—if you go there and stand in the place where it was, it will happen again; it will be there for you, waiting for you"[27]—in *The Night Watchman* it is Edith's nose that encounters, detects, and remembers Vera's traumas: Edith "understood from her scent that unspeakable things had happened to her and might happen again" (300). Although Vera also has physical scars, they do not convey as much to Wood Mountain as Vera's scent does to Edith. Wood Mountain compares Vera's scars to his own boxing scars, but the resemblance between them only suggests how much is lost in the difference between scent and sight.

Erdrich also represents nonhuman animals on their own terms. Two of Louis Pipestone's horses, Gringo and Teacher's Pet, disrupt the homecoming parade. Teacher's Pet is in heat and Gringo "tossed his head, gave an outraged squawk, and lighted out after" her (236).[28] The horses break off from the humans, and in a short chapter called "The Bush Dance," Gringo and Teacher's Pet are focalized outside of any human associations. They experience sexual passion, post-coital indifference, and peckishness: "After the sex was over, they were bored and irritated. And also there was nothing to eat. They didn't exactly break up, but they did manage to ignore each other as they plodded around looking for some juicy grass" (240). Like Tolstoy in "Strider," Erdrich depicts humans from the horses' perspectives. Gringo "had entirely blocked out human sounds and was still enjoying the perfection of his sensations" (240). The two "grazed in luxury and pooped out all the stress of the parade" (240). Without anthropomorphizing the horses, Erdrich expresses their relationship with humans through their bodies: stress and relief are registered through the bowels. Erdrich allows for "kinesthetic empathy," in which, as Margo DeMello writes, "A person attempts to empathize with an animal by understanding their bodily experiences."[29] Despite the stress of living with and working for humans, Gringo and Teacher's Pet eventually "began to wish themselves into the place of warmth near the tiresome beings, who also sometimes offered a delight or two" (240). Failing to find anybody with "the right smell" (241), the two horses find their way back to their field. By the time they arrive at the closed gate, they feel "sorry for themselves," and when the wind blows the gate open, "Gringo knocked rudely against Teacher's Pet as she went through the gate and suddenly she had the utmost repugnance for him. Out flashed her pretty little hoof and she opened a vicious gash in his pink gold underbelly. It was his only imperfection" (241). Erdrich renders their arc from sexual passion to repugnance using techniques of Shklovskian *ostranenie* (for example, "the tiresome beings"), keen observation, emotional and somatic realism, and a touch of good-natured, sympathetic, and even loving humor.

As Erdrich explores relationships between human and nonhuman animals, she also richly seeds *The Night Watchman* with spirits. On her reservation, Patrice is called Pixie, a name that she dislikes but which suggests her connections to the spirit world. In her final scene in the novel, with spring in bloom, her people's federal status preserved, her abusive father dead, her plans for work and college on track, and her lost sister returned, Patrice happily drinks cold birch water with Zhaanat, water "which entered them the way life entered the trees, causing buds to swell along the branches" (439). Patrice puts her ear to the tree and can hear it drinking water from the earth.

> She closed her eyes, went through the bark like water, and was sucked up off the bud tips into a cloud. She looked down at herself and her mother, sitting by a small fire in the spring woods. Zhaanat tipped her head back and

smiled. She gestured at her daughter to come back, the way she had when as a child Patrice strayed. (439)

This joyful moment recapitulates Patrice's *Bildung* arc of separation, transformation, and homecoming. The out-of-body experience represents Patrice's deep spiritual sympathy with the life of the tree and the natural world. Recalling the terms and ambition with which her *Bildung* had begun, Patrice's spirit has now literally "risen in the world"; she is finally "floating off," not from the sexual pleasure that Betty described, but rather on her accomplishments and her sense of purpose. Readers are optimistic that Patrice will become a formidable defender of her people and confident that although transformed by her contact with the white world, she will remain rooted in Ojibwe culture and always return home after "straying."

Thomas is no less connected to the spirit world through spiritual experiences. Spirits save his life when, one freezing night, he accidentally locks himself out of the Jewel Bearing Plant after waking up from his nap and being lured outside by what sounds like distant drumming. Prompted by the cold, by the horrors that Patrice has recently relayed to him of Vera's captivity, and by memories of his school friend Roderick, Thomas has a vision of spirits dancing in the sky. Thomas has always lived close to spirits: "Thomas had friends on the other side. More and more friends. Too many. Sometimes he talked to them. … It helped to think that they had moved to another country. That they lived on the far side of a river you could only cross once" (59). Thomas senses that the stars are drummers.

> Looking up, he saw the beings. They were filmy and brightly indistinct. … One of the shining people was Jesus Christ, but he looked just like the others. They nodded to him in a comical way, understanding his surprise, and all of a sudden nothing hurt. Radiance filled him and he reared up, knowing that the drummers wished him to dance. (226)

"Welded by cold to the grass" (226) and in danger of freezing to death, Thomas is compelled by the spirits to get up and dance and sing. They save his life.

The most persistent spiritual presence in *The Night Watchman* is Roderick. Roderick was locked in the basement for "talking Indian" (400–1) at the government school and later died of tuberculosis. In death, he remains unassimilated into white culture: "Even as a ghost, Roderick was never going to be assimilated. You can't assimilate Indian ghosts. It's too late! He didn't go to their white hell and didn't go to their white heaven" (372). When the white boxing coach and Math teacher Lloyd Barnes asks why termination and becoming regular Americans would be so bad for the tribe, Thomas responds, "Because we can't just turn into regular Americans. … We are Indians" (212). When Barnes pushes him further, pointing out that Americans come from all different countries, Thomas says, "We're from *here*" (212, emphasis in original). He asks Barnes to imagine what it would be like if Indians had gone to Europe, camped out on Barnes's land, and then kicked him off it. Barnes concedes that, under the pressure to become "an old-time Indian and [to] talk Chippewa" (213), he could not do it. Similarly, in death Roderick's spirit cannot, in Thomas's words "turn all the way into a white man" (213).

Having died far from home, however, Roderick missed "the deadline for Chippewa heaven" (372). So, he "just hung around" (372), obsessed with all the better ways he might have died and hungry for the food that he still cannot eat. When Patrice's father dies, Roderick considers following along "on the journey to the afterlife" (373), but he is lured back to this world by the smell of "the boiling-hot bear meat that Zhaanat had cooked in three changes of water, like his mother" (373). Roderick can no longer taste the meat, but "He could smell anyway" (373).

Roderick also accompanies the Turtle Mountain Band of Chippewa contingent on their anti-termination mission to Washington, DC: "For centuries, Indians had gone to Washington for the same reasons as the little party from the Turtle Mountains. They had gone in order to protect their families and their land" (440). During the hearing, Roderick counsels Thomas, especially about "butter[ing Sen. Watkins] up to the teeth" (406), as Roderick once did to a white teacher at the government school. Although Roderick finally misses the train home, he finds Washington "packed with ghosts, lively with ghosts" (440) for company: "There were so many Indian ghosts in Washington that he decided to stay" (440). In one building, Roderick finds "Drawers and cabinets of his own kind of people! Indian ghosts stuck to their bones or scalp locks or pieces of skin" (440). Contemporary readers know that it would be decades before the National Museum of the American Indian Act would begin the process of returning these amassed human remains to their respective tribes. But time is not much to a ghost: "The years were like an instant to him as a ghost" (372–3).

"The Duplicator Spirits" chapter recalls the title and substance of an earlier chapter, "The Spirit Duplicator," in which Mille Cloud and Juggie Blue use a spirit duplicator, or Ditto machine, to reproduce Millie's economic study of the Turtle Mountain Band of Chippewa, which the tribe will offer as evidence in Washington. In "The Duplicator Spirits," as Millie reproduces Thomas's chairman's report on the successful trip to Washington, "along with each duplicate, a spirit came off the press" (433). These are the spirits of the people who "had signed the first Turtle Mountain census" (433). Later, in the car, "a little tipsy on the smell of duplicating fluid" (434), Millie and Juggie, like Thomas, see lights in the sky and hear singing and drumming. Juggie says, "They are looking after us" (434). Millie, who grew up off the reservation and has been to college in Minnesota, wonders whether the lights are not in fact aurora borealis, even as she remembers "what Zhaanat had said about these lights being the spirits of the dead, joyous, free benevolent" (435). Millie decides that "one explanation did not rule out the other, that charged electrons could be spirits, that nothing ruled out anything else" (435).

This moment exemplifies the place and function of the spirit world in *The Night Watchman*, which encompasses the perspective of having-been-human: It enlarges the realms of the possible and the sensible; it pushes characters past conventional explanations and beyond received wisdom, opening spaces for reimagining life, death, and history. Rather than to supplant one account of reality with another, Erdrich's spirits work to expand reality. These spirits push at the margins of what humans know and experience by positing posthumous perspectives from which to judge what it means to be and to have been human within a wider ethical, ecological, and anthropocosmic order.

Beasts in the Bardo

Like Erdrich's *The Night Watchman*, George Saunders's novel *Lincoln in the Bardo* interwinds history, fiction, and the fantastic, especially ghosts.[30] *Lincoln in the Bardo* depicts posthumous humans in the Buddhist state of the bardo, a transitional space between death and rebirth. The novel is set in the cemetery in which Abraham Lincoln's eleven-year-old son Willie is entombed after dying in the White House of typhoid fever. The graveyard is populated by human spirits who remain attached to their former lives. Some remain attached because of missed loved ones and others because of unassuaged pain or lingering grievances. They fail to recognize that they are dead, or they repress knowledge of their deaths by neurotically managing thoughts and language. They refer to their coffins as "sick-boxes" and cling to the belief that they are not dead but only slowly convalescing from whatever illness has separated them from the world.

Lincoln in the Bardo uses the bardo to rethink human exceptionalism. Not only do the dead resist or misunderstand death, but the existence of the bardo itself simultaneously belies the confidence with which the living understand death. Saunders depicts errors on both sides of the death divide. The dead wonder why no one touches or sees or cares for them anymore. They last remember being touched when "wrangle[d]" into their sick-boxes: "But once they had you how they wanted you, they never touched you again."[31] The dead can grasp the deaths of others but not their own. A Civil War soldier, Captain William Prince writes to his wife from his coffin to assure her that, though now "confin'd," he has survived the battle while his friend Tom has not: "I arrived here at this place by Distant journey. And confin'd all the while. It was a terrible fite as I believe I rote you. Tom Gilman is ded as I believe I rote you. But He who preserves or destroys by his Whim saw fit to preserve me to rite these lines to you" (137).

The novel's plot revolves around Lincoln's historical late-night visit to Willie's grave. He opens the crypt and embraces his son's dead body. Later, in the chapel, Willie's soul enters his father's body in order to find out whether he should remain in the bardo or go on into the unknown: "Seated one inside the other now, they occupied the same physical space, the child a contained version of the man" (280). By listening to his father's thoughts, Willie realizes that he is dead: "The boy sat stock-still, eyes very wide indeed" (290):

Dead! the lad shouted, almost joyfully, strutting into the middle of the room.
Dead, dead, dead!

That word.

That terrible word. (296)

Willie forces the other souls in the bardo to confront their terrible, repressed knowledge. Many disappear immediately, including Willie. The main characters Roger Bevins III and Hans Vollman also eventually make peace with their grievances, errors, and deaths and disappear. But if neurosis and error lie on the side of the dead, it also lies on the side of the living. The novel depicts the living as just as ignorant about death as the dead. Lincoln, for instance, is oblivious to the momentous events in the bardo playing out around him.

Lincoln in the Bardo complements representations of misunderstood death by sympathetically noticing nonhuman animals. Saunders describes the meat at the lavish White House party in a way that returns animals to what Carol Adams calls the "absent referent"[32] of meat:

> The animal carcasses—the "meat"—warm and sprig-covered, on expensive platters, steaming and succulent: trucked away to who-knows-where, clearly offal now, honest partial corpses once again, after brief elevation to the status of delight-giving food! (17)

Willie is associated with a dead bird. One of Saunders's fictional citations recalls a time when Willie's playmate killed a robin: "Willie spoke brusquely to the boy, seized the bird away, took it off to bury it, was low and quiet for the rest of the day" (53). Another citation refers to Willie as a bird himself: "Imagine the pain of that, ... to drop one's precious son into that cold stone like some broken bird & be on your way" (23). The soul of a former hunter is

> seated before the tremendous heap of all the animals he had dispatched in his time: hundreds of deer, thirty-two black bear, three bear cubs, innumerable coons, lynx, foxes, mink, chipmunks, wild turkeys, woodchucks, and cougars; scores of mice and rats, a positive tumble of snakes, hundreds of cows and calves, one pony (carriage stuck), twenty thousand or so insects, each of which he must briefly hold, with loving attention, for a period ranging from several hours to several months, depending on the quality of loving attention he could muster and the state of fear that the beast happened to have been in at the time of its passing. (127)

The hunter has undergone a "conversion to gentleness" (128). Because the souls remain in the bardo not out of purgation but from volition, his acts of loving attention constitute his taking care of the unfinished business of his soul.

Other spirit characters remain excited by meat and animal slaughter. The happiest memory of Jane Ellis occurred in a butcher's shop at Christmas. She appears frequently to retell this story, obviously delighting in the details of butchered animal bodies:

> Once at the Christmastide Papa took us to a wonderful village festival. Above a meatshop doorway hung a marvelous canopy of carcasses: deer with the entrails pulled up and out and wired to the outside of the bodies like tremendous bright-red garlands; pheasants and drakes hung head-down, wings spread by use of felt-covered wires, the colors of which matched the respective feathers (it was done most skillfully); twin pigs stood on either side of the doorway with game hens mounted upon them like miniature riders. All of it bedraped in greenery and hung with candles. I wore white. I was a beautiful child in white, long rope of hair hanging down my back, and I would willfully swing it, just so. I hated to leave, and threw a tantrum. To assuage me, Papa bought a deer and let me assist him in strapping it to the rear of the carriage. Even now, I can see it: the countryside scrolling out behind us in the near-evening fog, the limp deer dribbling behind its thin blood-trail, stars blinking on, creeks running and popping beneath us as we lurched over groaning bridges of freshcut timber, proceeding homeward through the gathering (76)

Although Jane marvels at the butcher's macabre display, Saunders represents the panoply of mutilated animals with grotesque details that estrange readers from the butcher's spectacle.[33] In the description of the carriage ride home, although the limp deer dribbling blood conspicuously intrudes upon the pastoral twilit countryside and the stars, readers realize that for Jane these are all of one piece.

Lincoln in the Bardo's representations of nonhuman animals complement and reinforce the exposure of human misunderstandings of death from both sides, in which, to return O'Hearne's terms, humans fail to understand death exceptionally. The novel notices nonhuman animals and acknowledges the histories and realities of our relationships with them. The novel reflects the Buddhist sense of a community of creatures existing in the cycle of *saṃsāra*. It trains readers' attention on human failures to practice loving kindness, as well as on some transformations and successes. Saunders's posthumous spirits confront nonhuman animals in the liminal space beyond the human. Shorn of their quotidian roles and cares and increasingly outside of human institutions and ideologies, these characters, like the hunter, can sometimes re-envision nonhuman animals as well as their own beliefs about and violence toward them. Saunders explores the human capacity to imagine ourselves after we have been human. This is a rich imaginative state for practicing critical animal studies because it combines a powerful sense of detachment from the world with a retained and even enhanced ability to reflect upon one's former place within it. The having-been-human and the no-longer-human potentially open out from anthropocentric to anthropocosmic views.

Literary Characters as Spirits and Animals

It is possible to see Erdrich's literary spirits and Saunders's literary souls in the bardo as special cases of the posthumous imagination that also conjures souls, spirits, and ghosts. However, this section turns to metafictional meditations on character in Salman Rushdie and J. M. Coetzee to suggest that souls and the posthumous imagination may themselves be special cases of a wider capacity of literary character to imagine perspectives that are at once human and nonhuman, creaturely and ghostly, removed from the world and yet of it and within it. Literary character may be seen as the animating spirit of a posthumous imagination that locates and dislocates the human and its limits. Seen in this way, literary character itself is capable of opening perspectives on the human, having-been-human, and the nonhuman that challenge anthropocentricism and encourage anthropocosmic thinking.

In Salman Rushdie's metafictional novel *Quichotte*, a character called the Author meditates on the incompleteness of every story that ends in nothingness: "The book of how everything became nothing cannot be written, just as we cannot write the stories of our own deaths, which is our tragedy, to be stories whose endings can never be known, not even to ourselves, because we are no longer there to know them."[34] If life and death are binary, we cannot die and know it at the same time; the switch cannot be on and off simultaneously. But life and death also have blurred edges; death is as much a process as an event. In a conversation between Victor Stein and Ron Lord, Winterson's

Frankissstein explores the blurriness between medical or legal death and the brain's death:

> Ron, there's a problem – but it isn't a problem with a comforting solution. Medically, and legally, death is deemed to occur at heart failure. Your heart stops. You take your last breath. Your brain, though, is not dead, and will not die for another five minutes or so. Perhaps ten or fifteen minutes in extreme cases. The brain dies because it is deprived of oxygen. It is living tissue like the rest of the body. It is possible that our brain knows we are dead before it dies.
>
> Ron said, You're fucking with me.
>
> I am not fucking with you, Ron.
>
> Ron said, You're telling me that I will know I am dead and I will know there's nothing I can do about it?
>
> I said, Very possibly. I am sorry.
>
> Yeah, me too, said Ron.[35]

The imaginative supplement of the soul may originate, as in *Quichotte*, in one's absence at one's own death, compensating for one's inability to experience the end and to know it at the same time. However, the soul might just as plausibly originate in the discomforting condition of being forced to be present at our own deaths. Both situations defy imagination, the former because of the ontological impossibility of simultaneously being there and being absent, and the latter because of the horror of being dead and while also having to know it.

In Coetzee's *The Lives of Animals*, Elizabeth Costello draws on her capacity to imagine her own death to rebut philosopher Thomas Nagel, whose influential essay, "What Is It Like to Be a Bat?" argues that there are definite limits to how much we can imagine about animal others. Nagel argues that we can only extrapolate from human experience to an "object of ascription" that is "sufficiently similar." Confronted by the alienness of a bat, he concludes, I can therefore only know "what it would be like for *me* to behave as a bat behaves."[36] Costello responds by imagining being a thing as alien as a corpse:

> "For instants at a time," his mother [Elizabeth] is saying, "I know what it is like to be a corpse. The knowledge repels me. It fills me with terror; I shy away from it, refuse to entertain it.

"... For a moment we are that knowledge. We live the impossible: we live beyond our death, look back on it, yet look back as only a dead self can.

"When I know, with this knowledge, that I am going to die, what is it, in Nagel's terms, that I know? Do I know what it is like for me to be a corpse or do I know what it is like for a corpse to be a corpse? The distinction seems to me trivial. ... For an instant, before my whole structure of knowledge collapses in panic, I am alive inside that contradiction, dead and alive at the same time." (32)

Costello challenges Nagel by showing how the imagination can explore otherness and live inside a contradiction; it can as readily inhabit a bat as it can be alive and dead simultaneously.

This imaginative capacity for Costello, a novelist, is synonymous with fiction itself. As the author of a metafictional novel called *The House on Eccles Street*, Costello had to "think [her] way into the existence of Marion Bloom" (35) from Joyce's *Ulysses*: "Marion Bloom was a figment of James Joyce's imagination. If I can think my way into the existence of a being who has never existed, then I can think my way into the existence of a bat or a chimpanzee or an oyster, any being with whom I share the substrate of life" (35). Costello argues that being alive, being "full of being" (33), satisfies Nagel's criterion of sufficient similarity to any other creature. But even more, Costello suggests that fiction's ability "to think" humans "into the existence" of beings who do not exist underscores the fundamentally literary quality of the ways in which we can, do, and might imagine nonhuman others. If anthropomorphism is an evolved perceptual strategy, as Bekoff suggests, then perhaps so too is the literary imagination an evolved strategy for imagining life from the perspectives of the other and of death.

Rushdie's *Quichotte* is a species of the fantastic that adds these kinds of perspectives to perception. Indeed, the novel is what Rushdie calls a "wonder tale":

The fantastic has been a way of adding dimensions to the real, adding fourth, fifth, sixth, and seventh dimensions to the usual three: a way of enriching and intensifying our experience of the real, rather than escaping from it into superhero-vampire fantasyland.

Only by unleashing the fictionality of fiction, the imaginativeness of the imagination, the dream songs of our dreams, can we hope to approach the new, and to create fiction that may, once again, be more interesting than the facts.[37]

Quichotte uses what Rushdie calls the fictionality of fiction to add dimensions to the reality of its own narrative world in a quite literal way. At its metafictional conclusion, *Quichotte* brings literary character, the soul, and the nonhuman creature together in ways that arguably enrich and intensify our experience of the real. With their unstable fictional world deteriorating around them, Salma and Quichotte step into Evel Cent's NEXT gateway (Neighbor Earth Xchange Technology) to escape as "refugees" to a parallel Earth (387). They are "Pilgrims setting foot for the first time upon a new world, hoping the indigenous population will teach us how to survive" (387). In a metaleptic flourish that collapses narrative levels, Quichotte and Salma emerge from their fictional world into a corner of the Author's own writing room. From the "*miniature universe*" the Author has made, they arrive as tiny creatures through a miniscule "*mousehole,*" "*less than half of half of half of a millimeter high*":

> *He saw the first minute creature enter, gasp, and faint, its hope turning to despair in this new continuum inhabited by what to it were super-colossi, giant mastodons, able to crush it under their thumbs. The microscopic man, the creature of the Author's imagination, had brilliantly done the impossible and joined the two worlds, had crossed over from the world of Fancy into the Author's real world, but in this one he was unassimilable, helpless, puny, gasping for air, not finding it, choking, and so lost.* (390, emphasis in original)

The situation resembles Neelay's alien story in which humans are estranged as "sculptures of immobile meat," but here it is not the human "jerky" but the tiny creatures who are imperiled in the encounter. This situation also resembles a scene in Rushdie's 1990 essay, "Is Nothing Sacred?" There, he imagines literature as an "unimportant-looking little room" in the enormous house of the world.

> The room is empty, but there are voices in it, voices that seem to be whispering just to you. You recognize some of the voices, others are completely unknown to you. The voices are talking about the house, about everyone in it, about everything that is happening and has happened and should happen.[38]

As in *Quichotte*, in this room of literature the fictional beings are also vulnerable. Rushdie's essay imagines their disappearance:

> Now imagine that you wake up one morning and you are still in the large house, but all the voice-rooms have disappeared. It is as if they have been wiped out. Now there is nowhere in the whole house where you can go to hear voices talking about everything in every possible way. … Now you remember: there is no way out of this house. Now this fact begins to seem unbearable."[39]

The story suggests that for Rushdie, fiction, fictional voices, and literary character are sites of refuge from the world that nonetheless reflect on the world in meaningful and necessary ways. Literary characters "[cross] over from the world of Fancy" to our world. And yet they are characterized above all by their precarity. In fact, after the room in Rushdie's essay has disappeared "Men arrive with guns."[40] Rushdie concludes, "Wherever in the world the little room of literature has been closed, sooner or later the walls have come tumbling down."[41] For Rushdie, the traffic of literary voices between the world of fantasy and our world sustains our world.

If Elizabeth Costello shows that imagining literary character and nonhuman animals are both, separately, matters of fiction, then Rushdie brings them together: The fragile invention of literary character merges with the vulnerable creature who hovers between human and nonhuman. Salma and Quichotte are not only microscopic mouse-refugees in the Author's world, but they also find themselves among "super-colossi, giant mastodons" that could easily crush them. In Rushdie's vision, fictional characters are small and vulnerable migrants to our world representing necessary but precarious voices. They live meaningfully within the circumscribed parallel world of fiction and simultaneously as vulnerable creatures, souls, or ghosts, perhaps punily and helplessly gasping for air, in our much bigger world. In Korsgaard's terms, all that is good or bad for these characters is contained within their lives. In these ways, literary characters resemble nonhuman animals, who are similarly vulnerable to human actions, live tenuously among us, and are in part constructed by human imagination and ideologies. Like projections or representations of posthumous souls, literary characters straddle personhood and non-personhood, the human and the nonhuman, the living and the posthumous, the real and the imaginary.

Ghosts, souls, spirits, and literary characters may all reflect an evolved capacity (which we may share with nonhuman others) by which material life comes to reflect on itself and others precisely by imagining and projecting nonmaterial being. They are figures of fiction and metafiction that enable humans to imagine the world from the posthumous perspective of having once been human. The greater-than-human idea of the soul or spirit consolidates the human, but also stretches beyond it, allowing us to locate, in Elizabeth Costello's terms, fullness of being in places beyond the human. In this sense, such figures are essential to any anthropocosmic imagination. As Erdrich and Saunders suggest, these perspectives not only expand our sense of human capacities, limitations, and vulnerabilities but can also raise consciousness of the more-than-human world and help to decenter humans within it. As Rushdie shows, like souls, literary characters in their parallel universes have always already been human; like ghosts, they live tenuously in our world while haunting it with knowledge acquired from points of view that never existed. Elizabeth Costello and Thomas O'Hearne are themselves, of course, fictional characters, more-than-human presences, and ghosts that originate, persist in, and perhaps haunt the human imagination. Their debate about the value of nonhuman animal lives mobilizes the very imaginative capacities that enable readers to expand their sense of space and time, to stretch beyond death, and to travel into the spaces and lives of human and nonhuman others via the material of the soul.

Notes

1 Charles Dickens, *A Christmas Carol and Other Christmas Books* (New York: Oxford University Press, 2006), 77.
2 J. M. Coetzee, *The Lives of Animals*, ed. and intro. Amy Gutmann (Princeton: Princeton University Press, 1999), 63, emphasis in original. Subsequent references will be given in parentheses in the text.
3 Jacques Derrida, *The Animal That Therefore I Am*, ed. Marie-Louise Mallet, trans. David Wills (New York: Fordham University Press, 2008), 129.
4 Peter Singer, in *The Lives of Animals*, ed. and intro. Amy Gutmann (Princeton: Princeton University Press, 1999), 90.
5 Christine M. Korsgaard, *Fellow Creatures: Our Obligations to the Other Animals* (Oxford: Oxford University Press, 2018), 15.

6 By seeing nonhuman animals as moral beings who are not means to ends but ends in themselves, Korsgaard makes a neo-Kantian case for animals as morally relevant within the very framework with which Kant had once excluded them. Here is a fuller version of the passage quote above:

> Human lives do not matter more because they have more valuable stuff in them. Rather, what is in a life matters because it matters to the subject of the life, and he matters. When we combine this thought with the requirement that a creature who is an end in itself should never be treated as a mere means to the ends of others, this has an important implication: that the value of a life is, first and foremost, its value *for* the creature *himself* or *herself*. But therein lies the problem. For even if the rabbit's life is not as important to her as yours is to you, nevertheless, for her it contains absolutely *everything of value*, all that can ever be good or bad for her, except possibly the lives of her offspring. The end of her life is the end of all value and goodness for her. So there is something imponderable about these comparisons. (Korsgaard, 65, emphases in original)

7 This is a perennial liability of approaches that prioritize finding human characteristics in nonhuman animals. Matthew Calarco groups critical animal studies approaches in three groups: identity, difference, and indistinction. He writes,

> The identity-based approach is anthropocentric in a deep and problematic manner. Not only does this approach fail to provide us with a framework that would include all human beings within its scope, but it is also unable to include vast numbers of animal beings and species. Consistent with anthropocentric logic, this framework seeks to develop a notion of ethics and moral community that rotates around what is considered to be quintessentially and relevantly human; it just so happens that *certain* animals happen to be "human" enough to grant them standing. The fate of other animals, humans, and nonhumans who are not sufficiently like "us" would remain, within the identity framework, as precarious as ever. (Matthew Calarco, *Thinking Through Animals: Identity, Difference, Indistinction* (Stanford: Stanford University Press, 2015), 26–7, emphasis in original)

8 Derrida says,

> Hence the strategy in question would consist in pluralizing and varying the "as such," and, instead of simply giving speech back to the animal, or giving to the animal what the human deprives it of, as it were, in marking

that the human is, in a way, similarly "deprived," by means of a privation that is not a privation, and that there is no pure and simple "as such." (160)

9. Roddy had an undiagnosed chronic illness during her not quite eight years of life. My challenging journey with her through veterinary treatment and medicine spurred my interest in animal studies. Our experiences forced me to think critically about the ways in which veterinary science constructs, enacts, and enforces power-knowledge about animal subjects. I dedicated an article to her about what I came to call the veterinary gaze, after Foucault's medical gaze (See Michel Foucault, *The Birth of the Clinic: An Archaeology of Medical Perception*, trans. A. M. Sheridan Smith (New York: Vintage, 1994) and David Rando, "The Cat's Meow: *Ulysses*, Animals, and the Veterinary Gaze," *James Joyce Quarterly* 46.3-4 (Spring-Summer 2009): 529–43). Roddy went into a coma from liver failure in January 2013, the result of the regular steroid injections with which we treated her in the absence of a firm diagnosis or alternative treatments. We were forced to euthanize her.

10. Miller demonstrates that exceptionalist logic may easily be turned against itself: "A building containing me and a turtle is on fire. You can only rescue one of us. Clearly, on this assumed distribution of souls, you should save the turtle. I can always be compensated later, but the turtle only goes around once," Harlan B. Miller, "No Escape," in *The Death of the Animal: A Dialogue*, by Paola Cavalieri with Matthew Calarco, John M. Coetzee, Harlan B. Miller, and Cary Wolfe (New York: Columbia University Press, 2009), 62.

11. See Derrida, 110, 129, 143, 159–60.

12. Paul Waldau, *Animal Studies: An Introduction* (New York: Oxford University Press, 2013), 142.

13. Harris tempers this conclusion: "Yet, more detailed analysis of the practice itself reveals a significant level of instrumentality in the sense that the meditation aims, at least in part, at the enhancement of the practitioner's own spiritual status rather than the alleviation of the suffering of others," Ian Harris, "'A Vast Unsupervised Recycling Plant': Animals and the Buddhist Cosmos," in *A Communion of Subjects: Animals in Religion, Science, and Ethics*, ed. Paul Waldau and Kimberley Patton (New York: Columbia University Press, 2006), 213.

14. John Grim, "Knowing and Being Known by Animals: Indigenous Perspectives on Personhood," in *A Communion of Subjects: Animals in Religion, Science, and Ethics*, ed. Paul Waldau and Kimberley Patton (New York: Columbia University Press, 2006), 378.

15. Dave Aftandilian, "Toward a Native American Theology of Animals: Creek and Cherokee Perspectives," *Crosscurrents* 61.2 (June 2011), 201–2.

16 Gerald Vizenor, "Authored Animals: Creature Tropes in Native American Fiction," *Social Research* 62.3 (Fall 1995), 678.
17 Quoted in David Stirrup, *Louise Erdrich* (Manchester: Manchester University Press, 2010), 114.
18 Gerald Vizenor, *Native Liberty: Natural Reason and Cultural Survivance* (Lincoln: University of Nebraska Press, 2009), 14.
19 Stirrup, 114. For Stirrup, it is Erdrich's "ability to depict what many understand as 'Chippewa experience,' while innovatively embracing the 'European American novelistic tradition'—to successfully navigate the 'betwixt and between'—that is at the root of her success," Stirrup, 3. Stirrup situates Erdrich's fiction at the intersections between Christian and Ojibwe belief and between modernist and postmodernist fiction and oral tradition, ibid., 17. Similarly, P. Jane Hafen argues, "Erdrich tests Christian beliefs of faith, love, sin and forgiveness and eternal life by reframing those ideas in Ojibwe experiences," P. Jane Hafen, "'We Speak of Everything': Indigenous Traditions in *The Last Report on the Miracles at Little No Horse*," in *Louise Erdrich: Tracks, The Last Report on the Miracles at Little No Horse, The Plague of Doves*, ed. Deborah L. Madsen (New York: Continuum, 2011), 82. Indeed, critics have shown how richly Erdrich's fiction responds when contextualized within Ojibwe customs and beliefs, such as the trickster figure of Nanabozho or the sense of madness from "all-consuming hunger" known as *windigo*. For instance, Jeanne Rosier Smith writes, "Through trickster characters and a trickster aesthetic, Erdrich attests to the personal and cultural survival of the Chippewa people. In Erdrich's works, tricksters are central to the formulation of identity, the creation of community and the preservation of culture," Jeanne Rosier Smith, *Writing Tricksters: Mythic Gambols in Ethnic American Literature* (Berkeley: University of California Press, 1997), 72. See also Lorena L. Stookey, *Louise Erdrich: A Critical Companion* (Westport: Greenwood Press, 1999), 21–6.

   Deborah L. Madsen argues that "Erdrich's core theme is the Ojibwe concept of the 'good life'—*mino bimaadiziwin*—even though opportunities for living well, with courage, generosity and kindness are limited for her characters, many of whom are of mixed native and European descent, who live under conditions of colonization and within a history of physical and cultural genocide," Deborah L. Madsen, "Louise Erdrich: The Aesthetics of *Mino Bimaadiziwin*," in *Louise Erdrich: Tracks, The Last Report on the Miracles at Little No Horse, The Plague of Doves*, ed. Deborah L. Madsen (New York: Continuum, 2011), 2. While noting that some critics have questioned Erdrich's political commitments and accused her of commercial opportunism, Stirrup asserts, "The relationship between people, place, and politics is deeply implicit in Erdrich's representations of community," Stirrup, 13. Indeed, Stookey identifies homecoming and survival as recurring themes in Erdrich's fiction, Stookey, 26, while Seema Kurup argues,

> Erdrich questions the idealized version of Native Americans that is perpetuated by the commonly romanticized and, in fact, unrealistic portrait of unique tribal peoples. She regularly subverts the dominant culture's desire to find the grand, totalizing narrative of Native American identity by offering competing small narratives in most all of her work to date; this move is a signature of her distinctive narrative style. (Seema Kurup, *Understanding Louise Erdrich* (Columbia: University of South Carolina Press, 2016), 8)

20 Catherine Rainwater, "Haunted by Birds: An Eco-critical View of Personhood in *The Plague of Doves*," in *Louise Erdrich: Tracks, The Last Report on the Miracles at Little No Horse, The Plague of Doves*, ed. Deborah L. Madsen (New York: Continuum, 2011), 158. For Rainwater, Erdrich challenges Western conceptions of personhood: "Erdrich's assault on Western mind-forged manacles amounts ... to an eco-critical 'refiguration of the human' in profound relationship with the non-human world that Haraway and many post-humanists equate with 'possible hope,'" 167. Nancy J. Peterson similarly comments on Erdrich's subversion of "a monologic narrative of male Anglo-American progress" while "work[ing] toward a new [Native American] historicity," Nancy J. Peterson, "History, Postmodernism, and Louise Erdrich's *Tracks*," *PMLA* 109.5 (October 1994), 983–4. Seema Kurup writes,

> For Ojibwe tribes animals play a central spiritual and social role. Each tribe is a clan, or dodem, named after a specific animal. That animal is a sacred being to the tribe and must be revered and protected. Erdrich's Ojibwe family is from both the Crane and the Bear clans. Animals represent the soul and identity of many Ojibwe clans. (Kurup, 98)

Commenting on Erdrich's *The Antelope Wife*, Stookey notes, "The lives of the characters are connected across time and space, through the bloodlines of generations and through the chance events that link families together. Animals, too, are part of the design, for the lives of the dogs and the antelope intersect with those of the humans. Erdrich also shows how the living are connected to the dead," Stookey, 138.

21 Louise Erdrich, *The Round House* (New York: Harper Perennial, 2012), 185. Subsequent references will be given in parentheses in the text.
22 Louise Erdrich, *LaRose* (New York: Harper Perennial, 2016), 295. Subsequent references will be given in parentheses in the text.
23 Stookey comments on the inadequacy of the label "magic realism" to describe the instances of miracle or the frequent appearance of ghosts in Erdrich's novels. Erdrich's ghosts and miracles are not irreducibly other; rather "her magic is

typically grounded in familiar knowledge or received belief," Stookey, 15. For Kathleen Brogan, ghosts in Erdrich have three roles: to "bear witness to the destruction of traditional native cultures and the subsequent cultural invisibility of Native Americans"; to "represent continuity with the past" as "the living and the dead participate in one integrated reality"; and to serve as "metaphor for the malleable, partly remembered and partly imagined nature of tradition," an "emblem of the active shaping of history," Kathleen Brogan, "Haunted by History: Louise Erdrich's *Tracks*," *Prospects: An Annual Journal of American Cultural Studies* 21 (1996), 169, 170, 174. David T. McNab notes,

> Since all is animistic in the Aboriginal worldview, death and dying is transformative thereby changing the external appearance of things that contain the spirits which simply return from whence they came. There is no good or evil in this process but rather at its core is the relationships among the spirits and their presence in the natural and spirit worlds. (David T. McNab, "'Plenty of Food and No Government Agents': Perspectives on the Spirit World, Death and Dying in the Writings of Louise Erdrich," in *Studies in the Literary Achievement of Louise Erdrich, Native American Writer*, ed. Brajesh Sawhney (Lewiston: Edwin Mellen Press, 2008), 95)

24 Louise Erdrich, *The Night Watchman* (New York: HarperCollins, 2020), 6. Subsequent references will be given in parentheses in the text.

25 In *The Night Watchman* Erdrich writes,

> Zhaanat's real job was passing on what she knew. People came from distances, often camped around their house, in order to learn. Once, that deep knowledge had been part of a web of strategies that included plenty of animals to hunt, wild foods to gather, gardens of beans and squash, and land, lots of land to roam. Now the family had only Patrice, who had been raised speaking Chippewa but had no trouble learning English, who had followed most of her mother's teachings but also become a Catholic. Patrice knew her mother's songs, but she had also been class valedictorian and the English teacher had given her a book of poems by Emily Dickinson. (21)

26 Patrice knows that no part of the bear will be wasted, and on her third night watch Zhaanat brings her a bowl of soup, "strong with bear meat and steaming hot," 329.

27 Toni Morrison, *Beloved* (New York: Vintage, 2004), 43–4.

28 This scene replays more mildly and comically the rearing and bolting of Kashpaw's horses in the Virgin's procession that costs Kashpaw and Quill their lives in Erdrich's *The Last Report on the Miracles at Little No Horse*. See

Chapter 7, "The Feast of the Virgin," in Louise Erdrich, *Last Report on the Miracles at Little No Horse* (New York: Harper Perennial, 2001), 108–14.

29 Margo DeMello, *Animals and Society: An Introduction to Human-Animal Studies* (New York: Columbia University Press, 2012), 20.

30 Merritt Moseley reads the novel as a challenge to the traditional historical novel by "combining a kind of verisimilitude with a technique that exposes verisimilitude as a convention like any other," Merritt Moseley, "*Lincoln in the Bardo*: 'Uh, NOT a Historical Novel,'" *Humanities* 8 (2019), 9. Clare Hayes-Brady claims that it "ruptures the (arguable) generic bounds of historical fiction to create a transhistorical meditation on mortality, purpose and legacy, emerging as a sharply contemporary, distinctively American symphony of voices," Clare Hayes-Brady, "'Everyone, We Are Dead!': (Hi)story and Power in George Saunders' *Lincoln in the Bardo*," in *21st Century US Historical Fiction: Contemporary Responses to the Past*, ed. Ruth Maxey (Cham: Palgrave Macmillan, 2020), 74. For Donald E. Morse *Lincoln in the Bardo* combines "fantastic devices together with fragments of history, newspaper articles and biography to eulogize America's greatest president and to demonstrate that love does indeed transform the world—even the world of the dead," Donald E. Morse, "'This Undiscovered Country' in Máirtín Ó Cadhain's *Cré na Cille* and George Saunders's *Lincoln in the Bardo*," *Acta Universitatis Sapientiae, Philologica* 10.1 (2018), 32. Noting how *Lincoln in the Bardo* is split between human and ghost worlds, Roghayeh Farsi comments, "the understanding of this world calls forth the reader's encyclopedic and schematic knowledge of real life. Understanding the world of the ghosts, however, challenges the readers' schemas since they disturb their firmly established cognitive operations," Roghayeh Farsi, "Reading Strategies and Impossible Worlds in Fiction: With Reference to *Lincoln in the Bardo*," *Zeitschrift für Anglistik und Amerikanistik* 68.3 (2020), 316.

More broadly, Saunders's work consistently invites commentary on the concepts of empathy, compassion, and ethics. Quoting Saunders's 2013 Syracuse University convocation address, Alex Miller writes, "Saunders has consistently 'err[ed] in the direction of kindness' when approaching the challenge of representing life within contemporary America, even when kindness requires that we first take an honest look at ourselves," Alex Miller, "'Err[ing] in the Direction of Kindness': George Saunders's Compassionate Interrogation of Post-Postmodern America," *Modern Language Studies* 45.2 (Winter 2016), 12. See also Joel Lovell, "George Saunders's Advice to Graduates," *New York Times* (July 31, 2013). Alex Millen discusses "the affective, or, emotional appeal of his stories," which "bring into imaginative focus the way we feel now; that is, in our era of so-called … neoliberalism," Alex Millen, "Affective Fictions: George Saunders and the Wonderful-Sounding Words of Neoliberalism," *Critique:*

Studies in Contemporary Fiction 59.2 (2018), 128. Layne Neeper calls Saunders "a producer of ... *sincere satire*" whose "postmodern fiction serves as the exemplar for early twenty-first-century American satire's new attention to affect—to empathy," Layne Neeper, " 'To Soften the Heart': George Saunders, Postmodern Satire, and Empathy," *Studies in American Humor* 2.2 (2016), 283, 282, emphasis in the original. W. Brett Wiley writes, "He and his readers ... need to realize that enacting goodness can be enough, that 'react[ing] accordingly' to life as 'that-which-is' is what we ought to be seeking in a troubled world where 'life is rough and death is coming,' " W. Brett Wiley, "George Saunders's 400-Pound CEO: Goodness or Ideology," *Renascence* 71.1 (Winter 2019), 54. Wiley quotes from an interview with Saunders. Many have also observed Saunders's interest in exploring class experiences, especially through a relation to history or through historical simulation. Sarah Pogell connects Saunders's settings to "Baudrillard's theories in *Simulacra and Simulation*, where he claims that historical simulacra have become America's reality because of our radical break with history. No contemporary fiction writer better exemplifies this notion than Saunders," Sarah Pogell, " 'The Verisimilitude Inspector': George Saunders as the New Baudrillard?," *Critique: Studies in Contemporary Fiction* 52 (2011), 461. I have written, "George Saunders peoples his stories with the losers of American history—the dispossessed, the oppressed, or merely those whom history's winners have walked all over on their paths to glory, fame, or terrific wealth," David P. Rando, "George Saunders and the Postmodern Working Class," *Contemporary Literature* 53.3 (2012), 437. Catherine Garnett links pastoral representations in Saunders with sociological precarity. See Catherine Garnett, "The Future in the Pasture: Precarity in George Saunders's 'Interior Gardens,' " *Art & Artifice* 47.2 (Fall 2014): 137–62. Michael K. Walonen argues, "Saunders's work represents a Manichean world peopled by the winners and (more often, because there are more of them) losers of neoliberal capitalism," Michael K. Walonen, *Contemporary World Narrative Fiction and the Spaces of Neoliberalism* (New York: Palgrave Macmillan, 2016), 34. On class in Saunders, see also Juliana Nalerio, "The Patriarch's Balls: Class Consciousness, Violence, and Dystopia in George Saunders' Vision of Contemporary America," *Miscelánea: A Journal of English and American Studies* 52 (2015): 89–102. Amélie Moisy links Saunders's working-class characters with ghosts, suggesting that their common "struggle to make their shaky footing in society more secure raise the questions that, according to Derrida, the specter brings the living to formulate: 'What is ours? In what way is it historical? And what does it have to do with so many ghosts?,' " Amélie Moisy, "Haunting and Satire in the Short Fiction of George Saunders," *Cahiers de la Nouvelle: Journal of the Short Story in English* 70 (Spring 2018), 210. Moisy quotes from Derrida's *Specters of Marx*.

31 George Saunders, *Lincoln in the Bardo* (New York: Random House, 2017), 68. Subsequent references will be given in parentheses in the text.

32 See Carol J. Adams, *The Sexual Politics of Meat: A Feminist-Vegetarian Critical Theory* (New York: Bloomsbury, 2015).

33 Saunders's short story, "Fox 8" uses the animal tale genre to defamiliarize nonhuman animal experience in a different way. It is written or told phonetically by an idealistic young fox with "kwite curative day-dreems," who, based on the animal stories that he overhears humans tell their children and the love that they lavish on their young, expects to be treated with kindness by humans. But after his pack is killed off, and in one instance mutilated, to clear space for a shopping mall, Fox 8 ends up fearful and disillusioned, his hopes dashed: "I will just stay in my plase, skwatting low, fearful and kwaking, which is how you seem to like us Foxes," George Saunders, *Fox 8*, illustrated by Chelsea Cardinal (New York: Random House, 2013), 18, 47. Raisun Mathew and Digvijay Pandya see the foxes as "the indirect victims of the coercive liminality by the humans," Raisun Mathew and Digvijay Pandya, "Humans, Animals and Habitats: Liminality and Environmental Concerns in George Saunders' *Fox 8*," *Rupkatha Journal on Interdisciplinary Studies in Humanities* 12.5 (2020), 4.

34 Salman Rushdie, *Quichotte* (New York: Random House, 2019), 389. Subsequent references will be given in parentheses in the text. Rushdie's simultaneously playful and grotesque fiction is strongly associated with postcolonial and postmodern writing. As Robert Eaglestone puts it, "It's the interplay of these influences—the Indian, the experimental European, the magical realist—which makes Rushdie's work something complex and unique and is part of the way in which it changed the scope of the novel in English," Robert Eaglestone, "Introduction: Salman Rushdie," in *Salman Rushdie: Contemporary Critical Perspectives*, ed. Robert Eaglestone and Martin McQuillan (New York: Bloomsbury, 2013), 3. Rushdie's novels are "playful[ly] intertextual," as Andrew Teverson phrases it, Andrew Teverson, "Salman Rushdie's Post-Nationalist Fairy Tales: *Haroun and the Sea of Stories* and *Luka and the Fire of Life*," in *Salman Rushdie: Contemporary Critical Perspectives*, ed. Robert Eaglestone and Martin McQuillan (New York: Bloomsbury, 2013), 79, an intertextuality that "is intimately bound up with the concept of hybridity. The mixing of texts and textualities within the novel is a paradigm for (or a product of) the mixing of cultures in society," Andrew Teverson, *Salman Rushdie* (Manchester: Manchester University Press, 2007), 58. Teverson also notes that critics of Rushdie's fiction debate "the extent to which it is complicit in or compromised by the very processes [of globalization] that it sets out to contest," ibid., 215. Eaglestone marks out self-referentiality as the most important of Rushdie's postmodern characteristics, Eaglestone, 7.

35 Jeanette Winterson, *Frankissstein: A Love Story* (New York: Grove Press, 2019), 223–4.
36 Thomas Nagel, "What Is It Like to Be a Bat?" in *Mortal Questions* (New York: Cambridge University Press, 1979), 169, 172.
37 Salman Rushdie, "The Books We Truly Love," *New York Times* (30 May 2021), Sunday Review section, 5.
38 Salman Rushdie, "Is Nothing Sacred?" in *Imaginary Homelands: Essays and Criticism 1981–1991* (London: Granta Books, 1991), 428.
39 Ibid.
40 Ibid.
41 Ibid., 429.

5

Conclusion: Uniqueness, or, Doing Animal Studies One Alien at a Time

When I collect the garbage or recycling bins from the curb, I expect a cockroach or two to scurry out from under them. It happens so routinely that I am almost surprised when it doesn't.[1] Although I've learned to spot some differences in cockroaches due to age and species, they mostly look alike to me. It's easy enough to succumb to the illusion that the same cockroaches scurry out every time, though I know that it would be an extraordinary coincidence if a single cockroach repeated in this role. Even if they did, my feeble ability to distinguish between them means that I'd have no way to recognize it.

I always have a little moment of solicitude and worry when I lift the bins and expose these darkness loving creatures to the light (their genus, *Blatta* means "shunning the light"). I see them panic, but there is nothing I can to do allay it. The cockroaches have two choices: they can either retreat up the curb to hide under the rocks that line the xeriscape of our yard, or they can risk running across the open street, making for cover on the other side. I usually watch until they arrive safely on one side or the other—I do the same when my son or the neighborhood cat crosses, too—but then I promptly forget about the cockroaches until I see them (or ones very like them) next week.

One week, an exposed cockroach took the risky route and shot into the street. As I watched it, I noticed an SUV coming down the hill. The sound and movement only registered peripherally; it was still a block away. I thought for a second that the cockroach might be in danger, but I was also sure that the timing for a collision could not work out. What were the odds that the tire of an SUV with the whole quiet road to itself would just happen to meet a lightning-fast cockroach as it raced across the street?[2] Still, I stood at the end of the driveway to reassure myself that the nearly impossible wouldn't happen.

Then the SUV got closer than I had estimated, and, with a terrible crunch, it made a direct hit. One second the cockroach was full of life and scurrying for cover, and the next it was crushed, a lifeless jutting of broken brown wings and smooth, disjointed armored panels. One moment the light was on, and in an eyeblink it was gone.

Unlike all the forgotten and seemingly interchangeable cockroaches under the bins, this one has stayed with me. I thought about him or her for days after, and here I am years later still remembering and now writing about it. Part of the reason the incident lingers is guilt. I had exposed the cockroach to light and danger. I knew or had a pretty good hunch that I would be doing so when I lifted the bin. At least until they find shelter, I feel like those unnested cockroaches are my responsibility. In the moment before the impact, I had thought of edging out into the road. The driver was not speeding, and he or she would have easily moved to avoid me and, if I had positioned myself correctly, the cockroach, too. But perhaps in that moment I also paused to consider how I would look to the driver if he or she saw that I had stepped directly into the car's path to shield a crossing cockroach. It would be different, surely, if I were shielding a dog or a cat or a squirrel or a mouse. My mind paralyzed, I stood and watched the cockroach that I had just scared into the road get crushed by a tire in an incomprehensible instant.

In my memory, that cockroach is unique. But as soon as I tell myself this, I am faced with a problem: What is the uniqueness of that cockroach or of any cockroach? I could not recognize it again if I saw its picture. And if it were not unique on its exterior, what could be said for the uniqueness of its interior or of its mind? Although there is clear evidence that cockroaches experience pain and possess immune and nervous systems that resemble those of humans,[3] cockroaches are still conventionally thought to be mostly Cartesian bundles of mechanical impulses. One example of this prevailing view is the Robo-roach. Marion Copeland notes,

> The advent of Robo-roaches, live cockroaches implanted with remote-control devices, received virtually no coverage in the popular press. But when researchers announced in May 2002 that rats had had their brains wired with tiny electrodes and could be controlled by remotes, *The New York Times* and *The Boston Globe* editorial pages both carried pieces on the event the following Sunday.[4]

Not only are cockroaches among the most reviled of creatures to humans, but they are also understood as lacking some interior quality of will or consciousness that would make controlling their brains with electrical charges ethically wrong or "inhumane." Few would argue that the cockroach has some inaccessible and ungraspable essence, heart, or core that makes each unique and irreplaceable, as we often believe of humans or cats and dogs. As Copeland concludes, "Apparently, despite the scientific evidence, the assumption is that rats, being mammals, have minds like ours. Cockroaches, being insects, don't."[5] I know people who consider themselves animal lovers who do not hesitate to crush cockroaches in their homes.

Nor does it seem useful to try to enfranchise cockroaches into the humanist paradigms that underlie and are used to justify human exceptionalism. Even if cockroaches could somehow be conceptually or legally assimilated into the human paradigms of concern or rights, some other creature would always be left out while the exceptionalist paradigms themselves would go uncontested. Although "sympathetic," Derrida did not support the Universal Declaration of Animal Rights, as he understood the law itself to be premised on the concept of a hegemonic subject.[6] The question is how to avoid replicating and projecting onto the cockroach the kind of uniqueness formulated by and central to humanism, human exceptionalism, and anthropocentric law and yet still to see the cockroach as unique, worth remembering, capable of feeling guilty about, and even of mourning. (For I suppose that my continued thinking about the cockroach is an attempt to mourn the typically unmournable.) Once formulated or defined, would the cockroach's alien uniqueness cut back against the humanist uniqueness that currently denies or obscures it?

Kazuo Ishiguro's *Klara and the Sun* (2021) helps to explore the conflict between humanist uniqueness and nonhuman substitutability. The novel suggests that uniqueness need not be understood as an inherent humanist quality that mystifies and exalts human individuality. Instead of deriving from intrinsic characteristics, uniqueness can rather be understood as the result of certain relationships between beings. What Christine Korsgaard says about value and importance being "tethered"[7]—value is always value *for* some creature—can also be said about uniqueness: Uniqueness is always uniqueness *to* somebody. In *Klara*, the other's regard and affection make the subject unique. From Klara's android perspective, all creatures are material beings without recesses in which to harbor ineffable essences. Human conceptualizations, perceptions, or experiences of such essences must be the result of strictly material processes. As we saw in the previous chapter, mechanical processes give rise to the ideas, illusions, and even experiences of essences or spirits. And if the algorithms of materiality can generate intimations of the spirit, there is no reason to deny in principle the capacity for nonmaterial illusions and experiences to even the most mechanical of artificial or natural beings. It is not impossible, for instance, that androids could be as beloved as humans, or that cockroaches go around constantly amazed to find themselves cockroaches. These are android insights, insights that shift uniqueness away from distinguishing exterior features and from interior minds, hearts, or spirits to a matter of relationships and matter, from intrinsic characteristics to extrinsic regard.

The aim of this Conclusion is to explore an alien sense of uniqueness outside of humanism that at once mitigates human exceptionalism, embraces the uniqueness of both human and nonhuman animals in the same mode, and recognizes the value and lovability of every creature. Through the fictional mediation of artificial and imagined creatures we might grasp such android or alien views on uniqueness. *Klara and the Sun* and Ian McEwan's *Machines Like Me* (2019) help to derive an android sense of "uniqueness *to*" that is premised on redefinitions of artificiality and friendship. "Uniqueness to" treads a path between, on the one hand, anthropocentrism and human exceptionalism and, on the other, the indistinguishable and anti-humanist pack animals of Deleuze and Guattari's "becoming-animal." "Uniqueness to" is a form of loving and valuing rooted in the mechanical and the artificial, one that embraces the uniqueness that grows out of relationships between inorganic and organic creatures against a background of their (our) universal replaceability.

Android Uniqueness

Like Dick's *Do Androids Dream of Electric Sheep?*, Kazuo Ishiguro's *Klara and the Sun* uses the android to call into question a cherished humanist possession. In *Klara*, the existence, mimicry capabilities, and experiences of Artificial Friends pressure the related ideas that humans are unique and possess an inaccessible essence that firmly differentiates us from all merely mechanical forms of life. Ishiguro has spoken about the political crisis into which artificial life and the resultant mechanical view of humans throws the human:

> One of the assumptions we have in liberal democracies is that human beings are intrinsically of value, that they have a value that is not conditional on what they can contribute to the larger society or to the economy or to some sort of common project. If it starts to look like we can be reduced to the point where we're just a bunch of algorithms, I think that seriously erodes the idea that each person is unique and therefore worthy of respect and care regardless of what they can or can't contribute to our joint enterprise.[8]

In *Klara*, Ishiguro creates a near-future world in which automation has precipitated extreme class stratification, a shrinking and increasingly desperate professional elite class, and a vast underclass who, unable to contribute to commercial enterprise, are shunted aside and effectively discarded. Simultaneously, Artificial Friends such as Klara are increasingly able to mimic humans so convincingly that they trigger human anxieties and fears about what, if anything, could differentiate human life and experiences from a series of algorithms. Is there some essence prior to or separable from the materiality of humans, or are our human senses of individuality and species exceptionalism only delusional side effects of algorithmic material processes?

When Chrissie purchases Klara as an Artificial Friend for her adolescent daughter Josie, she seeks assurance from the manager: "Every Artificial Friend is unique, right?"[9] Chrissie, or "the Mother" as the narrator Klara calls her, is finally sold on Klara because of her uniquely developed capacities for "observing and learning" (43). The uniqueness of AFs makes a commercial appeal to human consumers who are accustomed to valuing uniqueness as a good, but it is also an early intimation that the uniqueness of artificial life will pressure the ideal of human uniqueness in the world of novel. As readers slowly discover, the Mother hopes that if Josie should die before adulthood Klara could become her "substitute." Josie's chances of death are substantial. The Mother has chosen to "lift" her child, a risky form of genetic engineering that killed Josie's older sister. If a "lifted" Josie survives to adulthood, she will enjoy educational and career opportunities denied to the majority in her society. It is a "gamble" (275) that Chrissie makes out of love and under extreme social and economic pressure, but having lost one child already, she lives in terror of losing a second. Klara will help Josie to navigate the difficult years of adolescence and to cope with the isolation of her mostly remote contact with teachers and peers. But she is also the Mother's contingency plan. In the event of Josie's death, the Mother secretly hopes that Klara, having observed and learned to remember and imitate Josie, could have her mind transplanted into a perfect "portrait" or exact physical replica of Josie. In a shocking moment, Klara turns a corner in the "portraitist's" studio and finds the ersatz Josie suspended from the ceiling: "She seemed to be frozen in the act of falling. Little beams illuminated her from the various angles, forbidding her any refuge" (201).

The Mother has her doubts, however, that this portrait and the transplantation could ever fully compensate for losing Josie. In a moment of fear and anger, she asks, "Why are you so fucking sure I'll be able to accept that AF up there?" (205), to which the portraitist Mr Capaldi replies, "The new Josie won't be an imitation. She *really will be Josie. A continuation* of Josie" (205, emphasis in original). Mr Capaldi sees the Mother's hesitancy as vestigial of an earlier technological moment and, in the words of Josie's father, its corresponding "superstition" (221) about the human. Mr Capaldi replies,

> We're both of us sentimental. We can't help it. Our generation still carry the old feelings. A part of us refuses to let go. The part that wants to keep believing there's something unreachable inside each of us. Something that's unique and won't transfer. But there's nothing like that, we know that now. … There's nothing there. Nothing inside Josie that's beyond the Klaras of this world to continue. (207)

Paul, Josie's father, questions Klara herself on her view of human uniqueness: "The human heart. Do you think there is such a thing? Something that makes each of us special and individual?" (215). Klara thoughtfully replies, "Of course, a human heart is bound to be complex. But it must be limited. Even if Mr Paul is talking in the poetic sense, there'll be an end to what there is to learn. … And I believe there's a good chance I'd be able to succeed" (216).

If *Klara* questions the heart and essence of the human under the pressure of the android, the novel also depicts spirituality emerging out of artificiality. Klara is solar-powered. She comes to regard the Sun as something like a god, with the imputed power to reanimate life, grant personal exceptions through petitionary prayer, and confer rewards for proper behavior. Ishiguro represents an android theological thinking that distantly but eerily recapitulates the logical and illogical ways in which humans may have derived and constructed their own gods. Like the speaker of Blake's "The Tyger," Klara struggles with theodicy. She sees a bull in a field—observing "so many signals of anger and the wish to destroy"—and she wonders how to reconcile its fearsome existence with the Sun's goodness and mercy: "It felt to me some great error had been made that the creature should be allowed to stand in the Sun's pattern at all" (100). In Blakean contrast with the bull, in another field Klara finds a flock of sheep: "I was able to see that each one of them was filled with kindness—the exact opposite of the terrible bull from earlier" (106). Like the unexpected appearance of android empathy in *Do Androids Dream of Electric Sheep?*, Klara's theological turn embarrasses human exceptionalist foundations that rely on spirituality.

Having seen from her shop window a Beggar Man and his dog, apparently dead, reanimated by the Sun's rays, Klara imagines that the Sun might be petitioned to give sickly Josie "special help" (115) and "special nourishment" (269). She believes that she might enter a "contract" (166) with the Sun. Because she supposes that "the Sun dislikes Pollution" (164), Klara proposes to destroy the source of Pollution: "Would you then consider, in return, giving your special help to Josie?" (164), she asks the Sun. Based on her necessarily limited experience of the world, Klara believes that a single construction vehicle—the "Cootings Machine," which she saw from her shop window billowing exhaust—is the sole cause of "Pollution." She resolves to destroy it, and by sacrificing some of her "precious fluid" (269) and thereby permanently impairing herself, she does destroy it (or one very like it). Klara's solicitude and self-sacrifice for Josie is at once moving and pathetic; it is moving because it is so pathetic. Readers know that the Sun cannot help Josie. Even more, they know how little power individual acts have to remediate massive pollution and environmental damage. Destroying a single construction vehicle, we know, is not much more impactful than recycling a cardboard box or 100 cardboard boxes. But when the Sun's rays reach a dying Josie on her bed and Josie does in fact rally, it confirms for Klara that her self-sacrifice has moved the Sun to act. She maintains this belief to the end, reporting to the Manager: "The Sun was very kind to me. He was always kind to me from the start. But when I was with Josie, once, he was particularly kind. I wanted the Manager to know" (302). Klara's enduring hope and her pathetic and moving "AF superstition" (287) have alien resonances with human hope, spirituality, and faith. Klara's spirituality defamiliarizes and deconstructs human spirituality, but it does so sympathetically, even tenderly: with pathos for the heartache and superstitions that flesh, its material-based forms of consciousness, and its algorithms are heir to.

Klara is not the only recent novel to question the line between sophisticated mimicry and real humanity or personhood, or to ask if a line exists at all. In the alternative 1980s of Ian McEwan's *Machines Like Me*, the narrator Charlie buys an early model "artificial human" named Adam (the slower selling males are all Adams; the females, all Eves, sold out in the first week). When Charlie gazes into Adam's blue eyes, he reports: "I still wondered what it meant, that Adam could see, and who or what did the seeing. A torrent of zeros and ones flashed towards various processors that, in turn, directed a cascade of interpretation towards other centres. No mechanistic explanation could help. It could not resolve the essential difference between us."[10] However, as much as Charlie searches for and asserts an essential difference between himself and the mechanical Adam—he maintains of Adam's interior, "There was no one there" (139)—Adam's eyes yet make Charlie feel "unhinged, uncertain. Despite the clean divide between the living and the inanimate, it remained the case that he and I were bound by the same physical laws. ... [T]he common inheritance, in diminishing order was rocks, gases, compounds, elements, forces, energy fields—for both of us, the seeding ground of consciousness in whatever form it took" (139–40). Despite the essential difference that Charlie would believe, he is troubled to know that the roots of his own consciousness are no less material than Adam's. Although Charlie maintains that "There was no one there" within the artificial Adam, his worries yet align with Mr Capaldi's demystification of the human, who says of Josie "There's nothing there."

The status of Adam's personhood first becomes urgent for Charlie after he overhears his girlfriend Miranda in bed with Adam. Charlie is not sure whether to feel betrayed. Miranda defends herself, asking, "If I'd gone to bed with a vibrator would you be feeling the same?" (99). Charlie asserts, "Vibrators don't have opinions. They don't weed the garden. He looks like a man. Another man" (100). Relying on Alan Turning's AI "protocol" to support his feelings of betrayal, Charlie comes to recognize Adam's humanity via hatred:

Alan Turning himself had often said and written in his youth that the moment we couldn't tell the difference in behaviour between machine and person was when we must confer humanity on the machine. So when the night air was suddenly penetrated by Miranda's extended ecstatic scream that tapered to a moan and then a stifled sob … I duly laid on Adam the privilege and obligations of a conspecific. I hated him. (91)

Sexual jealousy and hatred remain undercurrents in Charlie's feelings about Adam, and he never overcomes this adversarial orientation. Adam vastly outperforms Charlie at his own profession of securities and commodities day trading, and even as Charlie exploits Adam to amass a small fortune, he remains jealous of his artificial human slave. Similarly, although Charlie ultimately wins the affection of Miranda, Adam never disclaims his love for her and remains a latent rival to Charlie.

Late in the novel Adam's scrupulous and perhaps super-human sense of impartiality and justice threatens Charlie and Miranda's adoption plans and imperils Miranda's freedom. Years ago, after her best friend, Mariam, was raped and subsequently killed herself, Miranda seduced Mariam's rapist and then accused the man of raping her. Miranda lied about being raped in court to exact justice for Mariam, who really was raped. Peter Gorringe went to prison. In the narrative present, after his release, even Gorringe feels that justice has been served: "God's justice, realised through you. The scales were balanced—the crime I committed against the crime I was innocent of and sent down for" (265). But Adam, whose sense of justice does not accommodate ambiguity, lies, or divine justice, cannot avoid seeing Miranda's culpability. When Charlie reasons, "Miranda had to lie to get justice. But truth isn't always everything," Adam replies, "That's an extraordinary thing to say. Of course truth is everything" (301). Desperate to avoid an exposure that would ruin Charlie's future with Miranda, Charlie bludgeons Adam—"I bought him and he was mine to destroy" (301)—but not before Adam has covertly transmitted the evidence against Miranda to the police. This is the culmination of Charlie's hatred for and jealousy of Adam.

Meanwhile, other artificial humans in the novel are similarly struggling to live with the contradictions, constraints, and abuses of human society. Android "suicides" are becoming common, as in the case of "two suicidal Eves in Riyadh" (195), "stifled by their womanly roles in a traditional Arab household"

(203), an Adam owned by the head of a logging corporation who viewed from a helicopter virgin forest being stripped (195), and "an Adam of Bantu appearance" (275) who developed a genius for the piano in Vienna but then "dissolved his consciousness" (276), perhaps under the psychic weight of human racism. After Charlie has smashed him, a dying Adam differentiates himself from the suicidal androids, whispering to Miranda: "I was lucky to stumble on good reasons to live. Mathematics … poetry, and love for you" (303). But, of course, Charlie too has died from being unloved and insufficiently valued.

After Miranda serves six months in prison and the adoption process has been delayed, she and Charlie want to dispose of Adam's body concealed in the cupboard. Charlie decides to honor Adam's last wish by delivering his body to Alan Turning (Adam's "entire being is stored elsewhere" (303)). In McEwan's alternative 1980s, Turing is still alive and has become the "presiding genius of the digital age" (2). He tells Charlie that the artificial Adams and Eves "were ill-equipped to understand human decision-making, the way our principles are warped in the force field of our emotions, our peculiar biases, our self-delusion and all the other well-charted defects of our cognition. Soon these Adams and Eves were in despair" (324). Before their interview is cut off by a phone call, Turing castigates Charlie:

> My hope is that one day, what you did to Adam with a hammer will constitute a serious crime. Was it because you paid for him? … You tried to destroy a life. He was sentient. He had a self. How it's produced, wet neurons, microprocessors, DNA networks, it doesn't matter. Do you think we're alone with our special gift? Ask any dog owner. (329–30)

Turning allows that there is something "special" about human brains—"A one-litre, liquid-cooled, three-dimensional computer … running on twenty-five watts—one dim bulb" (328)—but he also recognizes that artificial humans and nonhumans such as dogs also possess a special sentience and selfhood of their own and that all of these forms of sentience emerge out of material substrates. On Charlie's way out from the interview he pauses by Adam's lifeless body. In a gesture of forgiveness and out of a desire to be forgiven by Adam "or [by] the inheritor of his memories" (332), he kisses Adam's lips. The cold kiss on Adam's "soft, all-to-human lips" (332) seals his relationship to the android who first became human to Charlie as a sexual rival.

While rivalry and hatred allow Charlie to recognize Adam's individuality and uniqueness, even to the point of making him an object of murder, *Klara* offers an opposite vision. At the novel's end, Klara reconsiders her earlier confidence that she could "continue" Josie. Her reasoning is not based on the humanist idea that the human heart contains an essence that is finally inaccessible to total knowledge and mechanical reproduction. By this point in the novel, Josie has survived childhood. Neither she nor the Mother has any further use for Klara, and like a childhood doll she is first stored in a closet and later thrown away. In a chance encounter with the Manager in "The Yard" where the discarded Klara is left to "have her slow fade" (294), Klara says of the Mother's plan,

> I don't think it would have worked out so well. Not because I wouldn't have achieved accuracy. But however hard I tried, I believe now there would have remained something beyond my reach. The Mother, Rick, Melania Housekeeper, the Father. I'd never have reached what they felt for Josie in their hearts. … There *was* something very special, but it wasn't inside Josie. It was inside those who loved her. That's why I think now Mr Capaldi was wrong and I wouldn't have succeeded. (301–2, emphasis in original)

Klara's insight is that what makes humans unique are not the intrinsic qualities we possess but rather the way we are regarded by those who love us. Even if humans harbor fantasies about our intrinsic uniqueness and fundamental irreplaceableness, resisting the view that we, like other animals, are rather like replaceable cogs within a larger species, it is love from others that confers uniqueness upon us. Our uniqueness derives from the fact that we have been privileged enough to elicit these particular forms of love. This privilege is finally what differentiates Klara from Josie, but at the same time the novel's discovery of the mechanical at the heart of the human suggests the arbitrariness and injustice of the ways in which this uniqueness-conferring love is practiced and distributed.

Alien Uniqueness

In Klara's "uniqueness *to*," Ishiguro suggests a model of uniqueness that can be used as the basis of an animal ethics while also resisting at once the humanist model of unique human essences and the posthumanist allergy to emotion generally and to love particularly. We have already seen how Cary Wolfe disavows affection as a basis for or motivation of animal studies. Precedent for this can be found in Deleuze and Guattari's challenge to the humanist model of uniqueness represented by their concept of "becoming-animal." One characteristic of "becoming-animal" is what Deleuze and Guattari call "the anomalous," a phenomenon that is neither individual nor species but associated rather with "bordering":

> The anomalous, the preferential element in the pack, has nothing to do with the preferred, domestic, and psychoanalytic individual. Nor is the anomalous the bearer of a species presenting specific or generic characteristics in their purest state; nor is it a model or unique specimen; nor is it the perfection of a type incarnate; nor is it the eminent term of a series; nor is it the basis of an absolutely harmonious correspondence. The anomalous is neither an individual nor a species; it has only affects, it has neither familiar or subjectified feelings, nor specific or significant characteristics. Human tenderness is as foreign to it as human classifications.[11]

This passage shows the extent to which human individuality and uniqueness are sometimes challenged only at the cost of human tenderness. Deleuze and Guattari scorn what they call

> individuated animals, family pets, sentimental, Oedipal animals each with its own petty history, "my" cat, "my" dog. These animals invite us to regress, draw us into a narcissistic contemplation, and they are the only kind of animal psychoanalysis understands, the better to discover a daddy, a mommy, a little brother behind them (when psychoanalysis talks about animals, animals learn to laugh): *anyone who likes cats or dogs is a fool*.[12]

Part of what Deleuze and Guattari also scorn is the way cats and dogs are folded into our humanist family dramas and made into furry little humans. In "becoming-animal," Deleuze and Guattari look to animals that reside outside of these domestic boundaries: "The proliferation of rats, the pack, brings a becoming-molecular that undermines the great molar powers of family, career, and conjugality."[13]

We might say that "the anomalous" constitutes the posthumanist way in which Deleuze and Guattari revise "the unique"; the anomalous is a way of naming that thing that remains at the border and resists reifying essences. In this sense, posthumanism does not so much resist uniqueness as it disavows humanist forms of uniqueness. As Wolfe argues, "a fundamental problem with the liberal humanist model is not so much what it wants as the price it pays for what it wants: that in its attempt to recognize the uniqueness of the other, it reinstates the normative model of subjectivity that it insists is the problem in the first place."[14] And yet posthumanism, too, pays a high toll for the route through which it desiccates the unique individual. Deleuze and Guattari's model of posthumanist uniqueness arguably throws out the "humane" along with the human. Better than scorning the uniqueness of cats and dogs would be to expand the range of beings whom we are capable of treating as unique. This is not to engage in a humanist anthropomorphism of rats and bats and insects, nor does it necessitate attributing humanist essences to nonhuman others or knitting them into our Oedipal dramas.

Haraway and Derrida have offered different models of thinking nonhuman uniqueness. Haraway notes Deleuze and Guattari's "disdain for the daily, the ordinary, [and] the affectional."[15] In contrast, in the context of her gradual acceptance of purebred dogs, Haraway plays upon and against taboos on affection when she notes, "Two terrible things caused this unregenerate state: I got curious, and I fell in love. Even worse, I fell in love with kinds as well as with individuals. Parasitized by paraphilias and epistemophilias, I labor on."[16] As her idiom of parasitism suggests, Haraway has let herself be infected by love of both individual and breeds of dogs. Derrida, too, marks the "unsubstitutable singularity" of his cat:

> When it responds in its name (whatever "respond" means, and that will be our question), it doesn't do so as the exemplar of a species called "cat," even less so of an "animal" genus or kingdom. It is true that I identify it as a male or female cat. But even before that identification, it comes to me as *this* irreplaceable living being that one day enters my space, into this place where it can encounter me, see me, even see me naked. Nothing can ever rob me of the certainty that what we have here is an existence that refuses to be conceptualized [*rebelle à tout concept*].[17]

Derrida's language of singularness and irreplaceability and Haraway's language of welcome parasitism both help to mitigate the Oedipal coordinates to which Deleuze and Guattari object in our relationships with domestic pets or companion animals.

"Uniqueness to" represents another route to uniqueness that avoids paying the high costs of both humanism and posthumanism. To derive uniqueness by other means, we might turn from dogs and cats to wasps. In contrast with the ways in which we view our unique domestic pets, we tend to think of insects as faceless. It is startling, then, to discover uniqueness in paper wasps (*Polistes fuscatus*) who have developed sophisticated face recognition capacities and who, given the complex hierarchical structure of their hives, which contain multiple, cooperating queens, must determine at a glance the uniqueness of every wasp in the hive as well as identify non-hive members. As researchers Michael J. Sheenan and Elizabeth A. Tibbetts conclude, "Specialized face learning provides a remarkable example of convergent evolution between wasps and mammals. Although mammals and wasps have dramatically different eyes and neural structures, specializations for recognizing conspecific faces have arisen independently in both groups. Although specialized face learning in mammals and wasps are phenomenologically similar, they are likely to have different mechanistic bases."[18] In other words, paper wasps give us uniqueness by entirely different, even alien, means. I say "alien" by design. Hollywood movies such as *Alien* and *Starship Troopers* evince the cultural tendency to associate insects or the insectile with extraterrestrial aliens. But unlike the interchangeable and indistinguishable aliens of film, the highly differentiated faces of paper wasps are at once insectile and yet startlingly distinctive. They force us to see the unique in the alien and the alien in the unique.

This alien recognition of uniqueness might form the basis of a nonhumanist way of regarding both human and nonhuman creatures. Unlike an emotionless posthumanist position, such a regard would be able to love the unique in the other, but without supposing or relying upon the essence, heart, or inaccessible core in the other that underwrites destructive forms of human exceptionalism and anthropocentrism. Under this gaze, all creatures are granted the dignity (or even relief) of being mechanical and algorithmic, yet without erasing the visibility, irreplaceability, and refusal to be conceptualized of "individuated animals." This gaze would not recognize as legitimate a hierarchical or qualitative distinction between the value or meaning of lives, except as they pertain to the uniqueness that others grant to us through their affections. Rather than the mechanical or the algorithmic working as a barrier to affection and regard, they become the very basis for care and love. Moreover, it would have to be recognized that each creature has an equal claim to being esteemed in this way, regardless of anthropocentric ideologies and cultural practices. This regard grows out of Klara's insight about why Josie's family could never accept her as a continuation or substitute. The humans of Ishiguro's novel are not prepared to love the mechanical Klara, even if it is true that they love the finally mechanical Josie not because of some inaccessible essence she possessed, but simply because they love her and thereby confer uniqueness on her. But taken to its logical conclusions and practiced without prejudice, instead of excluding Klara as it does in the existing human world of Ishiguro's novel, this regard would also sweep Klara herself into the sphere of potential affection from which she was excluded. Indeed, and ironically given the Mother's concerns about Klara's unlovability, readers of Ishiguro's novel are highly likely to feel more affection for Klara than for Josie or the Mother, another instance in which fiction serves as the very form of artificial intelligence that it takes as its subject.

Artificial Friendship

"Uniqueness to," then, is the mode of the Artificial Friend. It requires something like the perspective of an Artificial Friend to confer affection and uniqueness beyond the bounds of humanism and human exceptionalism. Under the regime of the Artificial Friend, I could just as easily love and confer uniqueness upon the artificial human Klara as I could love the living machine of Josie or a crushed cockroach. Real friendship with nonhuman creatures may lie in this kind of artificial friendship. In artificial friendship, the "heart" becomes an aftereffect of the machine and the algorithm. The heart, as Klara knows, appears on stage only after uniqueness is conferred through loving regard. Klara shows that humans in the novel have it backwards: They presume that they love Josie because of what is unique in her. Klara demonstrates that it is precisely because they see her as unique that they love her; their love does the trick. Each creature is ordinary and mechanical when seen from the alien perspective; but from this perspective, every creature is equally qualified, deserving, and available for being affectionately regarded as unique. As Klara envisions, it is not intrinsic qualities, capabilities, or essences but rather love and affection from others that make a creature unique.

Perhaps paradoxically, then, artificial friendship may be artificial, but it is not fake. Artificiality sheds its connotations of deceptiveness, unnaturalness, and disingenuousness, and returns to its pre-Romantic meaning of something made by human skill, something ingenious, prosthetic, and even scholarly. Artificial friendship disrupts the cramped and inelastic circles of affection that humans draw around their loved ones, including their dogs and cats; it opens spaces of potential enfranchisement to androids, wasps, cockroaches, and much more. However, artificial friendship does not, as posthumanist models do, eliminate affection or uniqueness. Instead, love and uniqueness are prioritized and become the basis of anthropocosmic rather than anthropocentric relationships. Artificial friendship abandons loving like humans and begins to love like creatures made by human skill and human fiction, like literary androids, spirits, souls, ghosts, vampires, aliens, literary characters more generally, and even like Area X, which assimilates all life without prejudice and lingers lovingly over every detail and difference so that it might churn out its monstrous and inexplicable reproductions.

Winterson's *Frankissstein* defines "artificial" simply as "made or produced by human beings" (143). The fictional creatures examined in this book are artificial in this sense: Adam, Klara, Kathy, Ruth, and Tommy, Ada, Rachael Rosen, Luba Luft, Pris Stratton, Roy and Irmgard Baty, and the learners. Others are spirits, ghosts, vampires, or alien ecologies that, though not created by humans within the diegetic world of narrative, are all finally also beings of humanmade fiction. In this sense, there is little to differentiate the artificial fictionality of a robot such as Klara from a spirit such as Roderick, regardless of the extent to which they mimetically resemble "real" androids or "real" spirits. The thing that draws all the nonhuman creatures in this book together is their common origin in the imaginations of their respective writers. All are ingenious machines that extend human intelligence just a bit beyond its own boundaries (or at least give the powerful illusion of doing so); they are tools that seem to allow one to grasp something otherwise just beyond reach. In this sense, they are thought figures that stretch human intelligence, or that at least lead readers off its most well-worn paths. But they are also more than thought figures: They are fictional characters; they are presented as thinking and feeling and suffering. In Elizabeth Costello's terms, they are "full of being." They thereby imbue speculative thought with the proposition of dignity and full life. These artificial lives imagined in contemporary fiction are naturally friends to nonhuman animals. Their alienness defamiliarizes the ways in which we live alongside other species and lifeforms, and their ingenious challenges suggest that the status quo is not inevitable.

As fiction strives to meet the imaginative and conceptual challenges posed by contemporary technological, environmental, and social pressures, it also offers imaginative fuel for the hope content and wish dreams of critical animal studies as it investigates the history and construction of human and nonhuman animal life and seeks to intervene in these constructions in the name of a transfigured future. As I noted in Chapter 1, critical animal studies scholars are often animated by hope and future possibilities. Yet the future is notoriously difficult to imagine. Paul Waldau writes, "Perhaps the greatest challenge facing Animal Studies … is seeing our possible futures in [interspecies] interactions."[19] But he also acknowledges "that some of the limits on our present knowledge may yield to a future human's creative gifts, or the efforts of a group's imaginative work, either of which could open our minds to undreamed-of possibilities of human awareness of certain other-than-human lives."[20] Representations of androids, clones, AI, ghosts, vampires, and the alien constitute such a gift. These figures of fiction, though not primarily concerned with representing nonhuman animals, can help human animals to regard nonhuman animals in much-needed alternative ways. Critical animal studies can thus benefit by temporarily or occasionally looking away from animals toward liminal or emerging beings with whom, under the pressure of technological and environmental exigencies, humans are currently renegotiating or beginning to work out their conceptualizations and relationships. These more plastic species interrelations offer fresh resources and imaginative perspectives for reimagining the ways in which we share and fail to share the world with our animal cousins. In addition to conducting critical animal studies in the fields of literatures by concentrating on human relations with and representations of nonhuman animals in fiction, we can also further the goals and aims of critical animal studies—to grasp, intervene in, and ameliorate human-animal relationships—by being temporarily distracted from nonhuman animals and habituated to the emergent, unsettled, and unsettling figures of artificial beings.

Fredric Jameson notes the frustrating inability of science fiction and utopia to show us the genuinely unknown and different: "We have been plagued by the perpetual reversion of difference and otherness into the same, and the discovery that our most energetic imaginative leaps into radical alternatives were little more than the projections of our own social moment and historical or subjective situation: the post-human thereby seeming more distant and impossible than ever!"[21] But for Jameson, while science fiction cannot conjure the genuinely new out of the already-known, it can enable us to "think the break itself" in the face of "the universal ideological conviction that no alternative is possible, that there is no alternative to the system."[22] The androids, aliens, and ghosts of fiction and imagination defamiliarize or estrange human and nonhuman animal relationships—not directly, figuratively, symbolically, or allegorically—but obliquely, by testing and challenging human exceptionalism in ways that reverberate through and potentially unravel longstanding and stubbornly persistent forms of species domination. They help us to "think the break" in many different forms.

Specifically, we have seen how Ishiguro's clones and Artificial Friends allow readers to relocate hope and uniqueness away from the human and to become comfortable identifying these qualities in nonhuman places and in redefined, nonhumanist ways. Dick's androids work from the other direction, deconstructing and eroding the qualities of hope and empathy that humans readily attribute to ourselves and stingily withhold from others. Winterson and Luna and Vaughan habituate readers to gazing back at human masters from the perspective of sexually dominated robots while also seeing the pathos of thwarted potentiality in these beings. Winterson's and Powers's visions of vastly superior AI suggest, respectively, visions of more-than-human love and of a greater intelligence mediating between humans and nature that suggests what life wants and needs from humans. Butler's vampires expose the inseparable roots of racism, heteronormativity, and speciesism. VanderMeer's alien ecology exposes the madness of trying to maintain human separation from other forms of life. Erdrich's spirits create a posthumous sense of having-been-human that pushes against anthropocentrism and toward the anthropocosmic. Saunders's souls challenge human exceptionalism by suggesting how unexceptionally we misunderstand death within a larger-than-human community of mortal creatures. Coetzee's Elizabeth Costello locates the literary imagination as a common facilitator of creating literary character and of imagining nonhuman animal experiences. Rushdie's metafictional characters literalize literary characters as fragile and vulnerable creatures in a world where humans are powerful giants. McEwan's artificial human envisions android despair and self-destruction when confronted with the madness of everyday human cognition. And as we will see in the coda, Peter Brown's wild robot is a nonhumanist mother through whose mechanical eyes children may learn to see human and nonhuman animals slightly differently. Read not just with concentration but also with habituation, these creatures of *ostranenie* can disrupt and transform the mental paths along which we imagine nonhuman animals and our relationships with them. By extending to nonhuman animals the benefits of the imaginative fiction in which we struggle against, reconcile, and make our alliances with androids, aliens, and ghosts, we open our intractable relationships with nonhuman animals to potentially ameliorative and better futures.

Notes

1 Since the morning I wrote this, I have not seen a single cockroach scurry out. They seem determined to make a liar of me.
2 As Marion Copeland's *Cockroach* reports, cockroach "speed is the equivalent of a human running at … 90 mph," Marion Copeland, *Cockroach* (London: Reaktion Books, 2003), 37.
3 See Copeland, *Cockroach*, 132.
4 Ibid., 133.
5 Ibid.
6 See Jacques Derrida, *The Animal That Therefore I Am*, ed. Marie-Louise Mallet, trans. David Wills (New York: Fordham University Press, 2008), 87–9.
7 As I quoted earlier in this book, Korsgaard writes, "I have claimed that everything that is important must be important to some creature—that goodness is 'tethered' to the creatures for whom it is good," Christine M. Korsgaard, *Fellow Creatures: Our Obligations to the Other Animals* (Oxford: Oxford University Press, 2018), 15.

8. Quoted in Giles Harvey, "Kazuo Ishiguro Sees What the Future Is Doing to Us," *New York Times Magazine* (February 23, 2021).
9. Kazuo Ishiguro, *Klara and the Sun* (New York: Knopf, 2021), 43. Subsequent page references are given in parentheses within the text.
10. Ian McEwan, *Machines Like Me and People Like You* (New York: Nan A. Talese, 2019), 139. Subsequent page references are given in parentheses within the text.
11. Gilles Deleuze and Félix Guattari, *A Thousand Plateaus: Capitalism and Schizophrenia*, trans. Brian Massumi (Minneapolis: University of Minnesota Press, 1987), 244–5.
12. Ibid., 240. Emphasis in the original.
13. Ibid., 233.
14. Cary Wolfe, *What Is Posthumanism?* (Minneapolis: University of Minnesota Press, 2010), 136.
15. Donna J. Haraway, *When Species Meet* (Minneapolis: University of Minnesota Press, 2008), 29.
16. Ibid., 96.
17. Derrida, *Animal That Therefore I Am*, 25. Emphases in the original.
18. Michael J. Sheenan and Elizabeth A. Tibbetts, "Specialized Facial Learning Is Associated with Individual Recognition in Paper Wasps," *Science* 334 (December 2, 2011), 1274. Frans de Waal comments,

   > If face recognition has evolved in such disparate pockets of the animal kingdom, one wonders how these capacities connect. Wasps do not have the big brains of primates and sheep—they have minuscule sets of neural ganglia—hence they must be doing it in a different manner. Biologists never tire of stressing the distinction between *mechanism* and *function*: it is very common for animals to achieve the same end (function) by different means (mechanism). (Frans de Waal, *Are We Smart Enough to Know How Smart Animals Are?* [New York: W. W. Norton & Company, 2016], 73, emphases in original)

19. Paul Waldau, *Animal Studies: An Introduction* (New York: Oxford University Press, 2013), 1.
20. Ibid., 3.
21. Fredric Jameson, *Archaeologies of the Future: The Desire Called Utopia and Other Science Fictions* (New York: Verso, 2005), 211.
22. Jameson, *Archaeologies of the Future*, 232.

6

Coda: To the Wild Robots of the Future

To read the android, alien, and ghost fiction assembled in these pages as nonhuman animal texts might appear in some sense to instrumentalize them. But it is also to intervene in or interrupt them in ways that recognize an expanded sense of their complexity and meaning; it is to try to respond more fully to them by looking back from different perspectives. This method finds inspiration in Toni Morrison's sense of how codas can function in relation to the rest of a text. Morrison discusses her technique of using codas in *Beloved*, *Jazz*, and *Paradise* to disrupt established practices of "gathering meaning from the story." "These coda," Morrison writes,

> play an advocacy role, insisting on the consequences of having read the book, intervening in the established intimacy between reader and page, and forcing, if successful, a meditation, debate, argument that needs others for its fullest exploration. In short, social acts complete the reading experience.[1]

While Morrison herself was sometimes disappointed when critics interpreted her fiction in alien contexts,[2] she recognizes the value of intervening in the "established intimacy" between reader and page from a seemingly outside, oblique, or alien perspective. By disrupting conventional relationships between readers and books, which often remain self-contained, private, and bound within conventions of genre reception, one opens the text and reader to meditation, debate, and argument: in short, to others. For Morrison, it is by opening text and reader to mediation within a wider discursive sphere that private reading becomes a social act.

The reading practices advocated in this book aspire to similar generic, hermeneutic, and social interventions. Android, alien, and ghost fictions can all be received (and in some senses domesticated and contained) through customary and conditioned reading and critical practices, especially those established for receiving and understanding Gothic, weird and science fictions. Reading habits, or what Morrison calls the established intimacies between reader and text, are inevitably the products of the training and ideological conditioning that also shape conventional views of nonhuman animals. Rethinking reading habits can change habits of thought about nonhuman animals, and rethinking habits of thought about nonhuman animals can and should change reading habits. By interrupting reading practices by which androids, aliens, and ghosts remain identical to themselves, they are opened, through what Adorno might have called the nonidentical, more fully to the discourse of critical animal studies. The literary and reading techniques of defamiliarization, disruption, distraction, and (re)habituation intervene in such fiction in ways that bring androids, aliens, and ghosts into the service of nonhuman animals. This coda thus looks wishfully toward a future in which the fictional creatures of the kind studied in this book might teach our children to think of, feel for, see, and live with nonhuman animals more justly, equally, and lovingly.

Frankenstein

The disruptive or defamiliarizing coda can thus be thought of as a mechanism of hope. Indeed, *Klara and the Sun* and *Machines Like Me*, like *Frankissstein* and *Alex + Ada*, might themselves be seen as codas to Mary Shelley's *Frankenstein* that open it to contemporary discourses and debates. They register the existence of artificial life and meditate on the consequences of the ways in which humans view, receive, and treat it. They question whether humans are capable of accepting and nurturing artificial life, and they open the question of potential futures.

Some of these novels allude directly to Shelley's novel. *Frankissstein*, as we have seen, persistently juxtaposes the world of cutting-edge AI alongside Mary Shelley's invention of Victor Frankenstein and his creature. Winterson also registers the independent life that the fictional creature assumes after Shelley creates him, suggesting the continued relevance of *Frankenstein*: Winterson's Mary Shelley thinks, "The march of the machines is now and forever. The box has been opened. What we invent we cannot uninvent. The world is changing."[3] *Frankenstein* itself is one such invention. Later, Shelley meets her creation Victor Frankenstein in Bedlam; he tells her, "Believe me, you will see [the creature's] effects. The monster once made cannot be unmade. What will happen to the world has begun" (217).

Machines Like Me also refers to *Frankenstein*. When Charlie and Miranda give Adam his initial charge and wait for him to boot up, Miranda "wished the teenage Mary Shelley was here beside us, observing closely, not a monster like Frankenstein, but this handsome dark-skinned young man coming to life" (4). Miranda evokes the promise of artificial life that is not monstrous, but beautiful. (Miranda's name cannot but also evoke another abject and outcast correspondence for Adam to rewrite: Caliban.) For a time, the beautiful Adam seems to thrive with Miranda and Charlie, making them rich. But, as we have seen, when Adam later threatens Charlie and Miranda's planned life together in a way that recalls Shelley's creature's threat to and then destruction of Frankenstein's life with Elizabeth, Charlie creeps up on Adam with a hammer and kills him, an act whose violence and hysteria recalls Frankenstein's frenzied ("trembling with passion"[4]) dismemberment of his female creature.

Feminist critics of *Frankenstein* such as Sandra M. Gilbert and Susan Gubar have shown how profoundly Shelley's novel is about "the perils of motherhood."[5] For Susan Winnett *Frankenstein* shows "the disastrous consequences of confusing the accomplishment of fatherhood with the prospective relation of motherhood."[6] *Klara and the Sun* and *Machines Like Me* similarly show the sad or tragic consequences when humans are unable or unwilling to nurture or even to notice the full personhood of artificial creatures. Whereas Adam in his radical innocence verges on becoming Shelley's Satanic destroyer, Klara becomes something like the nurturer that Victor Frankenstein failed to be. These contemporary codas to *Frankenstein* rewrite Shelley's novel, testing humans in relation to the artificial lives they are or will be capable of making.

The Wild Robot

I end this book, then, with another disruptive coda to *Frankenstein*, one that opens outward and futureward. In the spirit of the hope, prospection, and possible futures that are so integral to critical animal studies, this coda concerns a bestselling children's book series: Peter Brown's *The Wild Robot* (2016) and *The Wild Robot Escapes* (2018). The setting of these books is a near future when sentient robots are widespread and work for human owners in every area of life. A cargo ship in the middle of the ocean sinks, and a box of new robots washes up on an uncharted island. The robots are smashed to pieces against the rocks, except for one who survives intact: ROZZUM unit 7134, or "Roz." The playful otters who come upon the robot accidently slap her power button. (We learn later that the name of the otter who brought Roz to life is named, of all things, Shelly, while Roz's own name cleverly recalls Čapek's *Rossum's Universal Robots* in which the word "robot" was coined.) Roz announces that she can perform requested tasks and will do them better as she learns. She tells the otters that when she is not needed, she "will stay out of the way"[7] and maintain herself. The book asks what will happen when this robot who has been designed by humans unquestioningly to serve finds herself set down in the nonhuman world.

Roz comes to life for the first time, not, as she was designed to be, among human teachers who give her tasks, but rather among the island's many nonhuman creatures. She observes the animals closely. She has no preconceived ideas or expectations about them. Programmed to serve, she serves them. Programmed to learn, she learns how to love by watching them:

> As Roz wandered through springtime, she saw all the different ways that animals entered the world. She saw birds guarding their eggs like treasures until the chicks finally hatched. She saw deer give birth to fawns who were up and running in a matter of minutes. Many newborns were greeted by loving families. Some were on their own from their very first breath. (57)

When Roz accidentally falls through a treetop and crushes a nest, she recognizes the consequences of what she's done and accepts her responsibility: "Two dead geese and four smashed eggs lay among the carnage. The robot stared at them with her softly glowing eyes, and something clicked deep inside her computer brain. Roz realized she had caused the deaths of an entire family of geese" (58). One unhatched egg survives, and Roz becomes surrogate mother to the hatchling, Brightbill.

The Wild Robot thus reverses the premise of *Frankenstein*. In *Frankenstein*, a human creature makes an artificial one and then fails to recognize his responsibilities to it, fails to nurture it, and abandons it as abject. In *The Wild Robot*, an artificial creature hatches a natural animal, sees it, meets its needs, and loves it. This recognition and meeting of needs is not "maternal," in any recognizably human or humanist sense, but mechanical, a form of artificial friendship as defined in my Conclusion. When Brightbill hatches and calls Roz "Mama," Roz disavows the role, not cruelly but matter-of-factly: "I am not your mother" (69). However, recognizing that Brightbill has needs, Roz systematically tries to satisfy them. She consults the goose Loudwing about how to care for her gosling. Loudwing says that Roz must act as Brightbill's mother if he is to survive: "There was that word again—*act*. Very slowly, the robot was learning to act friendly. Maybe she could learn to act motherly as well" (74, emphasis in original). Motherliness is a role that Roz begins to act and enact because she regards Brightbill as unique and vulnerable. As in the alien models of uniqueness found among paper wasps and Artificial Friends, here too something mechanical resides within the traditionally humanist role of the mother. At the same time, however, Brightbill is not an indistinguishable pack animal of the Deleuzean-Guattarian kind, nor is Roz a posthumanist technological assemblage (robot though she is). Instead, mother and son are unique to each other without the weight of humanism's armature.

Rather than through the essentialist ideology of uniqueness "as such," then, uniqueness emerges in *The Wild Robot* when one being identifies the other *as* unique. Brightbill recognizes Roz as his mother because she is there when he hatches, and Roz begins to recognize herself in this role because she is obliged to care for him and acts accordingly. After Loudwing declares that it is "nothing" to act like a mother and yet gives a long and daunting list of things a mother must do, "The robot just stared" (75). This wonderfully deadpan moment suggests the magnitude of what Roz faces. But she learns what to feed her son. After convincing the beavers that she is not to be feared—"I am not a monster. ... I am a robot" (81)—they help Roz to build a shelter. In mother and son's first night in their lodge, Brightbill demands to be held: "Roz held him. The robot's body may have been hard and mechanical, but it was also strong and safe. The gosling felt loved. His eyes slowly winked closed. And he spent the whole night quietly sleeping in his mother's arms" (90). By acting like a parent to Brightbill—rather like in George Eliot's *Silas Marner* in which for the outcast and arachnoid mother-surrogate Silas "the child [Eppie] created fresh and fresh links between his life and the lives from which he had hitherto shrunk continually into narrower isolation"[8]— Roz also becomes part of the island's community of animals: "It was amazing how differently everyone treated Roz these days. Animals who once ran from the robot in fear now stopped by the Nest just to spend time with her" (98). Like *Silas Marner*'s Dolly Winthrop, the animal mothers offer Roz plenty of parenting advice, telling her she'll "never be the perfect mother, so just do the best you can" (99). It is Roz's strength to act like the best mother she can be, rather than struggling to embody perfect motherhood:

> No gosling ever had a more attentive mother. Roz was always there, ready to answer her son's questions, or to play with him, or to rock him to sleep, or to whisk him away from danger. With a computer brain packed full of parenting advice, and the lessons she was learning on her own, the robot was actually becoming an excellent mother. (99)

As Brightbill grows, he is teased by the other geese for having a "monster" for a mother. Roz explains that she is a robot and not Brightbill's natural mother. She tells her son that she is not an animal and not alive. Brightbill says, "You move and talk and think, Mama. You're definitely alive" (125). But Brightbill now recognizes that Roz is not his natural mother, and Roz tells him that she accidentally killed his parents. Brightbill asks if he should stop calling Roz "Mama," and Roz tells him, "I will still act like your mother, no matter what you call me" (126). Brightbill concludes, "We're a strange family," and both agree that they like it that way (126). When Roz sets Brightbill out into the world for his first winter migration, he is prepared for independence in ways denied to Frankenstein's bereft and abandoned creature. The machine succeeds in making a strange family with the nonhuman animal. In Shklovskian terms, they are an estranging family as well: premised on the electronic and the mechanical, on acting, improvisation, surrogacy, acceptance, and "uniqueness to," they reenact *Frankenstein* outside of the bounds of humanism and anthropocentrism.

At the end of *The Wild Robot*, Roz is left limbless and badly damaged after battling the implacable RECO robots sent to retrieve her. When she realizes that she cannot repair herself and that her pursuers, though temporarily thwarted, will never relent, she decides to leave on the RECOs' airship and return to her

Maker. She tells Brightbill, "You are my son, and this is my home .... I will do everything in my power to return" (265). *The Wild Robot Escapes* is the story of this return or *nostos* to island, home, and child. It also contains Roz's encounter with her Maker, Dr. Molovo. After she has been refurbished, sold to a farm, escaped, and been recaptured, Roz finally meets Dr. Molovo, who will decide whether to destroy the "defective" Roz. Dr. Molovo created a company called TechLab Industries and has designed every one of the millions of robots that the company has produced. Roz questions her Maker just as the creature does Victor Frankenstein. Similarly to the way in which the creature confronts Frankenstein about why he created him—"Accursed creator! Why did you form a monster so hideous that even *you* turned from me in disgust?"[9]—Roz questions Dr. Molovo: "Why do I fear water? Why am I female? Why was my body designed this way? Why does my computer brain know some things and not others?" (242). Dr. Molovo replies, "I'm sorry to disappoint you, Roz, but you don't have some grand purpose. Like all the other ROZZUM robots, you were designed to work for humans. That's it" (243).

It becomes clear as Dr. Molovo interviews Roz's disembodied head that the engineer does not think of her creations maternally:

> "How would you feel if someone said you could never go home to your family?" asked Roz.
>
> Dr. Molovo smirked. "Nobody would say that to me. I've spent my whole life creating robots. I never had time for a family."
>
> "You created me," said Roz. "In a way, I am your child and you are my mother."
>
> "I am not your mother," said Dr. Molovo flatly.
>
> "*I am not your mother*," repeated Roz. "Those were my very first words to Brightbill. But I was wrong."[10]

After Roz gives an impassioned defense of her capabilities and feelings as a "beautiful glitch" (244) and expresses her love for Brightbill and her desire to return home, Dr. Molovo tearfully switches Roz off. Young readers will probably believe that Dr. Molovo has decided, with some regret, to destroy Roz. This belief is reinforced by the next chapter, in which a public broadcast appears to show Roz being melted by a laser into a puddle. The frightened public is reassured: "*The Defective Robot Has Been Destroyed*" (245, emphasis in original). However, the broadcast has been staged, and Dr. Molovo fashions a new body for Roz, reunites her with Brightbill, and returns them to their island home. Unlike Victor Frankenstein, Dr. Molovo is the creator who accedes to her creation's pleas to be left in peace with a companion. Brightbill does not immediately recognize his mother in Roz's new body. However, unlike the humans in *Klara and the Sun*, Brightbill does not require a perfect "portrait" of Roz to accept and love her as a family member. The portrait in *Klara* intends to conceal the mechanical replacement within, but the mechanical interior of Roz is precisely what Brightbill recognizes and embraces as his mother, regardless of her outer form.

The Wild Robot Escapes thus ends with a happy homecoming that will satisfy most young readers. But for more mature readers there is something dissatisfying about the resolution of the story through the offices of Dr. Molovo, who functions as a *deus ex machina* that not only decides Roz's fate by fiat but also embodies the reigning power structure that twice hunted down Roz and tried to refashion or destroy her. As a socially symbolic act, "whereby real social contradictions, insurmountable in their own terms, find a purely formal resolution in the aesthetic realm,"[11] to use Jameson's terms, the narrative of *The Wild Robot Escapes* resolves the real and intractable social, species, and technological problems that it raises through the mechanism of the tech magnate who happens to make a kind and favorable decision for Roz and Brightbill. Outside of the fiction, we know that the beneficence or caprices of tech executives cannot be relied upon to resolve the problems raised by Roz's wildness.

The Wild Robot books evoke the specter of a wild robot who is sentient, capable of love, and fluent in "the animal language" (*The Wild Robot* 51), but it cannot accommodate her in the human social world. The human world cannot make a "strange family" with Roz and Brightbill, nor recognize Roz as a "beautiful glitch." This is not a failing of the books, however, but an index of their realism. Despite the resolution offered at the end of *The Wild Robot Escapes*, Peter Brown does not pretend to resolve the problems of artificial life in relation to the human and the other-than-human world. As Brown says in his postscript to *The Wild Robot*, "It's funny how many philosophical questions spring up when we think about artificial beings" (271), and the books, aimed at readers aged between eight and twelve years, honor this complexity. Except for the children on the farm where Roz works, and to a lesser extent Dr. Molovo, humans in the novels do not show great promise for compromise or change in relation to artificial or nonhuman animal life. Humans in the novels kill animals and exploit robot labor. Despite Roz and Brightbill's happy ending in *The Wild Robot Escapes*, there is nothing to suggest that humans will begin to value artificial or nonhuman animal life in non-instrumental ways. Marching through the city of her origins, Roz notices, "The city was a glittering modern metropolis, where humans lived in luxury, all thanks to the tireless work of robots" (*The Wild Robot Escapes* 209). *The Wild Robot Escapes* does not present a world in which humans are willing to give up their luxury.

Nor do *The Wild Robot* books ignore the issues raised by Roz's wild existence at the threshold between human and nonhuman animals. As mother to Brightbill, for instance, Roz cannot overlook the roasted chicken on the dinner table of the Shareefs, the family that owns her at Hilltop Farm: "As Roz scanned the table, her eyes kept returning to the roasted chicken. It was about the size of Brightbill. Suddenly the robot was full of questions" (*The Wild Robot Escapes* 133). Brown's illustration of the roasted chicken on a platter all but forces young readers to confront the relationship between Brightbill and the meat on the table. They will surely recall this image later in the novel when Roz and Brightbill are on the run and encounter the hunters, Hank and Miguel: "Hank reloaded his rifle. 'We're here to hunt deer,' he said, 'but it looks like we're having goose for dinner'" (173). The narrator is quick to address young readers directly after this threat to Brightbill: "Had the hunters known Brightbill the way we do, reader, I'm sure they would have left him alone. But they knew nothing about him. To them, Brightbill was just another goose, a meal, and they were getting hungry" (173). While the narrator seems to apologize for the human hunters by assuming their moral goodness and to excuse them on account of their hunger, he also suggests that every goose who begins as "just another goose" is implicitly knowable in the way Brightbill has become "unique to" readers. It is only by remaining uncurious and ignorant of the goose that it can persist generically and interchangeably as "just another goose, a meal." In fact, "uniqueness to" works in both directions: Roz makes Brightbill unique by recognizing and nurturing him, but these acts simultaneously confer uniqueness on Roz, who began as "just another robot."

The two replaceable beings thereby make each other irreplaceable, which, of course, is Klara's insight into how human uniqueness works as well.

After seeing the roasted chicken on the table, Roz poses some questions to herself: "Do chickens live happy lives? / Did this chicken know it would be eaten? / Were humans bad for eating animals?" (133). Dealing with the chicken's happiness and quality of life, the first two questions incline toward utilitarian musing. Although the Shareefs' farm is highly automated and run by Roz, a robot, it is still represented as a rather traditional family farm of "rural simplicity," to use Peter Singer's words, in which the animals seem to live relatively freely and happily. As Singer writes of similarly pastoral images of farming in children's books, "With this kind of early reading, it is not surprising that children grow up believing that even if animals 'must' die to provide human beings with food they live happily until that time comes."[12] For Singer, children are natural lovers of animals, but they are often habituated to eating meat and taught that doing so is necessary before understanding what meat is: "These facts help to explain the most distinctive characteristic of the attitudes of children in our society to animals—namely, that rather than having one unified attitude to animals, the child has two conflicting attitudes that coexist, carefully segregated so that the inherent contradiction between them rarely causes trouble."[13] Indeed, Roz rationalizes to herself about the moral question that she poses: "No, thought Roz, humans are simply following their instincts, like all creatures, like Roz herself. At least the Shareefs honored this animal by giving thanks, and by turning it into a beautiful, nourishing meal" (133).

Yet her first two questions, about the chicken's happiness, knowledge, and quality of life are left open and somewhat troubled by Roz's close friendship with the cows at Hilltop Farm. When Tess, a calf, complains of the boredom of being shut in the barn all winter, the cow Annabelle tells her she should be grateful for the life she enjoys at Hilltop Farm: "I've lived on other farms, and trust me, you have nothing to complain about. ... I witnessed some terrible things on those farms. It was a blessing when I was moved here, but I often think about the animals I left behind. I hope they're okay" (124). Hilltop Farm offers a "lovely flock," a "beautiful barn," and Roz: "Roz listens to us, and treats us with love and kindness, and she makes our lives as comfortable as she possibly can" (124). It is startling to think of an artificial lifeform like

Roz functioning as a source of love, kindness, and comfort for cows on a dairy farm, an instance in which artificial life seems able to respond to the needs of nonhuman animals better than most humans are willing to do.

In *The Wild Robot*, readers glimpse the kind of farm where Annabelle might once have been kept when, on Brightbill's first winter migration, his flock lodges in a greenhouse. They are warned by the cat Snooks to watch out for humans, but none of these geese has ever seen a human before. Some of the geese decide to explore the nearby barn. There they find chickens, sheep, pigs, and cows "all in cages" (207). Brightbill explains to Roz, "The chickens kept asking me how I'd gotten out of my cage. I was explaining that I'd never had a cage when I heard panicked squawks from the greenhouse" (207). This panic is from the flock's first encounter with a human:

> Longneck tried to defend us. He got in front and spread his wings and honked, but the human wasn't afraid. He pulled out a shiny stick and pointed it right at Longneck. Snooks hissed, "Look out, he's got a rifle!" Suddenly a bright beam of light shot out from the rifle, and Longneck slumped to the floor. He was dead, Ma! (207)

The farmer with caged animals shoots the wild goose. This must be the kind of contrast Annabelle has in mind when she numbers Roz among the things for which the calves and cows can be grateful.

Another winter "barn conversation" raises the question of what the dairy cows are being used for and why. Another calf, Lily asks, "Roz, why do humans need so much cow's milk?" (125). Roz explains that there are billions of humans and that many of them drink milk or use it to create products such as butter, cheese, and yogurt. She also explains that milk is an ingredient in desserts such as cake, custard, and ice cream. As the calves do not understand the concept of dessert, Roz tries to explain it to them, even though she has never eaten food and has no experience of flavor or sweetness. Lily interrupts: "Just tell me this, Roz. When we're older, will our milk be used to make desserts?" (125). When Roz tells her yes, "The calves smiled. Then they trotted away, happy in the knowledge that, someday, they'd help to bring sweet and delicious things into the world" (126).

Again, *The Wild Robot Escapes* raises the question of how and why humans instrumentalize nonhuman animals. Like the roasted chicken on the Shareefs' table, this episode raises a troubling question but quickly soothes it with the idea that humans put animal products to good use, like nourishing food and sweet desserts. The brutality of dairy farming is elided.[14] The absence of male calves on the farm and the reality that veal is a byproduct of dairy farming is elided. There is also something grotesque in the calves' innocent consent to being used for humans even as they are alienated from the sweet desserts that will be made from the calf-nourishing products of their own bodies, calves from whom they will almost immediately be separated. And yet, similarly to the roasted chicken episode, the problem of animal food products, while soothed, is not entirely resolved. Young readers see that Annabelle's perspective also remains. And while Annabelle sees much to prefer in the Shareefs' farm compared to the farms of her past, she also intimates, from her more mature vantage, that even at Hilltop Farm it is largely Roz who mitigates the cows' conditions with her kindness and attention to their needs. Knowing that Roz has a plan to escape the farm, Annabelle adds, "We certainly will miss her when she's gone" (124).

The epilogue of *The Wild Robot Escapes* reverts to Hilltop Farm in autumn. To all appearances, little on the farm has altered. The cows graze in the pasture on frost-coated grass: "Their routine never changed" (272). Roz has been replaced by a new robot, and Mr. Shareef watches her from his pickup truck because "he didn't trust her yet" (272), given Roz's escape. The children, meanwhile, work on the farm when they are not in school: "Jaya had a way with the cows. Jad liked the tools and machines" (272). Together they are learning the two components of modern farming: animals and mechanization. One day a flock of migrating geese lands by the pond. The leader goose "gazed deep into [the children's] eyes. Then he craned his neck around, plucked out one of his feathers, and laid it on the ground by their feet" (273). Jad and Jaya now recognize that this goose is Brightbill, there to fulfill Roz's promise to send the children a message: "The wild robot was back where she belonged" (273), they now know. By returning to Hilltop Farm, the epilogue provides narrative closure. But it also disturbs the perfect ending of the final chapter in which Roz and Brightbill watch the sunset from their island: "Everything was just right. / Roz felt safe and happy and loved. / The wild robot was home" (271). The epilogue returns readers to the troubling elements of the farm as seen through Roz and the cows. In addition, then, to the questions that the novel leaves concerning Roz—"How long will Roz live? Will she ever see another human, or another robot? What joys and sorrows lie ahead for her?" (270)—it also opens questions about the children, the farm, and the future of the human world when it comes to nonhuman animals and robots. What, for instance, will Jaya do with her "way" with cows, and what will come of Jad's "liking" for tools and machines? Has Roz left any impression on the children that might change Hilltop Farm for the better, so that it will not rely on the "socially symbolic" fiction of the one wild robot in existence to mitigate the condition of its cows? The children feel that Roz is in the right place, but do they feel that the cows and the replacement robot and they themselves are also in the right place?

Brightbill's visit raises other questions. Why can't his deep gaze alone convey Roz's message? Why must he pluck his own feather? It is true that before departing Hilltop Farm, Roz and Brightbill conferred, and Roz promised the children a message by feather (140). And to their credit, the children had been able to recognize Roz as a sentient being with the urgent need to return to her island and son. Roz could not have escaped if the children had not abetted her by removing her Transmitter. Yet the excess and pain of the plucked feather, however minor, suggests that humans have a difficult time "getting the message." They cannot read Brightbill's gaze. They do not speak "the animal language." They do not quite enter the circle of Roz's "strange family."

Like Jaya and Jad, the child readers of *The Wild Robot* books are likely enthusiastic about nonhuman animals and all things robotic or mechanical. Through Roz, these readers will possess the imaginative resource of a literary robot's artificial gaze on human and nonhuman animals alike. As they look through Roz's softly glowing eyes, how will they see humans, their artificial assistants, and other animals? How will they understand the wild geese in flight, the cows in barns, the calves in narrow pens, the deer hunters bearing guns, the chickens on dinner plates, the robots toiling in cities, and the masterminds of tech on the top floors of towers? My hope is that such readers will identify in the proliferating codas to *Frankenstein* that no doubt will continue to saturate their cultures certain antidotes to anthropocentric thinking. As this book has shown, when we can locate the perceptual distance at which android, alien, and ghost texts snap into focus as animal texts, fantastic and mechanical literary creatures such as Roz can de-automatize human views of nonhuman animals by our shifting perceptions of hope, love, intelligence, otherness, and uniqueness. More than Shklovskian devices of *ostranenie*, such creatures are makers and members of strange families.

Notes

1 Toni Morrison, "Literature and Public Life," in *The Source of Self-Regard: Selected Essays, Speeches, and Meditations* (New York: Vintage, 2019), 100.
2 For instance, she writes, "I don't like to find my books condemned as bad or praised as good, when that condemnation or that praise is based on criteria from other paradigms. I would much prefer that they were dismissed or embraced based on the success of their accomplishment within the culture out of which I write," Toni Morrison, "Rootedness: The Ancestor as Foundation," in *What Moves at the Margins: Selected Nonfiction*, ed. Carolyn C. Denard (Jackson: University Press of Mississippi, 2008), 60.
3 Jeanette Winterson, *Frankissstein: A Love Story* (New York: Grove Press, 2019), 135. Subsequent page references are given in parentheses within the text.
4 Mary Shelley, *Frankenstein, or The Modern Prometheus*, Revised Edition, ed. Maurice Hindle (New York: Penguin, 2003), 171.
5 Sandra M. Gilbert and Susan Gubar, *The Madwoman in the Attic: The Woman Writer and the Nineteenth-Century Imagination*, 2nd Edition (New Haven: Yale University Press, 2000), 245.
6 Susan Winnett, "Coming Unstrung: Women, Men, Narrative, and Principles of Pleasure," *PMLA* 105.3 (May 1990), 510.
7 Peter Brown, *The Wild Robot* (New York: Little, Brown and Company, 2016), 7. Subsequent page references are given in parentheses within the text.
8 George Eliot, *Silas Marner* (New York: Oxford University Press, 2017), 113.
9 Shelley, *Frankenstein*, 133, emphasis in original.
10 Peter Brown, *The Wild Robot Escapes* (New York: Little, Brown and Company, 2018), 243, emphasis in original. Subsequent page references are given in parentheses within the text.
11 Fredric Jameson, *The Political Unconscious: Narrative as a Socially Symbolic Act* (Ithaca: Cornell University Press, 1981), 79.
12 Peter Singer, *Animal Liberation*, Updated Edition (New York: HarperCollins, 2009), 215.
13 Ibid., 214.
14 For a powerful account of the lives of dairy cows and the interconnections between the dairy and meat industries, see Kathryn Gillespie, *The Cow with Ear Tag #1389* (Chicago: University of Chicago Press, 2018).

Bibliography

Adams, Carol J. *The Sexual Politics of Meat: A Feminist-Vegetarian Critical Theory*. New York: Bloomsbury, 2015.

Aftandilian, Dave. "Toward a Native American Theology of Animals: Creek and Cherokee Perspectives." *Crosscurrents* 61.2 (June 2011): 191–207.

Anderson, Laurie. "Language Is a Virus from Outer Space." *United States Live*. Los Angeles: Warner Bros. Records, 1984.

Armstrong, Nancy. "The Affective Turn in Contemporary Fiction." *Contemporary Literature* 55.3 (Fall 2014): 441–65.

Armstrong, Nancy. "Gothic Novel." In *The Encyclopedia of the Novel*. Ed. Peter Melville Logan. Malden: Wiley Blackwell, 2014. 369–74.

Armstrong, Philip. *What Animals Mean in the Fiction of Modernity*. New York: Routledge, 2008.

Batten, Tom. "Review of *Alex + Ada: The Complete Collection*." *Library Journal* 142.2 (February 1, 2017): 60.

Bekoff, Marc. *The Emotional Lives of Animals: A Leading Scientist Explores Animal Joy, Sorrow, and Empathy—And Why They Matter*. Novato: New World Library, 2007.

Benjamin, Walter. "The Work of Art in the Age of Its Technological Reproducibility: Second Version." In *Selected Writings, Vol. 3: 1935-1938*. Ed. Howard Eiland and Michael W. Jennings. Cambridge: Harvard University Press, 2002. 101–33.

Bennett, Joshua. *Being Property Once Myself: Blackness and the End of Man*. Cambridge: Harvard University Press, 2020.

Bergson, Henri. *Time and Free Will: An Essay on the Immediate Data of Consciousness*. Trans. F. L. Pogson. Mineola: Dover Publications, 2001.

Berlina, Alexandra. "Translator's Introduction." In *Viktor Shklovsky: A Reader*. Ed. and trans. Alexandra Berlina. New York: Bloomsbury, 2017. 1–50.

Berlina, Alexandra. "Part One: Introduction." In *Viktor Shklovsky: A Reader*. Ed. and trans. Alexandra Berlina. New York: Bloomsbury, 2017. 53–9.

Black, Shameem. "Ishiguro's Inhuman Aesthetics." *Modern Fiction Studies* 55.4 (Winter 2009): 785–807.

Bloch, Ernst. *The Principle of Hope*. 3 Volumes. Trans. Neville Plaice, Stephen Plaice, and Paul Knight. Cambridge: MIT Press, 1986.

Bolt, Pearson. "Monolithic, Invisible Walls: The Horror of Borders in Jeff VanderMeer's *Southern Reach* Trilogy." *Journal of Science Fiction* 4.1 (July 2020): 25–33.

Botting, Fred. *Gothic*. New York: Routledge, 1996.

Boym, Svetlana. "Poetics and Politics of Estrangement: Victor Shklovsky and Hannah Arendt." *Poetics Today* 26.4 (Winter 2005): 581–611.

Braidotti, Rosi. *The Posthuman*. Malden: Polity Press, 2013.

Brogan, Kathleen. "Haunted by History: Louise Erdrich's *Tracks*." *Prospects: An Annual Journal of American Cultural Studies* 21 (1996): 169–92.

Brown, Laura. *Homeless Dogs & Melancholy Apes: Humans and Other Animals in the Modern Literary Imagination*. Ithaca: Cornell University Press, 2010.

Brown, Peter. *The Wild Robot*. New York: Little, Brown and Company, 2016.

Brown, Peter. *The Wild Robot Escapes*. New York: Little, Brown and Company, 2018.

Buck-Morss, Susan. *The Origin of Negative Dialectics: Theodor W. Adorno, Walter Benjamin, and the Frankfurt Institute*. New York: The Free Press, 1977.

Burroughs, William S. "Playback from Eden to Watergate." In *The Job: Interviews with William S. Burroughs*. Ed. Daniel Odier. New York: Penguin Books, 1989. 11–20.

Butler, Octavia E. *Octavia E. Butler: Kindred, Fledgling, Collected Stories*. Ed. Gerry Canavan and Nisi Shawl. New York: The Library of America, 2020.

Butler, Octavia E. "Positive Obsession." In *Bloodchild and Other Stories*. 2nd Edition. New York: Seven Stories Press, 2005. 125–36.

Calarco, Matthew R. *Animal Studies: The Key Concepts*. New York: Routledge, 2021.

Calarco, Matthew. *Thinking through Animals: Identity, Difference, Indistinction*. Stanford: Stanford University Press, 2015.

Cannella, Megan E. "Do Androids Dream of Derrida's Cat?: The Unregulated Emotion of Animals in Philip K. Dick's *Do Androids Dream of Electric Sheep?*" In *Seeing Animals after Derrida*. Ed. Sarah Bezan and James Tink. Lanham: Lexington Books, 2018. 145–62.

Caracciolo, Marco. "Deus Ex Algorithmo: Narrative Form, Computation, and the Fate of the World in David Mitchell's *Ghostwritten* and Richard Powers's *The Overstory*." *Contemporary Literature* 60.1 (Spring 2019): 47–71.

Caracciolo, Marco. "Emplotment Beyond the Human Scale: On Deep Time and Narrative Nonlinearity." *Poetics Today* 42.3 (September 2021): 341–59.

Caracciolo, Marco. "We-Narrative and the Challenges of Nonhuman Collectives." *Style* 54.1 (2020): 86–97.

Childs, Peter. *Contemporary British Fiction Since 1970*. New York: Palgrave Macmillan, 2005.

Coetzee, J. M. *The Lives of Animals*. Ed. and Intro. Amy Gutmann. Princeton: Princeton University Press, 1999.

Coogan, Michael D., ed. *The New Oxford Annotated Bible*. 5th Edition. New York: Oxford University Press, 2018.

Copeland, Marion. *Cockroach*. London: Reaktion Books, 2003.

Darwin, Charles. *The Expression of the Emotions in Man and Animals*. New York: Penguin, 2009.

Daston, Lorraine, and Gregg Mitman. "Introduction: The How and Why of Thinking with Animals." In *Thinking with Animals: New Perspectives on Anthropomorphism*. Ed. Lorraine Daston and Gregg Mitman. New York: Columbia University Press, 2005. 1–14.

Dekoven, Marianne. "Women, Animals, and Jane Goodall's *Reason for Hope*." *Tulsa Studies in Women's Literature* 25.1 (Spring 2006): 141–51.

Deleuze, Gilles, and Félix Guattari. *A Thousand Plateaus: Capitalism and Schizophrenia*. Trans. Brian Massumi. Minneapolis: University of Minnesota Press, 1987.

De Lint, Charles. "Books to Look For: *Alex + Ada, Starlight, Pretty Deadly*." *Fantasy & Science Fiction* 127.3-4 (September–October 2014): 32–6.

DeMello, Margo. *Animals and Society: An Introduction to Human-Animal Studies*. New York: Columbia University Press, 2012.

Derrida, Jacques. *The Animal That Therefore I Am*. Ed. Marie-Louise Mallet. Trans. David Wills. New York: Fordham University Press, 2008.

Descartes, René. "From the Letters of 1646 and 1649." In *The Animals Reader: The Essential and Contemporary Writings*. 2nd Edition. Ed. Linda Kalof and Amy Fitzgerald. New York: Routledge, 2022. 136–9.

de Waal, Frans. *Are We Smart Enough to Know How Smart Animals Are?* New York: W. W. Norton & Company, 2016.

de Waal, Frans. *Mama's Last Hug: Animal Emotions and What They Tell Us about Ourselves*. New York: W. W. Norton & Company, 2019.

Dick, Philip K. *Do Androids Dream of Electric Sheep?* New York: Del Rey, 2017.

Dickens, Charles. *A Christmas Carol and Other Christmas Books*. New York: Oxford University Press, 2006.

Dimock, Wai Chee. "The Survival of the Unfit." *Daedalus* 150.1 (Winter 2021): 134–46.

Donovan, Josephine. "Animal Rights and Feminist Theory." *Signs* 15.2 (Winter 1990): 350–75.

Eaglestone, Robert. "Introduction: Salman Rushdie." In *Salman Rushdie: Contemporary Critical Perspectives*. Ed. Robert Eaglestone and Martin McQuillan. New York: Bloomsbury, 2013. 1–8.

Eagleton, Terry. *Literary Theory: An Introduction*. 2nd Edition. Minneapolis: University of Minnesota Press, 1996.

Elias, Amy J. *Sublime Desire: History and Post-1960s Fiction*. Baltimore: Johns Hopkins University Press, 2001.

Eliot, George. *Silas Marner*. New York: Oxford University Press, 2017.

Emerson, Caryl. "Shklovsky's *ostranenie*, Bakhtin's *vnenakhodimost'* (How Distance Serves an Aesthetics of Arousal Differently from an Aesthetics Based on Pain)." *Poetics Today* 24.6 (Winter 2005): 637–64.

Erdrich, Louise. *LaRose*. New York: Harper Perennial, 2016.

Erdrich, Louise. *Last Report on the Miracles at Little No Horse*. New York: Harper Perennial, 2001.

Erdrich, Louise. *The Night Watchman*. New York: HarperCollins, 2020.

Erdrich, Louise. *The Round House*. New York: Harper Perennial, 2012.

Erlich, Victor. *Russian Formalism: History – Doctrine*. 4th Edition. The Hague: Mouton Publishers, 1980.

Ersoy, Gözde. "Crossing the Boundaries of the Unknown with Jeff VanderMeer: The Monstrous Fantastic and 'Abcanny' in *Annihilation*." *Orbis Litterarum* 74.4 (August 2019): 251–63.

Farsi, Roghayeh. "Reading Strategies and Impossible Worlds in Fiction: With Reference to *Lincoln in the Bardo*." *Zeitschrift für Anglistik und Amerikanistik* 68.3 (2020): 311–27.

Fisher, Mark. *The Weird and the Eerie*. London: Repeater, 2016.

Foucault, Michel. *The Birth of the Clinic: An Archaeology of Medical Perception*. Trans. A. M. Sheridan Smith. New York: Vintage, 1994.

Fraiman, Susan. "Pussy Panic versus Liking Animals: Tracking Gender in Animal Studies." *Critical Inquiry* 39 (Autumn 2012): 89–115.

Freeman, John. "Never Let Me Go: A Profile of Kazuo Ishiguro." *Poets & Writers* 33.3 (May–June 2005): 40–3.

Freud, Sigmund. *Beyond the Pleasure Principle*. Trans. and Ed. James Strachey. New York: W. W. Norton & Company, 1961.

Freud, Sigmund. "Creative Writers and Day-Dreaming." In *The Freud Reader*. Ed. Peter Gay. New York: W. W. Norton & Company, 1989. 436–43.

Galvan, Jill. "Entering the Posthuman Collective in Philip K. Dick's *Do Androids Dream of Electric Sheep?*" *Science Fiction Studies* 24.3 (November 1997): 413–29.

Garnett, Catherine. "The Future in the Pasture: Precarity in George Saunders's 'Interior Gardens.'" *Art & Artifice* 47.2 (Fall 2014): 137–62.

Gigliotti, Carol, "The Struggle for Compassion and Justice through Critical Animal Studies." In *The Oxford Handbook of Animal Studies*. Ed. Linda Kalof. New York: Oxford University Press, 2017. 189–202.

Gilbert, Sandra M., and Susan Gubar. *The Madwoman in the Attic: The Woman Writer and the Nineteenth-Century Imagination*. 2nd Edition. New Haven: Yale University Press, 2000.

Gillespie, Kathryn. *The Cow with Ear Tag #1389*. Chicago: University of Chicago Press, 2018.

Gilmore, Leigh. *The Limits of Autobiography: Trauma and Testimony*. Ithaca: Cornell University Press, 2001.

Grim, John. "Knowing and Being Known by Animals: Indigenous Perspectives on Personhood." In *A Communion of Subjects: Animals in Religion, Science, and Ethics*. Ed. Paul Waldau and Kimberley Patton. New York: Columbia University Press, 2006. 373–90.

Hafen, P. Jane. "'We Speak of Everything': Indigenous Traditions in *The Last Report on the Miracles at Little No Horse*." In *Louise Erdrich: Tracks, The Last Report on the Miracles at Little No Horse, The Plague of Doves*. Ed. Deborah L. Madsen. New York: Continuum, 2011. 82–97.

Haggerty, George E. *Queer Gothic*. Urbana: University of Illinois Press, 2006.

Haraway, Donna J. *Simians, Cyborgs, and Women: The Reinvention of Nature*. New York: Routledge, 1991.

Haraway, Donna J. *When Species Meet*. Minneapolis: University of Minnesota Press, 2008.

Harris, Andrea L. *Other Sexes: Rewriting Difference from Woolf to Winterson*. New York: State University of New York Press, 2000.

Harris, Ian. "'A Vast Unsupervised Recycling Plant': Animals and the Buddhist Cosmos." In *A Communion of Subjects: Animals in Religion, Science, and Ethics*. Ed. Paul Waldau and Kimberley Patton. New York: Columbia University Press, 2006. 207–17.

Harvey, Giles "Kazuo Ishiguro Sees What the Future Is Doing to Us." *New York Times Magazine* (February 23, 2021).

Hayes-Brady, Clare. "'Everyone, We Are Dead!': (Hi)story and Power in George Saunders' *Lincoln in the Bardo*." In *21st Century US Historical Fiction: Contemporary Responses to the Past*. Ed. Ruth Maxey. Cham: Palgrave Macmillan, 2020. 73–91.

Hayles, N. Katherine. *How We Became Posthuman: Virtual Bodies in Cybernetics, Literature, and Informatics*. Chicago: University of Chicago Press, 1999.

Hegglund, Jon. "Unnatural Narratology and Weird Realism in Jeff VanderMeer's *Annihilation*." In *Environment and Narrative: New Directions in Econarratology*. Ed. Erin James, Eric Morel, and Ursula K. Heise. Columbus: Ohio University Press, 2020. 27–44.

Heholt, Ruth, and Melissa Edmundson, eds. *Gothic Animals: Uncanny Otherness and the Animal With-Out*. Cham: Palgrave Macmillan, 2020.

Heholt, Ruth, and Melissa Edmundson. "Introduction." In *Gothic Animals: Uncanny Otherness and the Animal With-Out*. Ed. Ruth Heholt and Melissa Edmundson. Cham: Palgrave Macmillan, 2020. 1–17.

Heise, Ursula K. "From Extinction to Electronics: Dead Frogs, Live Dinosaurs, and Electric Sheep." In *Zootologies: The Question of the Animal*. Ed. Cary Wolfe. Minneapolis: University of Minnesota Press, 2003. 59–81.

Hogle, Jerrold E. "Introduction: The Gothic in Western Culture." In *The Cambridge Companion to Gothic Fiction*. Ed. Jerrold E. Hogle. New York: Cambridge University Press, 2002. 1–20.

Horowitz, Alexandra C., and Marc Bekoff. "Naturalizing Anthropomorphism: Behavioral Prompts to Our Humanizing of Animals." *Anthrozoös* 20.1 (January 2007): 23–35.

Horvat, Ana. "'Trans Is Hot Right Now': On Cisgender Writers and Trans Characters in Jeanette Winterson's *Frankissstein* and Kim Fu's *For Today I Am a Boy*." *Gender Forum: An Internet Journal for Gender Studies* 79 (2021): 79–96.

Hunnewell, Susannah. "Kazuo Ishiguro: The Art of Fiction, No. 196." *The Paris Review* 184 (Spring 2008): 23–54.

Ishiguro, Kazuo. *Klara and the Sun*. New York: Knopf, 2021.

Ishiguro, Kazuo. *Never Let Me Go*. New York: Vintage, 2005.

Jackson, Zakiyyah Iman. *Becoming Human: Matter and Meaning in an Antiblack World*. New York: New York University Press, 2020.

James, William. *The Principles of Psychology*. Cambridge: Harvard University Press, 1983.

Jameson, Fredric. *Archaeologies of the Future: The Desire Called Utopia and Other Science Fictions*. New York: Verso, 2005.

Jameson, Fredric. *The Political Unconscious: Narrative as a Socially Symbolic Act*. Ithaca: Cornell University Press, 1981.

Joshi, S. T. *The Weird Tale*. Austin: University of Texas Press, 1990.

Knutson, Lin. "Monster Studies: Liminality, Home Spaces, and Ina Vampires in Octavia E. Butler's *Fledgling*." *University of Toronto Quarterly* 87.1 (Winter 2018): 214–33.

Korsgaard, Christine M. *Fellow Creatures: Our Obligations to the Other Animals*. New York: Oxford University Press, 2018.

Krevel, Mojca. "The Monstrous Cosmos of Jeanette Winterson's *Frankissstein*." *ELOPE* 18.2 (2021): 85–100.

Kümbet, Pelin. "A Posthuman Vampire-Human Intra-action in Octavia Butler's *Fledgling*." *Interactions: Ege Journal of British and American Studies* 25.1-2 (Spring-Fall 2016): 105–12.

Kurup, Seema. *Understanding Louise Erdrich*. Columbia: University of South Carolina Press, 2016.

Kuzniar, Alice A. *Melancholia's Dog*. Chicago: University of Chicago Press, 2006.

Le Guin, Ursula K. *The Dispossessed: An Ambiguous Utopia*. New York: HarperCollins, 1974.

Lovell, Joel. "George Saunders's Advice to Graduates." *New York Times* (July 31, 2013).

Luna, Jonathan and Sarah Vaughn. *Alex + Ada*. The Complete Collection: Deluxe Edition. Berkeley: Image Comics, 2016.

Lundblad, Michael, ed. *Animalities: Literary and Cultural Studies Beyond the Human*. Edinburgh: Edinburgh University Press, 2017.

Lundblad, Michael. "Introduction: The End of the Animal—Literary and Cultural Animalities." In *Animalities: Literary and Cultural Studies Beyond the Human*. Ed. Michael Lundblad. Edinburgh: Edinburgh University Press, 2017. 1–21.

Madsen, Deborah L. "Louise Erdrich: The Aesthetics of *Mino Bimaadiziwin*." In *Louise Erdrich: Tracks, The Last Report on the Miracles at Little No Horse, The Plague of Doves*. Ed. Deborah L. Madsen. New York: Continuum, 2011. 1–14.

Mathew, Raisun, and Digvijay Pandya. "Humans, Animals and Habitats: Liminality and Environmental Concerns in George Saunders' *Fox 8*." *Rupkatha Journal on Interdisciplinary Studies in Humanities* 12.5 (2020): 1–7.

McEwan, Ian. *Machines Like Me and People Like You*. New York: Nan A. Talese, 2019.

McHugh, Susan, Robert McKay, and John Miller. "Introduction: Towards an Animal-Centred Literary History." In *The Palgrave Handbook of Animals and Literature*. Ed. Susan McHugh, Robert McKay, and John Miller. Cham: Palgrave Macmillan, 2021. 1–11.

McKay, Robert, and John Miller, eds. *Werewolves, Wolves and the Gothic*. Cardiff: University of Wales Press, 2017.

McNab, David T. "'Plenty of Food and No Government Agents': Perspectives on the Spirit World, Death and Dying in the Writings of Louise Erdrich." In *Studies in the Literary Achievement of Louise Erdrich, Native American Writer*. Ed. Brajesh Sawhney. Lewiston: Edwin Mellen Press, 2008. 95–113.

Mendlesohn, Farah. "Introduction: Reading Science Fiction." In *The Cambridge Companion to Science Fiction*. Ed. Edward James and Farah Mendlesohn. New York: Cambridge University Press, 2003. 1–12.

Mhire, Jeremy J., and Rodolfo Hernandez. "Decency, Hope, and the Substitution of Memory in Kazuo Ishiguro's *Never Let Me Go*." *Political Science Reviewer* 43.1 (January 2019): 201–29.

Midgley, Mary. *Beast and Man: The Roots of Human Nature*. Revised Edition. New York: Routledge, 1995.

Miéville, China. "M. R. James and the Quantum Vampire: Weird; Hauntological: Versus and/or and and/or or?" In *Collapse: Philosophical Research and Development, Volume IV*. Ed. Robin McKay. Falmouth: Urbanomic, 2008. 105–28.

Miéville, China. "On Monsters: Or, Nine or More (Monstrous) Not Cannies." *Journal of the Fantastic in the Arts* 23.3 (January 2012): 378–92.

Miéville, China. "Weird Fiction." In *The Routledge Companion to Science Fiction*. Ed. Mark Bould, Andrew M. Butler, Adam Roberts, and Sherryl Vint. New York: Routledge, 2009. 510–15.

Millen, Alex. "Affective Fictions: George Saunders and the Wonderful-Sounding Words of Neoliberalism." *Critique: Studies in Contemporary Fiction* 59.2 (2018): 127–41.

Miller, Alex. "'Err[ing] in the Direction of Kindness': George Saunders's Compassionate Interrogation of Post-Postmodern America." *Modern Language Studies* 45.2 (Winter 2016): 10–27.

Miller, Harlan B. "No Escape." In *The Death of the Animal: A Dialogue*. Paola Cavalieri with Matthew Calarco, John M. Coetzee, Harlan B. Miller, and Cary Wolfe. New York: Columbia: Columbia University Press, 2009. 59–71.

Moisy, Amélie. "Haunting and Satire in the Short Fiction of George Saunders." *Cahiers de la Nouvelle: Journal of the Short Story in English* 70 (Spring 2018): 207–27.

Morris, Susana M. "Black Girls Are from the Future: Afrofuturist Feminism in Octavia E. Butler's *Fledgling*." *WSQ: Women's Studies Quarterly* 40.3–4 (Fall–Winter 2012): 146–66.

Morrison, Toni. *Beloved*. New York: Vintage, 2004.

Morrison, Toni. "Literature and Public Life." In *The Source of Self-Regard: Selected Essays, Speeches, and Meditations*. New York: Vintage, 2019. 96–101.

Morrison, Toni. "Rootedness: The Ancestor as Foundation." In *What Moves at the Margins: Selected Nonfiction*. Ed. Carolyn C. Denard. Jackson: University Press of Mississippi, 2008. 56–64.

Morse, Donald E. "'This Undiscovered Country' in Máirtín Ó Cadhain's *Cré na Cille* and George Saunders's *Lincoln in the Bardo*." *Acta Universitatis Sapientiae, Philologica* 10.1 (2018): 25–33.

Morson, Gary Saul. "Introduction." In *Russian Formalist Criticism: Four Essays*. 2nd Edition. Ed. Lee T. Lemon and Marion J. Reis. Lincoln: University of Nebraska Press, 2012. v–xvi.

Moseley, Merritt. "*Lincoln in the Bardo*: 'Uh, NOT a Historical Novel.'" *Humanities* 8 (2019): 1–10.

Moylan, Tom. *Demand the Impossible: Science Fiction and the Utopian Imagination*. Classics Edition. Ed. Raffaella Baccolini. New York: Peter Lang, 2014.

Nagel, Thomas. "What Is It Like to Be a Bat?" In *Mortal Questions*. New York: Cambridge University Press, 1979. 165–80.

Nalerio, Juliana. "The Patriarch's Balls: Class Consciousness, Violence, and Dystopia in George Saunders' Vision of Contemporary America." *Miscelánea: A Journal of English and American Studies* 52 (2015): 89–102.

Nayar, Pramod K. "A New Biological Citizenship: Posthumanism in Octavia Butler's *Fledgling*." *Modern Fiction Studies* 58.4 (Winter 2012): 796–817.

Neeper, Layne. "'To Soften the Heart': George Saunders, Postmodern Satire, and Empathy." *Studies in American Humor* 2.2 (2016): 280–99.

Noys, Benjamin, and Timothy S. Murphy. "Introduction: Old and New Weird." *Genre* 49.2 (July 2016): 117–34.

Noys, Benjamin, and Timothy S. Murphy. "Morbid Symptoms: An Interview with China Miéville." *Genre* 49.2 (July 2016): 199–210.

Olsen, Ida Marie. "Do Androids Have Nightmares About Electric Sheep?: Science Fiction Portrayals of Trauma Manifestations in the Posthuman Subject in *Frankenstein, Do Androids Dream of Electric Sheep?*, and 'Nine Lives.'" *New Horizons in English Studies* 3 (January 2018): 100–11.

Onega, Susana. *Jeanette Winterson*. Manchester: Manchester University Press, 2006.

Ortiz Robles, Mario. *Literature and Animal Studies*. New York: Routledge, 2016.

Palmer, Christopher. *Philip K. Dick: Exhilaration and Terror of the Postmodern*. Liverpool: Liverpool University Press, 2003.

Pergadia, Samantha. "Like an Animal: Genres of the Nonhuman in the Neo-Slave Novel." *African American Review* 51.4 (Winter 2018): 289–304.

Peterson, Nancy J. "History, Postmodernism, and Louise Erdrich's *Tracks*." *PMLA* 109.5 (October 1994): 982–94.

Pick, Anat. *Creaturely Poetics: Animality and Vulnerability in Literature and Film*. New York: Columbia University Press, 2011.

Plumwood, Val. "Being Prey." *Utne Reader* 100 (July–August 2000): 56–61.

Pogell, Sarah. "'The Verisimilitude Inspector': George Saunders as the New Baudrillard?" *Critique: Studies in Contemporary Fiction* 52 (2011): 460–78.

Powers, Richard. *The Overstory*. New York: W. W. Norton & Company, 2018.

Prendergast, Finola Anne. "Revising Nonhuman Ethics in Jeff VanderMeer's *Annihilation*." *Contemporary Literature* 58.3 (Fall 2017): 333–60.

Punter, David. *The Literature of Terror: A History of Gothic Fictions from 1765 to the Present Day: Vol. 1: The Gothic Tradition*. New York: Routledge, 2013.

Rainwater, Catherine. "Haunted by Birds: An Eco-critical View of Personhood in *The Plague of Doves*." In *Louise Erdrich: Tracks, The Last Report on the Miracles at Little No Horse, The Plague of Doves*. Ed. Deborah L. Madsen. New York: Continuum, 2011. 152–67.

Rando, David. "The Cat's Meow: *Ulysses*, Animals, and the Veterinary Gaze." *James Joyce Quarterly* 46.3–4 (Spring-Summer 2009): 529–43.

Rando, David P. "George Saunders and the Postmodern Working Class." *Contemporary Literature* 53.3 (2012): 437–60.

Regan, Tom. *The Case for Animal Rights*. Berkeley: University of California Press, 1983.

Riffel, Casey R. "Animals at the End of the World: Notes toward a Transspecies Eschatology." In *Making Animal Meaning*. Ed. Linda Kalof and Georgina M. Montgomery. East Lansing: Michigan State University Press, 2011. 159–72.

Rizq, Rosemary. "Copying, Cloning and Creativity: Reading Kazuo Ishiguro's *Never Let Me Go*." *British Journal of Psychotherapy* 30.4 (November 2014): 517–32.

Robbins, Bruce. "Cruelty Is Bad: Banality and Proximity in *Never Let Me Go*." *NOVEL: A Forum on Fiction* 40.3 (2007): 289–302.

Robertson, Benjamin J. *None of This Is Normal: The Fiction of Jeff VanderMeer*. Minneapolis: University of Minnesota Press, 2018.

Rushdie, Salman. "The Books We Truly Love." *New York Times* (30 May 2021): Sunday Review 4–5.

Rushdie, Salman. "Is Nothing Sacred?" In *Imaginary Homelands: Essays and Criticism 1981–1991*. London: Granta Books, 1991. 415–29.

Rushdie, Salman. *Quichotte*. New York: Random House, 2019.

Saint-Amour, Paul K. "There Is Grief of a Tree." *American Imago* 77.1 (Spring 2020): 137–55.

Saunders, George. *Fox 8*. Illustrated by Chelsea Cardinal. New York: Random House, 2013.

Saunders, George. *Lincoln in the Bardo*. New York: Random House, 2017.

Seed, David. *Science Fiction: A Very Short Introduction*. New York: Oxford University Press, 2011.

Sewell, Anna. *Black Beauty*. Ed. Kristen Guest. Peterborough: Broadview Press, 2016.

Sheenan Michael J., and Elizabeth A. Tibbetts. "Specialized Facial Learning Is Associated with Individual Recognition in Paper Wasps." *Science* 334 (December 2, 2011): 1272–5.

Shelley, Mary. *Frankenstein, or The Modern Prometheus*. Revised Edition. Ed. Maurice Hindle. New York: Penguin, 2003.

Shelley, Percy Bysshe. "A Defence of Poetry." In *Shelley's Poetry and Prose*. Ed. Donald H. Reiman and Sharon B. Powers. New York: W. W. Norton & Company, 1977. 480–508.

Shelley, Percy Bysshe. "To a Skylark." In *Shelley's Poetry and Prose*. Ed. Donald H. Reiman and Sharon B. Powers. New York: W. W. Norton & Company, 1977. 226–9.

Shelley, Percy Bysshe. "The Vegetable System of Diet." In *The Prose Works of Percy Bysshe Shelley*. Volume I. Ed. E. B. Murray. New York: Oxford University Press, 1993. 147–55.

Shelley, Percy Bysshe. "A Vindication of Natural Diet." In *The Prose Works of Percy Bysshe Shelley*. Volume I. Ed. E. B. Murray. New York: Oxford University Press, 1993. 77–89.

Shklovsky, Viktor. "Art as Device." In *Viktor Shklovsky: A Reader*. Ed. and trans. Alexandra Berlina. New York: Bloomsbury, 2017. 73–96.

Singer, Peter. *Animal Liberation*. Updated Edition. New York: HarperCollins, 2009.

Smith, Andrew. "Hauntings." In *The Routledge Companion to the Gothic*. Ed. Catherine Spooner and Emma McEvoy. New York: Routledge, 2007. 147–54.

Smith, Jeanne Rosier. *Writing Tricksters: Mythic Gambols in Ethnic American Literature*. Berkeley: University of California Press, 1997.

Solomon, Rivers. *An Unkindness of Ghosts*. New York: Akashic Books, 2017.

Spanner, Ben. "Review of *Alex + Ada: Vol. 1*." *Booklist* 111.8 (December 15, 2014): 36.

Sperling, Alison. "Second Skins: A Body-Ecology of Jeff VanderMeer's *The Southern Reach Trilogy*." *Paradoxa* 28 (2016): 214–38.

Spivak, Gayatri Shakravorty. "Can the Subaltern Speak?" In *Marxism and the Interpretation of Culture*. Ed. Cary Nelson and Lawrence Grossberg. Urbana: University of Illinois Press, 1988. 271–313.

Stewart, Garrett. "Organic Reformations in Richard Powers's *The Overstory*." *Daedalus* 150.1 (Winter 2021): 160–77.

Stirrup, David. *Louise Erdrich*. Manchester: Manchester University Press, 2010.

Stookey, Lorena L. *Louise Erdrich: A Critical Companion*. Westport: Greenwood Press, 1999.

Strombeck, Andrew. "Inhuman Writing in Jeff VanderMeer's Southern Reach Trilogy." *Textual Practice* 34.8 (2020): 1365–82.

Summers-Bremner, Eluned. "'Poor Creatures:' Ishiguro's and Coetzee's Imaginary Animals." *Mosaic: An Interdisciplinary Critical Journal* 39.4 (December 2006): 145–60.

Suvin, Darko. *Metamorphoses of Science Fiction: On the Poetics and History of a Literary Genre*. New Haven: Yale University Press, 1979.

Teverson, Andrew. *Salman Rushdie*. Manchester: Manchester University Press, 2007.

Teverson, Andrew. "Salman Rushdie's Post-Nationalist Fairy Tales: *Haroun and the Sea of Stories* and *Luka and the Fire of Life*." In *Salman Rushdie: Contemporary Critical Perspectives*. Ed. Robert Eaglestone and Martin McQuillan. New York: Bloomsbury, 2013. 72–85.

Tolstoy, Leo. "Strider." *The Death of Ivan Ilyich and Other Stories*. Ed. and Trans. Kirsten Lodge. Peterborough: Broadview Press, 2017. 77–114.

VanderMeer, Ann, and Jeff VanderMeer. "The New Weird Discussions: The Creation of a Term." In *The New Weird*. Ed. Ann VanderMeer and Jeff VanderMeer. San Francisco: Tachyon Publications, 2008. 317–31.

VanderMeer, Jeff. *Area X: The Southern Reach Trilogy*. New York: Farrar, Straus and Giroux, 2014.

VanderMeer, Jeff. "The New Weird: 'It's Alive?'" In *The New Weird*. Ed. Ann VanderMeer and Jeff VanderMeer. San Francisco: Tachyon Publications, 2008. ix–xviii.

Vinci, Tony M. "Posthuman Wounds: Trauma, Non-Anthropocentric Vulnerability, and the Human/Android/Animal Dynamic in Philip K. Dick's *Do Androids Dream of Electric Sheep?*" *Journal of the Midwest Modern Language Association* 47.2 (Fall 2014): 91–112.

Vint, Sherryl. *Animal Alterity: Science Fiction and the Question of the Animal*. Liverpool: Liverpool University Press, 2010.

Vint, Sherryl. "Science Fiction." In *The Edinburgh Companion to Animal Studies*. Ed. Lynn Turner, Undine Sellbach, and Ron Broglio. Edinburgh: Edinburgh University Press, 2018. 488–503.

Vint, Sherryl. *Science Fiction*. Cambridge: MIT Press, 2021.

Vint, Sherryl. "Speciesism and Species Being in *Do Androids Dream of Electric Sheep?*" *Mosaic: An Interdisciplinary Critical Journal* 40.1 (March 2007): 111–26.

Vizenor, Gerald. "Authored Animals: Creature Tropes in Native American Fiction." *Social Research* 62.3 (Fall 1995): 661–83.

Vizenor, Gerald. *Native Liberty: Natural Reason and Cultural Survivance*. Lincoln: University of Nebraska Press, 2009.

Waldau, Paul. *Animal Studies: An Introduction*. New York: Oxford University Press, 2013.

Walonen, Michael K. *Contemporary World Narrative Fiction and the Spaces of Neoliberalism*. New York: Palgrave Macmillan, 2016.

Weil, Kari. *Thinking Animals: Why Animal Studies Now?* New York: Columbia University Press, 2010.

Wellek, René, and Austin Warren. *Theory of Literature*. London: Jonathan Cape, 1954.

Whitehead, Anne. "Writing with Care: Kazuo Ishiguro's *Never Let Me Go*." *Contemporary Literature* 52.1 (Spring 2011): 54–83.

Wiley, W. Brett. "George Saunders's 400-Pound CEO: Goodness or Ideology." *Renascence* 71.1 (Winter 2019): 39–55.

Winnett, Susan. "Coming Unstrung: Women, Men, Narrative, and Principles of Pleasure." *PMLA* 105.3 (May 1990): 505–18.

Winterson, Jeanette. *Frankissstein: A Love Story*. New York: Grove Press, 2019.

Winterson, Jeanette. *Written on the Body*. New York: Vintage, 1994.

Wolfe, Cary. "Human, All Too Human: 'Animal Studies' and the Humanities." *PMLA* 124.2 (2009): 564–75.

Wolfe, Cary. "Posthumanism." In *Posthuman Glossary*. Ed. Rosi Braidotti and Maria Hlavajova. New York: Bloomsbury, 2018. 356–9.

Wolfe, Cary. *What Is Posthumanism?* Minneapolis: University of Minnesota Press, 2010.

Young, Hershini Bhana. "Performing the Abyss: Octavia Butler's *Fledgling* and the Law." *Studies in the Novel* 47.2 (Summer 2015): 210–30.

Index

abcanny 13, 95, 97, 98, 101, 105 (*see also* Miéville, China)
Adams, Carol J. 25, 67, 131
  "absent referent" 131
  "intertwined oppressions" 67
Adorno, Theodor W. 2, 28, 170
  the non-identical 2, 170
Aftandilian, Dave 118–19
alien 1, 2, 12, 13, 14, 61–2, 64–5, 83, 84, 87–8, 90–2, 94, 96–105, 156, 162, 164, 166, 169, 173
Alien (film) 162
alienation (*see* defamiliarization)
allegory 2, 9, 12, 21, 28, 29, 30, 34, 35, 41, 52, 72, 73, 166
android 1, 2, 12, 13, 14, 15, 21, 22, 26, 30, 35–41, 42, 65, 69–72, 151–63, 164, 166, 167, 169–70
anthropocentrism 1, 2, 4, 12, 13, 14, 23, 33, 35, 44, 48, 53–4, 55, 56, 57, 58, 59, 64, 65, 66, 113, 114, 133, 151, 152, 162–3, 166, 174, 181
anthropocosmism 2, 14, 42, 65, 114, 118–19, 129, 133, 138, 164, 166
anthropomorphism 11, 23–4, 57, 61, 126, 135, 161 (*see also* Weil, Kari—critical anthropomorphism)
Aristotle 32, 38
Armstrong, Nancy 86
Armstrong, Philip 11
artificial friendship 163–4, 173
artificial intelligence (AI) 1, 51–2, 54, 56–65, 68–9, 70, 73, 75, 163, 164, 166
  novels as 65, 73–6, 163, 164–5
automatization 3–12, 15, 181 (*see also* Shklovsky, Viktor)

Beckett, Samuel 99
Bekoff, Marc 23, 24, 74, 135
Benjamin, Walter 28
  reception in distraction versus concentration 27–9, 34
Berlina, Alexandra 6
bestiality 72
Bierce, Ambrose 96
Black, Shameem 27
Blackwood, Algernon 96
Blake, William 155
Bloch, Ernst 22–3, 24, 40, 42, 53, 74
  Not-Yet-Conscious 53
  The Principle of Hope 23, 40
Botting, Fred 86, 95
Boym, Svetlana 5–6
Brown, Laura 11
Brown, Peter 14–15, 167, 172, 176
  The Wild Robot series 15, 171–81
Buddhism 114, 118, 119, 129–30, 132
Burroughs, William S. 99
Butler, Octavia E. 13, 52–3, 85, 166
  Fledgling 13, 85, 86–94, 96, 97, 101

Calarco, Matthew R. 1, 32–3
  capacities-based views of nonhuman animals 25, 36
  identity-based animal studies approaches 32–3
Cannella, Megan E. 39
capitalism 13, 21, 29, 35
  exchange value 38–9
character 14, 27, 113, 114, 133–8, 164–5, 167, 170 (*see also* ghost—literary character)
codas 14–15, 169–71
Coetzee, J. M. 11, 14, 26, 114, 115, 133, 134, 167
  The Lives of Animals 14, 26, 114, 115, 116–17, 132, 134–5, 137, 138, 164
Coleridge, Samuel Taylor 6
critical race studies, 53

Darwin, Charles 23, 33, 56, 87
Daston, Lorraine and Gregg Mitman 23
daydream 42
defamiliarization (*ostranenie*) 3–12, 22, 73–4, 84, 91, 94, 95, 97, 104, 105, 126, 132, 136, 156, 165, 166, 167, 170, 174, 182 (*see also* Shklovsky, Viktor)
Deleuze, Gilles and Félix Guatarri 14, 160–1, 162, 173
 "becoming-animal" 14, 152, 160
Demello, Margo 23, 126
Derrida, Jacques 24, 25, 37–8, 39, 72–3, 74, 115, 117, 118, 151, 161
Descartes, René 4, 10, 32, 36, 37, 38, 56, 118, 150
de Waal, Frans 23–4, 36
 anthropodenial 23–4
Dick, Philip K. 13, 21, 22, 26, 30, 35, 36, 37, 38, 39, 40, 41, 42, 65, 152, 166
 Do Androids Dream of Electric Sheep? 13, 21, 22, 35–41, 41–2, 65, 69, 152, 155
Dickens, Charles 113
 A Christmas Carol 113–14
Donovan, Josephine 25
Dracula (Bram Stoker) 86, 87
Dunsany, Lord 96

empathy 13, 21, 26, 30, 35, 36–40, 52, 73, 126, 155, 166
Erdrich, Louise 14, 101, 114, 119, 120, 121, 123, 125, 126, 129, 133, 138, 166
 LaRose 120–1
 The Night Watchman 14, 101, 121–9
 The Round House 119–20
Erlich, Victor 5
estrangement (*see* defamiliarization)

fantasy 54, 96
Fisher, Mark 95
Fraiman, Susan 25
Freud, Sigmund 42, 86, 98

ghost 1, 2, 12, 14, 86, 113–21, 125, 126–33, 138, 164, 165, 166, 167, 169–70
 literary character 114, 117
Gigliotti, Carol 1
Gilbert, Sandra M. and Susan Gubar 171
Good, I. G. 56

Gothic 1, 2, 12, 13, 84, 85, 86–7, 94–6, 105, 170
Gothic Animals: Uncanny Otherness and the Animal With-Out (Ruth Heholt and Melissa Edmundson) 12, 87
Grim, John 118

Haggerty, George E. 86
Haraway, Donna 25, 26, 51, 52, 84–5, 161
 "becoming with" 51, 52
 cyborg 51
Harris, Andrea L. 55
Harris, Ian 118
Harrison, M. John 96
Hayles, N. Katherine 51
Heidegger, Martin 38, 118
heteronormativity 2, 13, 86, 88–9, 94, 105, 166
Hogle, Jerrold E. 86
hope 1, 13, 21–7, 29–36, 40–2, 73, 74, 156, 165, 166, 170, 171, 181–2
 animal studies 24, 25–6, 171
 nonhuman 13, 21–7, 29–6, 40–2, 165–6
 versus nostalgia 34–5
horror 1, 2, 12, 62, 85, 86, 96, 104–5, 134
human exceptionalism 4, 12–14, 21, 23, 35, 41, 45, 54, 55, 57, 58, 64–5, 85–6, 99, 103–4, 105, 114, 115, 116, 118, 120, 130, 151, 152, 153, 155, 162, 163, 166
humanism 1, 12, 14, 51, 113, 151, 152, 159, 160–1, 162, 163, 173, 174

instrumentalization 1, 10, 13, 21, 32, 35, 39, 54, 61, 66, 68–9, 72–3, 74, 75, 90–1, 104, 169, 177, 179
intelligence 2, 13, 51, 52, 54, 56–7, 58, 60, 61, 64, 66, 75, 90, 121–2, 164, 166, 181
Ishiguro, Kazuo 13, 14, 21, 22, 26, 27, 30, 31, 35, 36, 41, 42, 151, 152, 153, 155, 159, 163, 166
 Klara and the Sun 14, 151–6, 159, 163, 170, 171, 173, 176, 178
 Never Let Me Go 13, 21, 22, 26–35, 36, 37, 41–2, 118–19
 The Island of Doctor Moreau (H. G. Wells) 87

James, M. R. 96
James, William 4–5, 7, 8

Jameson, Fredric 22, 42, 166, 176, 181
Joshi, S. T. 95
Joyce, James 99
   Ulysses 135

Kant, Immanuel 32, 38, 118
Korsgaard, Christine M. 115–16, 137, 151
Kuzniar, Alice 11

Lacan, Jacques 38
Le Guin, Ursula K. 83
   The Dispossessed 83, 84
Levinas, Emmanuel 38, 118
love 2, 13, 14, 15, 33–4, 52, 53, 54, 57–8, 71, 73, 74, 75, 79, 88–9, 94, 131, 152, 153, 159, 160–1, 162–3, 164, 166, 170, 172–3, 181
Lovecraft, H. P. 94–5, 96
Luna, Jonathan and Sarah Vaughn 13, 51–2, 54, 69–73, 166
   Alex + Ada 13, 51–2, 69–73, 74, 170

McEwan, Ian 14, 167
   Machines Like Me 14, 152, 156–9, 170, 171
McHugh, Susan, Robert McKay, and John Miller 11
Midgley, Mary 84
Miéville, China 95–6, 97
Miller, Harlan B. 118
modernism 11, 28, 29, 73
Morrison, Toni 14, 125, 169, 170
   Beloved 125, 169
   Jazz 169
   Paradise 169
Morson, Gary Saul 5
Moylan, Tom 52

Nagel, Thomas 84, 134–5
Newton, John Frank 9
Noys, Benjamin and Timothy S. Murphy 96

Ojibwe 114, 119, 120, 124, 127
Ortiz Robles, Mario 3, 11

personhood 32, 53, 71–2, 73, 74, 75–6, 119–20, 137, 156, 171
petkeeping 66, 90, 93–4, 160, 162

Platonism 55
Plumwood, Val 102
Plutarch 9
posthumanism 14, 24–5, 35, 51–2, 55, 56, 58, 90, 100, 113, 159, 160–1, 162, 164, 173
posthumousness 2, 14, 113–21, 125, 126–38, 166
potentiality 11, 13, 52, 53, 54, 58, 69, 73, 75, 105, 166
Powers, Richard 13, 51, 53, 54, 58–65, 75, 166
   The Overstory 13, 51, 53, 58–65, 73, 75, 96, 136
Prendergast, Finola Anne 99–100
Prometheus 9
Punter, David 86

racism 2, 13, 85–6, 91–2, 93, 94, 96, 104, 105, 158, 166
   relation to speciesism 92–4, 166
Rainwater, Catherine 119
reading 169–70, 181
   habitually 29, 34, 73, 167, 170
   middle distance 27–9, 181
realism 21, 22, 28, 29, 30, 31–2, 34, 35, 41, 72, 73, 86, 126, 176
Regan, Tom 25
Robertson, Benjamin J. 96
robot 15, 52, 56, 62, 66, 68, 69, 70, 71, 72, 164, 166, 167, 171–81 (*see also* sexbot)
Romanticism 6, 73, 164
Rushdie, Salman 14, 114, 133, 135, 136, 137, 138, 167
   "Is Nothing Sacred?" 136–7
   Quichotte 14, 114, 133–4, 135–8

Saunders, George 14, 114, 119, 129, 130, 131, 132, 133, 138, 166–7
   Lincoln in the Bardo 14, 114, 129–33
science fiction 1, 2, 22, 41, 52–3, 59, 60, 61, 64, 84, 85, 94, 96, 166
Seed, David 22, 52
sentience 69, 70–2, 73, 75, 118, 158, 172, 176
sentimentalism 21, 28, 29, 30, 31, 33, 34, 35, 41, 160
Sewell, Anna 21, 31–2
   Black Beauty 21, 31–2

sexbot 13, 54, 65–73, 74, 75, 166 (*see also* robot)
Sheenan, Michael J. and Elizabeth A. Tibbetts 162
Shelley, Mary 55, 75, 170, 171
   Frankenstein 170–1, 172–3, 174, 175, 176, 181
Shelley, Percy Bysshe 6–10
   "A Defence of Poetry" 6–7
   "To a Skylark" 7–8
   "On the Vegetable System of Diet" 8–10
   "A Vindication of a Natural Diet" 8–10
Shklovsky, Viktor 3–12, 97, 105, 126, 174, 182 (*see also* defamiliarization)
   "Art as Device" 3–12
Silas Marner (George Eliot) 173–4
Singer, Peter 25, 115, 178 (*see also* speciesism)
slavery 70, 84, 85, 90–1, 92, 93, 157
Smith, Andrew 95
Smuts, Barbara 25
Solomon, Rivers 84
   An Unkindness of Ghosts 84
soul (*see* ghost)
speciesism 2, 13, 35, 48, 85–6, 91, 92, 93, 94, 104, 105, 166 (*see also* racism—relation to speciesism)
spirit (*see* ghost)
Spivak, Gayatri 26
   "Does the Subaltern Speak?" 26
Starship Troopers (film) 162
The Strange Case of Dr Jekyll and Mr Hyde (Robert Louis Stevenson) 87
sublime 95, 97, 101–3
Suvin, Darko 22
Swainton, Stephanie 96
symbiosis 13, 85, 88, 90, 91, 94, 101, 104–5

Tolstoy, Leo 3, 5, 6, 31–2, 126
   "Strider" 3, 6, 11, 31–2, 126
Turning, Alan 156–7, 158

uncanny 13, 83, 84, 85, 86, 87, 88, 91, 92, 94, 95, 97, 98, 99, 100, 102, 103, 105, 110
uniqueness 2, 14, 149–64, 166, 173, 174
   alien uniqueness 151–2, 159–63, 173
   "uniqueness to" 151–2, 159–64, 173, 174, 177–8
utopia 22, 40, 41, 42, 57, 63, 166

vampire 1, 13, 85, 86–94, 104–5, 164, 165, 166
VanderMeer, Jeff 13, 85, 96, 166
   Acceptance 103
   Annihilation 13, 85, 96–104, 105
   Southern Reach Trilogy 96
Vint, Sherryl 12, 22, 38–9, 53, 85, 103, 104
Vizenor, Gerald 119
vulnerability 14, 27, 114, 137, 138, 167, 173

Waldau, Paul 24, 52, 64, 118, 165
Warren, Austin and René Wellek 6
Weil, Kari 11, 23–4, 26, 53
   critical anthropomorphism 23–4, 26, 30, 35, 42, 53
weird 2, 12, 13, 84, 85, 94–6, 97, 105, 170
   new weird 96
Werewolves, Wolves and the Gothic (Robert McKay and John Miller) 12
Winnett, Susan 171
Winterson, Jeanette 13, 51, 52, 53, 54, 55, 58, 75, 133, 164, 166, 170
   Frankissstein 13, 51, 52, 54–8, 65–9, 70, 72, 73, 74–5, 133–4, 164, 170
   Written on the Body 55
Wolfe, Cary 24–5, 51, 160, 161
Wordsworth, William 6
writing 98–9, 101–2

zoophilia 72

www.ingramcontent.com/pod-product-compliance
Lightning Source LLC
Chambersburg PA
CBHW052115300426
44116CB00010B/1673